KU-734-964

CHRIST CHURCH
COLLEGE
CANTERBURY

AUTHOR. BERGONZI, B.

TITLE. The turn of a century

CLASS NO. 820.9   COPY. B

WITHDRAWN

THE TURN OF A CENTURY

By the same author

THE EARLY H. G. WELLS
HEROES' TWILIGHT
THE SITUATION OF THE NOVEL
ANTHONY POWELL
T. S. ELIOT (Masters of World Literature series)

H. G. WELLS'S TONO-BUNGAY (editor)
GEORGE GISSING'S NEW GRUB STREET (editor)
INNOVATIONS: ESSAYS ON ART AND IDEAS (editor)
T. S. ELIOT: FOUR QUARTETS (Casebook series) (editor)
THE TWENTIETH CENTURY (Vol. 7 of the *Sphere History of Literature in the English Language*) (editor)

THE TURN OF
A CENTURY

*Essays on Victorian and
Modern English Literature*

BERNARD BERGONZI

Macmillan

© Bernard Bergonzi 1973

All rights reserved. No part of this publication may be
reproduced or transmitted, in any form or by any means,
without permission.

First published 1973 by
THE MACMILLAN PRESS LTD
London and Basingstoke
Associated companies in New York Toronto
Dublin Melbourne Johannesburg and Madras

SBN 333 14636 0

Printed in Great Britain by
RICHARD CLAY (THE CHAUCER PRESS) LTD
Bungay, Suffolk

820.8

33001

820.9
B

171442

Contents

Contents

Preface

These essays were first published between 1959 and 1972 and are on a variety of authors – all British by birth or assimilation, and all now dead – who were writing during the second half of the nineteenth century and the first half of the twentieth. The major emphasis of the book falls on the literature of the decades immediately before and after the turn of the century in 1901: the *fin de siècle* period, the Edwardian years, the First World War and the 1920s. The first essay, however, looks back to an early-Victorian poem, Tennyson's *The Princess*, which seems to me to contain interesting anticipations of twentieth-century sensibility and problems; while the last essay is on a young poet killed in the Second World War, Keith Douglas, whose work offers a significant contrast to the poetry of the First. An agreeable if accidental symmetry may be seen in the fact that nearly all the works I discuss appeared within the span of a single century, ranging from the first edition of *The Princess* in 1847 to the posthumous publication of Douglas's *Alamein to Zem-Zem* in 1946.

It is always risky for a critic to suggest that essays published separately blend into unity when put together into a book. I would not want to claim anything so grand as unity for these essays, but I think they offer a fair degree of continuity in subject-matter and theme. A recurring topic is the interrelation between the literature of the late nineteenth century and that of the twentieth. Here one is in an area of paradoxes and shifting categories. In one sense the Modern Movement of Pound and Eliot and Joyce was in full reaction against the literature of the last years of Victoria's reign; yet that literature contained within itself the seeds of the subsequent modernist achievement. Again, it is a commonplace of literary history to contrast the fiction of Edwardian realists like

Wells and Galsworthy with the more imaginatively advanced
work of the innovators. Yet Wells and Galsworthy show, in
their best fiction, a deep awareness of the crisis of confidence
that overtook the national culture by the turn of the century,
however superficially vigorous and assertive it appeared.
From one point of view, Victorianism remained triumphant
until the almost simultaneous advent of the Modern Movement and the First World War; but in a different perspective
the significant transformation can be seen thirty or even forty
years before.

Other subjects that I return to include the ideology of
modernism; the slightly exotic contribution of Roman Catholic writers like Chesterton and Belloc and Roy Campbell to
English literary culture; and the literature of two World
Wars. In some essays the emphasis is primarily critical, in
others literary-historical, though in some measure the two
must, I believe, always go together (and here I shall pay a
passing tribute to my one-time tutor, F. W. Bateson, who
showed me the possibility of combining original criticism
with accurate literary history). The 1960s and 1970s have seen
a remarkable revival of interest in the years spanning the
turn of the century, apparent in such things as the cult of
Aubrey Beardsley and *art nouveau*; television adaptations of
Galsworthy or Henry James; the fascination, partly mocking,
partly affectionate, with the zenith of the British Empire; and
the complex mixture of pathos and nostalgia that continues
to be aroused by the First World War. I hope these essays
may be of some interest in documenting the literary activity
of those years.

Acknowledgements

These essays mostly remain in the state in which they were
first published, though I have made occasional revisions in the
interest of greater amenity of phrasing or accuracy of expression, and have changed some of the titles. Particulars of original publication are as follows: appropriate acknowledgements
are made to the editors and publishers in question.

1. 'Feminism and Femininity in *The Princess*': *The Major
   Victorian Poets: Reconsiderations*, ed. Isobel Armstrong
   (Routledge & Kegan Paul, 1969).
2. 'Fin de Siècle': *The Victorians* (vol. 6 of *The Sphere History of Literature in the English Language*), ed. Arthur
   Pollard (Sphere Books, 1970).
3. 'R.L.S.': *New York Review of Books*, 26 Jan. 1967.
4. 'New Grub Street': Introduction to Penguin English
   Library edition (Penguin Books, 1968).
5. 'The Correspondence of Gissing and Wells': *Essays in
   Criticism* (summer 1962).
6. '*Tono-Bungay*': Introduction to Riverside Edition
   (Houghton Mifflin, 1966).
7. 'Wells, Fiction and Politics': *The Politics of Twentieth
   Century Novelists*, ed. G. A. Panichas (Hawthorn Books,
   1971).
8. 'John Gray': Introduction to *Park: A Fantastic Story* by
   John Gray (St Albert's Press, 1966).
9. 'Chesterton and/or Belloc': *Critical Quarterly* (spring
   1959).
10. 'Man as Property': *Spectator*, 15 Feb. 1963.
11. 'The Reputation of Ford Madox Ford': *New Blackfriars*
    (Apr. 1967).
12. 'Georgians in Peace and War': *New York Review of
    Books*, 30 Sep. 1965.

13. 'Kipling and the First World War': *Rudyard Kipling*, ed. John Gross (Weidenfeld & Nicolson, 1972).

14. 'The Huxley Line' (originally 'Little Aldous and the Cockroach Man'): *Hudson Review* (summer 1970).

15. 'The *Waste Land* Manuscripts': *Encounter* (Apr. 1972).

16. 'Modern Reactionaries': *London Magazine* (Nov. 1966).

17. 'Wyndham Lewis' (originally 'Black Cartesian'): *Hudson Review* (autumn 1969).

18. 'Roy Campbell: Outsider on the Right': *Journal of Contemporary History* (Apr. 1967).

19. 'Keith Douglas': *London Magazine* (Feb. 1968).

1 Feminism and Femininity in *The Princess*

Tennyson, despite Mr Auden's notorious observation, was not a stupid poet. Although, like most poets, he was not an original thinker, he was certainly capable of thinking, as T. S. Eliot once reluctantly admitted ('Tennyson and Browning are poets, and they think . . .'): he was aware of the major ideas of his age, and was excited and sometimes confused by them. Ideas got into his poems, though not always to the advantage of the poetry; one must admit that Eliot was right in saying that Tennyson was not among the poets who 'feel their thought as immediately as the odour of a rose', though one might also add that the intellectual preoccupations of the Victorians were possibly not of a kind to lend themselves to such attractively immediate apprehension. *The Princess* is, I suppose, the strangest of Tennyson's well-known poems, and it is also, in a literal sense, one of his most thoughtful: ideas got into the poem more successfully here than elsewhere, and I want to suggest that the eccentricity of its form was dictated by Tennyson's desire to entertain and contemplate ideas, some of them rather disturbing ideas, to which he was not prepared to be formally committed.

In the opening lines of *The Princess* Tennyson unfolds a substantial amount of information and shows that the poem's sub-title – 'A Medley' – is relevant from the very beginning. The narrator is staying at Vivian Place, the mansion of Sir Walter Vivian, together with five other young men, as the guests of their fellow-student, Walter junior. Also in the party are Walter's young sister, Lilia, and her maiden-aunt companion. The occasion is a summer day when Sir Walter has thrown his grounds open to the people of the district: his

tenants and their families, and the members of the local
Mechanics' Institute. In the second paragraph of the poem
the narrator describes the interior of Vivian Place:

> And me that morning Walter show'd the house,
> Greek, set with busts: from vases in the hall
> Flowers of all heavens, and lovelier than their names,
> Grew side by side; and on the pavement lay
> Carved stones of the Abbey-ruin in the park,
> Huge Ammonites, and the first bones of Time;
> And on the tables every clime and age
> Jumbled together; celts and calumets,
> Claymore and snowshoe, toys in lava, fans
> Of sandal, amber, ancient rosaries,
> Laborious orient ivory sphere in sphere,
> The cursed Malayan crease, and battle-clubs
> From the isles of palm: and higher on the walls,
> Betwixt the monstrous horns of elk and deer,
> His own forefathers' arms and armour hung.

As description, this passage catches a particular moment in
the development of early-Victorian taste. The architectural
context may still be neo-classical – 'Greek, set with busts' –
but it has already been invaded by an energetically promis-
cuous connoisseurship, which ranges over the entire globe
and back through time to prehistory in pursuit of cultural
objects. The interior description is balanced by the succeeding fine account of the outdoor scene, where the working
people in the park indulge in recreative pursuits that combine sober pleasure with scientific instruction, in a manner
no less characteristic of the period. Within the poem itself,
this veritable 'medley' looks forward to the fantastic adventures in the long central section, where every kind of exoticism is mingled with allusions to geometry, astronomy and
palaeontology.

The narrator goes on to look at the family portraits, and is
shown an ancient chronicle which records the exploits in
medieval times of the Vivians' illustrious ancestors. He is
particularly struck by the account of a valiant lady knight
who, in the manner of Boadicea or Joan of Arc, 'Had beat her

foes with slaughter from her walls'. Here we are introduced
to the theme of feminism which dominates the poem: it is
amplified when, after the narrator and his host have joined
the rest of the party at the near-by ruined Abbey, Lilia,
despite the mockery of her brother and his friends, delivers
herself of ardently feminist sentiments. Her ideas are to be
given copious expression, both discursively and dramatically,
in the succeeding section, but she focuses the debate in a
single, vivid image when she ties her coloured scarf round a
statue of one of the Vivians' sternest feudal ancestors, the
knight Sir Ralph:

> and there was Ralph himself,
> A broken statue propt against the wall,
> As gay as any. Lilia, wild with sport,
> Half child half woman as she was, had wound
> A scarf of orange round the stony helm,
> And robed the shoulders in a rosy silk,
> That made the old warrior from his ivied nook
> Glow like a sunbeam.

A charming and yet a disturbing picture, at least to those
whose attitudes are rooted in traditional masculine attitudes:
'the feudal warrior lady-clad' provides an ideogrammatic
juxtaposition of opposed values, and hints at a time when the
familiar differences between the sexes will be much less clear-
cut, and may even vanish altogether. Modern readers of these
lines may find echoing in their heads other, more recent
phrases, where the splendours of a vanished past are symbolised by a broken statue or defaced hero: a 'broken Corio-
lanus' or 'two gross of broken statues'. *The Princess* is, in fact,
a surprisingly modern poem: as Marshall McLuhan has
shown, Tennyson often anticipates symbolist and post-symbo-
list techniques.[1] With this in mind, we may regard the lines
about the interior of Vivian Place as more than just a piece of
accurate descriptive verse: they have something of the quality of 'These fragments I have shored against my ruins',
where the dislocated modern consciousness moves freely and
uneasily amid the *disjecta membra* of cultural and historical
relativism: 'every clime and age / jumbled together'. Tenny-

son's 'first bones of Time' may present a more assured and
hopeful picture than Eliot's 'withered stumps of time', but
they seem to belong to the same universe. Such anticipations
may look un-Tennysonian, but they are certainly not un-
Victorian; whilst Tennyson was working over the final version of *The Princess*, Matthew Arnold was making his brave
and painful exploration of that most familiar of twentieth-
century disorders, 'the dialogue of the mind with itself', and
was lamenting:

> this strange disease of modern life,
> With its sick hurry, and divided aims.

Returning to the narrative of the opening section of *The
Princess*, we move through the light-hearted badinage between Lilia and the youths concerning her scheme for a
ladies' college, until we are ready for the transition to the
central 'story' of the poem, which is to be improvised in turn
by the seven young men. This narrative, when we come to it,
reads as a kind of dream-sequence, and Tennyson is remarkably explicit about the elements that will, as it were, compose
its manifest content. Lilia is to be the Princess, of almost
absurdly heroic stature: 'six feet high, / Grand, epic, homici-
dal', whilst the narrator is to be the Prince who will win her,
thus suggesting that the flirtation and possible courtship of
the two young people provides a sub-plot underneath the
poem's more grandiose themes.

> Heroic seems our Princess as required –
> But something made to suit with Time and place,
> A Gothic ruin and a Grecian house,
> A talk of college and of ladies' rights,
> A feudal knight in silken masquerade,
> And, yonder, shrieks and strange experiments
> For which the good Sir Ralph had burnt them all –
> This *were* a medley! we should have him back
> Who told the 'Winter's tale' to do it for us.

These are the elements which, informed by the unfinished
argument about women's rights and education, are trans-

muted into the lengthy fantastic narrative that is to follow.
At this point I shall refer to Mr John Killham's admirable
study of the sources and intellectual background of *The
Princess*, from which I have greatly profited.[2] Among other
things, Mr Killham shows that the connection between the
things mentioned in the opening of *The Princess* is less arbi-
trary than one might at first suppose; he points out, in particular, that there were close links between the feminist
movement and the movements for the advancement and
education of the working class, so that the educative outing of
a Mechanics' Institute is a not inappropriate background for a
dramatic debate about the future of women. We can also consult Mr Killham for a full account of the feminist movements
of the 1840s, and the extent to which Tennyson was interested in them, although such knowledge is not essential for
a basic understanding of the poem. But it is, I think, important to realise that its central narrative is a dream-transforma-
tion of a sober debate, and that many of its more singular
characteristics arise from Tennyson's desire to make a full
imaginative exploration of questions which, at the same time,
are kept intellectually distanced. The transformation of Lilia
into Princess Ida has something in common with Lewis
Carroll's successive transformations of Alice, culminating in
the 'Queen Alice' of *Through the Looking-Glass*.

II

The central story, about the three young men – the Prince,
Cyril and Florian – who disguise themselves as girls in order
to enrol in the ladies' university, has a fine air of *opera buffa*
absurdity. After the dense social specificity of the opening of
the poem we are immersed in a colourful but vague fairy-tale
world, and the ladies' college is set in the kind of dream-
landscape that tends to recur, though usually in more menacing forms, in Victorian poetry: one thinks of 'Childe Roland'
or *The City of Dreadful Night*. The adventures of the three
young men proceed energetically but smoothly, and one has
to make a certain deliberate effort to recall that each section
is supposedly improvised by one of the seven young men,
whilst the songs – which Tennyson inserted into the final

edition of the poem – are contributed by Lilia and her aunt.
A successively improvised consciousness, such as the Prince's
is supposed to be, can have little substantive reality, and we
cannot be sure about the relation between the Prince's 'voice'
and that of each of the seven successive narrators. In the
'Conclusion' of *The Princess*, however, Tennyson tries to re-
solve the difficulty by asserting that the story we have just
read has, in fact, been 'written up' by the narrator; he goes on
to discuss the difficulties he found in establishing consistency
of tone. Rarely can a poem have discussed with such frankness its own process of composition:

> So closed our tale, of which I give you all
> The random scheme as wildly as it rose:
> The words are mostly mine; for when we ceased
> There came a moment's pause, and Walter said,
> 'I wish she had not yielded!' then to me,
> 'What, if you drest it up poetically!'
> So pray'd the men, the women: I gave assent:
> Yet how to bind the scatter'd scheme of seven
> Together in one sheaf? What style could suit?
> The men required that I should give throughout
> The sort of mock-heroic gigantesque,
> With which we banter'd little Lilia first:
> The women – and perhaps they felt their power,
> For something in the ballads which they sang,
> Or in their silent influence as they sat,
> Had ever seem'd to wrestle with burlesque,
> And drove us, last, to quite a solemn close –
> They hated banter, wish'd for something real,
> A gallant fight, a noble princess – why
> Not make her true-heroic – true-sublime?
> Or all, they said, as earnest as the close?
> Which yet with such a framework scarce could be.
> Then rose a little feud betwixt the two,
> Betwixt the mockers and the realists:
> And I, betwixt them both, to please them both,
> And yet to give the story as it rose,
> I moved as in a strange diagonal,
> And maybe neither pleased myself nor them.

Readers of Wayne C. Booth's *The Rhetoric of Fiction* will be familiar with the idea that the 'implicit voice' of the author will always be present in a novel, no matter how deliberately impersonal and self-containedly dramatised; and what is true of fiction is also true in many respects of Victorian narrative poems. One problem in *The Princess* is to distinguish between (*a*) Tennyson's own implicit voice; (*b*) that of the principal narrator; (*c*) those of the six other narrators in the central section; and (*d*) those of the Prince. Having raised this question, we can leave it; certainly there is no point in pursuing it with scholastic exactitude, since with such an avowedly 'random scheme' as *The Princess* one is hardly likely to discover any consistent distinctions. But such indirection in the narrative technique is, I think, another index of *The Princess*'s modernity of form; it looks forward to the characteristic fictional complexity of Conrad and Ford.

In practice, this uncertainty about the relation between the various narrative levels tends to heighten the sense of unreality that surrounds the Prince. And the unreality is emphasised in a fairly unsubtle way when we are shown the Prince falling, at regular intervals, in a cataleptic fit, in which all his surroundings become ghostly and insubstantial:

> On a sudden in the midst of man and day,
> And while I walk'd and talk'd as heretofore,
> I seem'd to move among a world of ghosts,
> And feel myself the shadow of a dream.

These periodic reminders of the potential insubstantiality, not only of the Prince but of those who surround him, prevent us from becoming too intently absorbed in the adventures of the Prince and his companions: unreality must remain unreality, and the profoundly serious is constantly held in check by the mock-heroic.

What is serious about the underlying debate, and what most involves Tennyson (or his narrator), is outlined in the preliminary exchange between Lilia and her brothers: are women fundamentally different – and in practice inferior – beings from men, or are the apparent differences simply the result of a long period of cultural and environmental conditioning? Lilia emphatically asserts the latter opinion: 'It is but bringing up; no more than that.' In our own day this position has been stated with greater rigour by such writers as Simone de Beauvoir and Betty Friedan, who see women as scarcely yet emancipated from the helotage of a male-dominated world; their position can be summed up in Simone de Beauvoir's phrase: 'One is not born, but becomes a woman.' Against this, one may set the traditional view of woman as the *Ewig-Weibliche*, a biologically differentiated creature, whose child-bearing role makes her fundamentally different from men; as Freud put it, 'anatomy is a woman's destiny'. This is a fascinating debate, and one which is never likely to be resolved on the level of theory, since there is no possibility of common ground between the contestants, and not even a common terminology. And so far the division has taken a predictable shape: almost all the professional opinion that sees women as an 'environmentally differentiated' being has come from women writers, and most (but by no means all) of the claims that she is 'biologically' different have been expressed by men. In practice, opinion tends to adopt various compromises, often not very rational ones, somewhere between the extremes represented by Freud and Simone de Beauvoir. A work such as Doris Lessing's *The Golden Notebook* shows, very movingly, how a modern woman can achieve a degree of intellectual, professional and sexual emancipation infinitely far beyond anything dreamed of by the young ladies of *The Princess*, and well in advance of the aspirations of the heroines of Ibsen and Shaw, and still remain a prey to her own emotions: to this extent she remains a victim of male exploitation.

In the central section of *The Princess*, Tennyson uses the utterances of Princess Ida and her companions, and the reflections of the Prince, in order to examine some of the major possible attitudes to the 'position of women' question; at the same time, the dramatic working-out of his fantasy tends to undercut any easy repose in a purely intellectual solution. When Princess Ida welcomes the three supposed students to the college she sternly urges them to forget about men and thoughts of marriage. Not, indeed, for good (Ida avoids the

pathological anti-masculinism of some of the later suffra-
gettes), but for a long time to come:

> Some future time, if so indeed you will,
> You may with those self-styled our lords ally
> Your fortunes, justlier balanced, scale with scale.

One of the most traditional and extreme ways of seeing
women as a biologically differentiated creature is to regard
her primarily as a sexual object, the plaything (or playmate)
of the male. This position has always been rightly repudiated
by feminists, and Ida refers to it only to dismiss it:

> Look, our hall!
> Our statues! – not of those that men desire,
> Sleek Odalisques, or oracles of mode,
> Nor stunted squaws of West or East . . .

The statues are, instead, of notable female warriors, rulers
and builders of antiquity. The view of women as sexual objects reappears in Section V, when the old king, the Princess's
father, asserts it in lines whose terseness strikingly expresses
the brutality of their sentiments:

> Man is the hunter; woman is his game;
> The sleek and shining creatures of the chase,
> We hunt them for the beauty of their skins;
> They love us for it, and we ride them down.

He goes on to emphasise the absolute opposition of sexual
roles in a series of crashing antitheses:

> Man for the field and woman for the hearth:
> Man for the sword and for the needle she:
> Man with the head and woman with the heart:
> Man to command and woman to obey;
> All else confusion.

It is, of course, a matter of everlasting annoyance to feminists
that such sentiments are by no means confined to the male

sex: for very many women, even today, they provide a perfectly acceptable self-image. And this attitude finds a certain
support in a kind of sentimental Jungianism, which posits an
absolute distinction between *animus* and *anima*, and sees
woman only as a tender, complacent, yielding, maternal (and
yet withal mysterious) creature, who is wholly complementary to man. That this over-simple dichotomy is false both to
the facts of experience and literature is shown, not only by
Ida's opinions, but by her role. The archetypes of the Good
Angel and the Mother have always represented one aspect
only of the feminine nature; against them one must set all the
traditional images of woman as militant or destructive. The
most extreme example is, perhaps, the black Hindu goddess
Kali, the bloodthirsty wife of Shiva; one might equally mention Clytemnestra, or the various vampire figures beloved of
the nineteenth-century Decadence. Of a more benign order
there are such famous Old Testament heroines as Judith and
Jael; the medieval St Joan, and in Renaissance epic, Ariosto's
Bradamante and Spenser's Britomart. (A debased version of
the type is still in universal circulation as the Britannia of
our coinage, complete with helmet, trident and shield.)
Princess Ida sees herself, and is presented to us, as a figure in
this tradition of the militant female.

The Prince does not share his father's brutally clear-cut
sentiments; he is very sympathetic to the feminist cause, and
throughout the narrative he responds rather like the worried,
open-minded liberal who is such a common character in
twentieth-century fiction. At the end of the narrative he is to
suggest a possible evolutionary solution of the feminine di-
lemma. Meanwhile, after the Princess's introductory remarks,
he and his friends listen to a lecture by the Lady Psyche, a
young widow who has solved the problem of the working
mother with enviable ease by letting her baby sleep beside
her in the classroom. The lecture begins with a passage that
shows the assurance with which Tennyson could transform
scientific speculation into excellent poetry; at the same time,
it dwells on the topic of evolution, which forms a major strand
in the poem – appearing initially in the early reference to
'the first bones of Time' – and which recurs in such things as
the near-by spectacle of 'the bones of some vast bulk that

lived and roar'd / Before man was' or the geological expedition.

> This world was once a fluid haze of light,
> Till toward the centre set the starry tides,
> And eddied into suns, that wheeling cast
> The planets: then the monster, then the man;
> Tattoo'd or woaded, winter-clad in skins,
> Raw from the prime, and crushing down his mate;
> As yet we find in barbarous isles, and here
> Among the lowest.

Psyche traces the role and treatment of women through the ages, and ends with a soaring vision of a possible future:

> At last
> She rose upon a wind of prophecy
> Dilating on the future; 'everywhere
> Two heads in council, two beside the hearth,
> Two in the tangled business of the world,
> Two in the liberal offices of life,
> Two plummets dropt for one to sound the abyss
> Of science, and the secrets of the mind:
> Musician, painter, sculptor, critic, more:
> And everywhere the broad and bounteous Earth
> Should bear a double growth of those rare souls,
> Poets, whose thoughts enrich the blood of the world.'

This presupposes a dual monarchy of the sexes, ruling as complementary equals. In its context it is revolutionary enough; but it stops short of according women total autonomy, inasmuch as they are still supposed to exist in some kind of inescapable relationship with man; they are still to be, literally, 'the opposite sex'. The seeds of the problem that Lawrence was to anatomise in *Women in Love* have been sown.

Shortly after this lecture, the male identity of the three disguised intruders is made known, and the harmony of the women's university is overthrown. Its equilibrium is seen to have been indeed precarious, and its instability is shown in such factors as the jealousy and bitchiness of the Lady Blanche, and Psyche's deep maternal anguish about her child. We have already been shown that many of the inmates of the college are unhappy with their enforced seclusion:

> others lay about the lawns,
> Of the older sort, and murmur'd that their May
> Was passing: what was learning unto them?
> They wish'd to marry; they could rule a house;
> Men hated learned women . . .

Ida's injunction that the women may marry one day, but that they must wait until the female sex had been brought to a pitch of true equality with the male, is not, in the event, found very helpful. *The Princess* is very much about the business of 'role-playing', and a central topic is the fatal ease with which the role of the *Ewig-Weibliche* thrusts aside the consciously pursued goal of the woman who has overcome her cultural disabilities and grown into the educated equal and companion of the male. This is clearly seen when, after the battle, the ladies of the college rapidly become ministering angels and tend the wounded men. Here one can only admit that Tennyson has focused on an observable psychological truth, even though the radical feminist may deplore it.

The interpolated songs contain the most celebrated poetry of *The Princess*; although they are supposedly sung by Lilia and her aunt as interludes in the seven-part improvised narrative of Walter and his friends, they occur as anonymous outbursts of pure lyricism, moments of emotional stasis in the midst of the unruly narrative action. In 'Tears, idle tears', Tennyson's verse reaches one of its sublime heights, and its unalloyed lyrical seriousness almost destroys the mock-heroic setting into which it is inserted. The equally exquisite though less profound 'Now sleeps the crimson petal' reflects, as Mr Killham reminds us, Tennyson's interest in Persian poetry. Yet the songs provide more than a delightful anthology rather arbitrarily inserted into the narrative of *The Princess*. They are, I believe, reassurances to the reader that despite everything the *Ewig-Weibliche* will still dominate: their references to motherhood and erotic love provide familiar points of reference in a world seemingly disorientated by Princess Ida's pursuit of feminine equality. (Just as, in the preamble, Lilia, after her feminist outburst, is gently eased back into a more appropriate role by being asked to sing.) The songs themselves, with their intensity of feeling and static, self-contained quality, provide emblems of what the feminine nature is conventionally supposed to be.

But if Tennyson seemingly undermines the conceptions of feminism by showing the instability of an institution run according to its principles, and by setting against feminism the attractive and traditional femininity symbolised by the songs, the Prince takes a more sympathetic position. In his final address to the Princess he generously embraces her standpoint:

> Henceforth thou hast a helper, me, that know
> The woman's cause is man's: they rise or sink
> Together, dwarf'd or godlike, bond or free:

He develops his picture of the liberation of woman, though stressing the need to preserve her essential femininity: 'to live and learn and be / All that not harms distinctive womanhood'. He is being cautious here, for similar arguments were for a long time used to deny civic rights to women (and still are in Switzerland). The Prince, indeed, seems to be reasserting the traditional notion of biological differentiation:

> For woman is not undevelopt man,
> But diverse: could we make her as the man,
> Sweet Love were slain: his dearest bond is this,
> Not like to like, but like in difference.

But he continues with an interesting evolutionary speculation:

> Yet in the long years liker must they grow;
> The man be more of woman, she of man;
> He gain in sweetness and in moral height,
> Nor lose the wrestling thews that throw the world;
> She mental breadth, nor fail in childward care,
> Nor lose the childlike in the larger mind.

It is a beguiling notion, and one which is unlikely to be disturbing if simply confined to moral qualities. But its deeper
implications seem to entertain the androgynous, a certain
blurring of the sexes, which we have already had foreshadowed
in the figure of the 'feudal warrior lady-clad'. It is indeed
arguable that as civilisation continues to evolve, many traditional sexual attributes may become unnecessary, such as the
aggressive masculinity of the old king, and that a mingling of
sexual characteristics may become evident. According to some
commentators, this condition has already been reached: 'All
around us, young males are beginning to retrieve for themselves the cavalier role once piously and class-consciously sur-
rendered to women: *that of being beautiful and being
loved*.'[3] Having allowed this possibility to present itself, the
Prince concludes his speech with a stirring account of ideal
marriage, in which questions of equality and inequality will
not arise, and in which each sex will perfectly complement
the other, until they become 'The single pure and perfect
animal', almost as if the halves of the bisexual animal described in Plato's fable were reunited. It is a moving picture,
but an evasive one: we are not told whether this process of
evolutionary improvement is to involve any voluntary element, and whether the goal of intellectual and cultural
equality with men that Ida worked for is to be regarded as a
mistake, or at best unnecessary. In the last analysis, *The
Princess* is a timid poem: Tennyson has raised implications
that must necessarily have been upsetting to the habitual
assumptions of many of his readers, even if the mock-heroic,
spasmodic mode of treatment kept the pressure low; and he
damps them down when they look like becoming too exigent.
Nevertheless, the fact that they are raised at all places *The
Princess* at the beginning of a line whose later exemplars include *The Doll's House*, *Women in Love* and *The Golden
Notebook*.

After the narrated adventures we return to the solidity of
Vivian Place, and Lilia and the young men. The extravaganza is over, and the festivities in the park are also coming to
an end: we meet Sir Walter, 'A great broad-shoulder'd genial
Englishman', a reassuring figure with both feet firmly on the
ground, who makes an instant contrast to the Prince, with his

frail consciousnesss and cataleptic tendencies. The party sit on in the gathering darkness, 'rapt in nameless reverie, / Perchance upon the future man'. Then, at last, Lilia removes the silk scarf from the statue of Sir Ralph, and they make their way homeward.

III

It may reasonably be objected that in this discussion I have been too little concerned with *The Princess* as a poem, and too much with its intellectual content and its place in the history of ideas. If this charge has any validity, I can only reply that what is happening in the central part of the poem is a debate, in no matter how extravagant and oblique a form; and if we are not to read it as a mere extravaganza (and to do so would, I think, make *The Princess* a remarkably thin and boring work), then it is as well to have some concept of what the debate is about, and how the ideas, in whatever disguised or distorted form, work in the poem.

Considered as verse, *The Princess*, apart from a few of the songs, seems to me to refine on without strikingly developing the techniques of the 1842 *Poems*; and considered as a structure, it is open to all the faults of inconsistencies of tone, and shifts of direction, to which the poet disarmingly draws attention (and hopes to justify) in the passage which I have already quoted. If we are to read *The Princess* with any hope of grasping its essential qualities, then we have to read it in a deliberately *ad hoc* fashion, just as we do with that celebrated later 'medley', *The Waste Land*. If there are faults, they are to be found in the excessive *longueurs* of some of the discursive narrative passages; and, more interestingly, in Tennyson's failure adequately to characterise the Princess herself. A comparison with Spenser's Britomart will make the nature of this failure clear: there is simply too little of the militant female in Ida's make-up; one can imagine her striking heroic gestures in a piece of Victorian allegorical statuary, but not plunging into a fight with the genuine relish of a Bradamante or Britomart. In this respect, Tennyson is part of his age; notoriously, with the exception of Becky Sharp (and she is not officially a heroine), the girls in Victorian fiction seem very lacking when compared with the vivacious heroines of Shakespeare's comedies: for whatever reason, the Victorian consciousness had difficulty in imagining women who possessed other than a narrow range of feminine qualities, and a reluctance to attribute sexual awareness to women clearly contributed to this difficulty. Beyond this, we can say the Victorian ideal of the feminine, as illustrated in Pre-Raphaelite painting as well as in fiction, was too much fixated on a frail version of the *Ewig-Weibliche*, the passive, yielding, tender, feminine image, and was too little aware of the militant aspects of femininity. *The Princess*, though it undoubtedly suffers because of this fixation, may be regarded at the same time as an attempt to redress its deficiencies.

1969

2 *Fin de Siècle*

Towards the end of the nineteenth century many writers felt
that literature and art had moved into a new phase, and that
even though Queen Victoria continued to be very much
alive, the Victorian era was already passing away. Although
there was, and is, agreement that the change took place,
critics remain divided about the best way of describing this
phase of cultural history, and about the point in time when it
began to emerge. To talk simply of the 'nineties' is tempting: the period was indeed remarkably compact, with a very
characteristic literary flavour, and its mythology has survived
for over seventy years. The 'nineties', whether qualified as
'naughty' or 'mauve' or 'yellow', can still exert a striking
appeal, as is evident in the recent vogue for Beardsley prints
and *art nouveau* decoration. And yet to refer to a single decade in this way can be misleading, since many of the essential attitudes of the nineties had their roots in the eighties or
even the seventies; specifically, the Aesthetic Movement,
which is sometimes referred to as though it were synonymous
with the innovations of the nineties, was essentially a manifestation of the previous decade; as early as 1881 Oscar Wilde
was caricatured in the Gilbert and Sullivan opera, *Patience*.
The word 'Decadence' has a broader application, but suffers
from its ambiguity; some of the time it suggests a combination of physical lassitude and psychological and moral perversity – as exemplified for instance in J.-K. Huysman's novel,
A Rebours, which was much admired in the nineties – although more properly it should refer only to language.
Arthur Symons wrote in the Introduction to *The Symbolist
Movement in Literature* (1899): 'the term is in its place only
when applied to style; to that ingenious deformation of the
language, in Mallarmé, for instance, which can be compared
with what we are accustomed to call the Greek and Latin of

the Decadence.' A few years before, Symons had been happy to use 'decadence' in the broader and looser sense, as in his poem, 'Intermezzo', which describes the dancer 'Nini Patte-en-l'Air' as the 'Maenad of the Decadence'.

I have decided in this essay to use the phrase *fin de siècle*, which clearly points to the preoccupations of the last years of the nineteenth century, without being limited to a single decade, and which can cover such particular manifestations as 'aestheticism' and 'decadence'. From the early nineties onward, *fin de siècle* was something of a catch-phrase; there is a characteristic instance in Wilde's *The Picture of Dorian Gray*, published in 1891:

> '*Fin de siècle*,' murmured Lord Henry.
> '*Fin du globe*,' answered his hostess.
> 'I wish it were *fin du globe*,' said Dorian with a sigh.
> 'Life is a great disappointment.' (chapter xv)

In the poem just referred to, Symons attributes to Nini Patte-en-l'Air

> The art of knowing how to be
> Part lewd, aesthetical in part
> And *fin-de-siècle* essentially.

Holbrook Jackson quotes various other entertaining instances of the phrase in his book, *The Eighteen Nineties* (first published in 1913 and still an indispensable guide to the period). It occurs most portentously in Max Nordau's *Degeneration*, of which the English translation appeared in 1895; writing with ponderous, pseudo-scientific assurance, Nordau uses the phrase *fin de siècle* to define and dismiss practically everything that was significant in late nineteenth-century art and literature: Wagner, Ibsen, Zola, the French symbolists, were all seen as symptomatic of a prevalent mental and physical degeneration. The English translation of *Degeneration* was something of a *succès de scandale*; it ran through several impressions in 1895, no doubt because it coincided with the trials of Oscar Wilde, but was quickly forgotten. Bernard Shaw attacked the book at length in *The Sanity of Art*.

The phrase *fin de siècle* was applied to a wide range of
trivial behaviour, provided it was sufficiently perverse or
paradoxical or shocking. Yet in so far as *fin de siècle* refers to
a serious and consistent cultural attitude, it has two essential
characteristics: the conviction that all established forms of
intellectual and moral and social certainty were vanishing,
and that the new situation required new attitudes in life and
art; and the related belief that art and morality were separate
realms, and that the former must be regarded as wholly
autonomous; hence, the aesthetic doctrine of 'art for art's
sake'. As I have remarked, it is difficult to define the point at
which these attitudes begin clearly to emerge. If the *fin de
siècle* represented a break with established Victorian attitudes, then the break was not particularly clean: in a literary
sense there are lines of development that link the *fin de siècle*
poets with the major Romantics; with Blake, with Coleridge
and with Keats. Arthur Hallam's review of Tennyson's early
poems – whose influence was acknowledged by Yeats – was an
important intermediary: Hallam praised a poetry of pure
images, without any admixture of rhetoric, in a thoroughly
proto-symbolist fashion. One writer has attempted to pin
down the emergence of the doctrine of aestheticism:

The actual doctrine appears first in Swinburne's review of
Baudelaire's *Fleurs du Mal* in the *Spectator* for September
6th, 1862 (reprinted in Swinburne's *Works*, volume XIII,
p. 419) and in Pater's essay on Winckelmann, which was
published in the *Westminster Gazette* in 1867. Swinburne's
William Blake (1868) gave prominence to the phrase 'art
for art's sake' and five years later the phrase was embodied
in the provocatively enigmatic conclusion to Pater's *Renaissance*.[1]

The mention of Walter Pater takes us clearly within the
ambience of the *fin de siècle*. For over thirty years Pater was
one of the most influential of English writers, both for his
manner of writing and for what was supposed to be his essential message. Oscar Wilde, in *De Profundis*, refers to reading
Pater's *The Renaissance* (originally entitled, in the first
edition of 1873, *Studies in the History of the Renaissance*) in

his first term at Oxford, calling it 'that book which has had such a strange influence over my life'. Arthur Symons, in a memorial essay written after Pater's death, said that *The Renaissance* 'even with the rest of Pater to choose from, seems to me sometimes the most beautiful book of prose in our literature'. James Joyce, in many passages in his early books, *Dubliners* and *A Portrait of the Artist as a Young Man,* reveals a consciousness that has been saturated in Pater's prose. W. B. Yeats, looking back in the 1920s to his companions of the nineties, wrote:

> If Rossetti was a subconscious influence, and perhaps the most powerful of all, we looked consciously to Pater for our philosophy. Three or four years ago I re-read *Marius the Epicurean*, expecting to find I cared for it no longer, but it still seemed to me, as I think it seemed to us all, the only great prose in modern English. . . .[2]

Such valuations are hard for the present-day reader to accept, since he is accustomed to a prose that is expressive rather than musical, and he is likely to echo Max Beerbohm's complaint about Pater, with its illustrative parody.

> I was angry that he should treat English as a dead language, bored by that sedulous ritual wherewith he laid out every sentence as in a shroud – hanging like a widower, long over its marmoreal beauty or ever he could lay it at length in his book, its sepulchre.[3]

Beerbohm's point is well taken, and yet it is in a sense unfair to Pater; his prose makes its effects cumulatively, and its appeal can grow with familiarity; one also becomes aware of a curious counterpointing between Pater's elaborately cadenced, ritualistic prose, and his sceptical, relativistic, even iconoclastic intelligence. G. S. Fraser has recently published an instructive article on the method of Pater's prose.[4]

From an art-historical point of view, *The Renaissance* is an important work, since Pater was one of the first English writers to deal in an analytical and historically conscious

fashion with some of the major artists of the Italian Renaissance, thus anticipating the later, more systematic research of
Berenson and other scholars. At the same time Pater ranges
widely, in a way that illustrates the cultural time-travelling
and eclecticism that typified the Aesthetic Movement of the
seventies and eighties. At one end of the scale he writes about
two thirteenth-century French stories, and at the other he dis-
cusses the eighteenth-century German antiquarian, Johann
Winckelmann. The most famous lines in *The Renaissance* –
indeed, in all Pater's work – form the celebrated purple passage about the Mona Lisa, which Yeats rather perversely
arranged in *vers libre* to print as the first exhibit in the
Oxford Book of Modern Verse. It is unfortunate that this
passage has come to be regarded merely as a virtuoso stylistic
exercise; it occurs as the climax of Pater's essay on Leonardo,
and is carefully led up to and prepared for by the developing
strategy of the essay. Furthermore, what Pater says about the
Mona Lisa is at least as important as the way he says it. For
him she is a symbol of the modern consciousness that is burdened by a multiplicity of knowledge and experience; she is an
embodiment of the timeless frequenting of many cultures
that modern historical knowledge has made possible; she
anticipates *The Waste Land* and the *Musée Imaginaire*:

She is older than the rocks among which she sits; like the
vampire, she has been dead many times, and learned the
secrets of the grave; and has been a diver in deep seas, and
keeps their fallen day about her; and trafficked for strange
webs with Eastern merchants: and, as Leda, was the
mother of Helen of Troy, and, as Saint Anne, the mother
of Mary; and all this has been to her but as the sound of
lyres and flutes, and lives only in the delicacy with which it
has moulded the changing lineaments, and tinged the eye-
lids and the hands. The fancy of a perpetual life, sweeping
together ten thousand experiences is an old one; and
modern philosophy has conceived the idea of humanity as
wrought upon by, and summing up in itself, all modes of
thought and life. Certainly Lady Lisa might stand as the
embodiment of the old fancy, the symbol of the modern
idea.

In the almost equally celebrated 'Conclusion' to *The Renaissance*, Pater continues to stress the 'modern idea': 'to regard all things and principles of things as inconstant modes or fashions has more and more become the tendency of modern thought'. Here we see the authentically *fin de siècle* note. As a historical relativist, Pater was sceptical about the possibility of ultimate values and truths; human life was fleeting and uncertain, and instead of pursuing abstractions, man should constantly strive to refine and purify his sensations and impressions:

Every moment some form grows perfect in hand or face; some tone on the hills or the sea is choicer than the rest; some mood of passion or insight or intellectual excitement is irresistibly real and attractive to us, – for that moment only. Not the fruit of experience, but experience itself, is the end. A counted number of pulses only is given to us of a variegated, dramatic life. How may we see in them all that is to be seen in them by the finest senses? How shall we pass most swiftly from point to point, and be present always at the focus where the greatest number of vital forces unite in their purest energy?

To burn always with this hard, gemlike flame, to maintain this ecstasy is success in life. In a sense it might even be said that our failure is to form habits: for, after all, habit is relative to a stereotyped world, and meantime it is only the roughness of the eye that makes any two persons, things, situations, seem alike. While all melts under our feet, we may well grasp at any exquisite passion, or any contribution to knowledge that seems by a lifted horizon to set the spirit free for a moment, or any stirring of the senses, strange dyes, strange colours, and curious odours, or work of the artist's hands, or the face of one's friend. Not to discriminate every moment some passionate attitude in those about us, and in the very brilliancy of their gifts some tragic dividing of forces on their ways is, on this short day of frost and sun, to sleep before evening.

The traditional *carpe diem* theme is reinforced by a profound, modern scepticism which rejects any 'theory or idea or system which requires of us the sacrifice of any part of this experience'. The moral antinomianism that Pater's 'Conclusion' seemed to be advancing was found deeply subversive; and Pater, who in his personal life was an orderly, withdrawn, somewhat timid scholar, removed it from the second edition of *The Renaissance*: 'As I conceived it might possibly mislead some of those young men into whose hands it might fall.' He finally restored the 'Conclusion', slightly modified, to the third edition of his book, with the added comment: 'I have dealt more fully in *Marius the Epicurean* with the thoughts suggested by it.'

Marius the Epicurean, published in 1885, is nominally a novel, but Pater's talents for fiction were limited, and there is little sense of character or dramatic interplay in *Marius*. The central figure is a Roman gentleman living in the second century A.D., a conscientious, rather solemn young man, who attempts to live according to the best principles of paganism, as outlined in the Epicurean philosophy. *Marius the Epicurean* is sub-titled 'His Sensations and Ideas', and although Marius' attitude to life is continuous with that presented in the 'Conclusion' to *The Renaissance*, his Epicureanism is a very high-minded affair, far removed from mere sensuous hedonism; Marius cultivates the pleasures of the mind and spirit rather than of the senses. But the insufficiency of Epicureanism weighs increasingly on Marius, and he is drawn to an enchanting community of early Christians. He is captivated by the beauty of their ritual, and the sweetness and light of their beliefs, and he dies in their care, without having been formally converted. Provided one does not expect the normal satisfactions of fiction from *Marius*, and gives oneself time to adapt to its infinitely leisurely cadences, *Marius* can be read as a work of a genuine if muted charm, where action is at a minimum, but where the reader is slowly borne along by the billowing movement of Pater's prose and caught up by degrees into Marius' unfolding consciousness. Although Pater endeavours to make the historical detail correct, it is evident that an earnest nineteenth-century inquirer lies beneath Marius' Roman exterior, and that the Roman Empire of the Antonines thinly conceals the late-Victorian British Empire. The book develops at length the historical superimpositions

B

hinted at in the description of the Mona Lisa.

Pater's major writings reveal another crucial element in the *fin de siècle* state of mind: the mistrust of theory and system, and the corresponding stress on sensation and impression, led in the nineties to a taste for the brief, concentrated lyric, and, in prose, for the short story. In the twentieth century the tendency became more systematic, in the 'images' and 'epiphanies' and other moments of fragmentary illumination in the literature of the Modern Movement. *Marius* had a more immediate effect in projecting the attractiveness of ritual as a way of life, independently of religious affiliation. Yeats remarked of it:

> I began to wonder if it, or the attitude of mind of which it was the noblest expression, had not caused the disaster of my friends. It taught us to walk upon a rope tightly stretched through serene air, and we were left to keep our feet upon a swaying rope in a storm.[5]

There was one writer who absorbed Pater's lesson not wisely but too well, who achieved a tragic celebrity with relatively slender talents, and whose name is still a veritable symbol for the whole *fin de siècle* period and state of mind. This, of course, is Oscar Wilde: he is difficult to place in literary history, since, as he admitted, he devoted his genius to his life rather than his art. Wilde survives as a figure of pure and fascinating mythology, where the works inevitably seem secondary to the legend of the man. The essential judgements were made, sharply but justly, soon after Wilde's death by Arthur Symons, who was the finest critic of his day:

> His intellect was dramatic, and the whole man was not so much a personality as an attitude. Without being a sage, he maintained the attitude of a sage; without being a poet, he maintained the attitude of a poet; without being an artist, he maintained the attitude of an artist, and it was precisely in his attitudes that he was most sincere.[6]

Admittedly, Wilde wrote copiously in verse and prose, but the more one reads through his collected works, the more one

is conscious of its largely derivative quality. Most of the verse
draws heavily on a variety of Victorian poets, while his most
famous piece of fiction, *The Picture of Dorian Gray*, though a
lively story, is a pale imitation of Huysmans's *A Rebours*. The
dialogues first published in Wilde's book, *Intentions*, 'The
Critic as Artist' and 'The Decay of Lying', offer a witty and
accessible source of ideas about art that were fundamental to
symbolist aesthetics, and which have been developed in the
literature and criticism of the twentieth century. Yet they are
all taken over from other critics: 'Reading *Intentions* one
finds here a bit of Arnold, here a patch of Pater or William
Morris, and, in this unlikely company, even Carlyle.'[7]

If one wishes to find what is most enduring in Wilde's
work, one is likely to turn to his comedies, *Lady Winder-
mere's Fan*, *A Woman of No Importance*, *An Ideal Husband*
and *The Importance of Being Earnest*, which were produced
betweeen 1892 and 1895. All are excellent pieces of theatre
and splendidly witty. Yet the first three tend to be melodramatic and contain a rather uneasy mixture of farce and
morality; *The Importance of Being Earnest* is Wilde's comic
masterpiece, and indeed one of the great comedies of the
English theatre. Its qualities have been well described by Ian
Gregor in an important article on Wilde's comedies;[8] he says
of this play: 'what he gives us is a completely realised idyll,
offering itself as something irrevocably *other* than life, not a
wish-fulfilment of life as it might be lived'. For the rest, some
of Wilde's shorter tales preserve their self-conscious charm;
and among the poems, 'The Ballad of Reading Gaol' stands
out as an impressive achievement, although it is over-long
and suffers from Wilde's tendency to turn the elements of
tragedy into a repetitive decoration. To quote Symons again:

In this poem, where a style formed on other lines seems
startled at finding itself used for such new purposes, we see
a great spectacular intellect, to which, at last, pity and
terror have come in their own person, and no longer as
puppets in a play.[9]

Symons himself was one of the most interesting figures of
the *fin de siècle* period. He was born in 1865 and emerged in

the eighties as a self-taught but learned young literary man, who was widely read in several languages. In addition to his distinction as a critic, he was a prolific minor poet, a translator, an essayist on all forms of art and an entrepreneur of foreign literary influences. In this last respect Symons was of crucial importance, notably as the author of *The Symbolist Movement in Literature* (1899), a book which discussed the work of such French poets as Rimbaud, Verlaine, Laforgue and Mallarmé. This book had a decisive influence on the development of twentieth-century poetry in English. It was dedicated to Yeats, who became a close friend of Symons in the nineties; Symons, who was very much at home in Paris literary circles, introduced Yeats to Mallarmé and other French symbolists, and to their work, thereby expanding and reinforcing Yeats's existing interest in poetic symbolism, which he had developed from his reading of Blake and his dabblings in magic and the occult. Yeats himself influenced Symons away from mere 'decadence' as a literary concept, towards a quasi-occult understanding of symbolism, reinforced with a Paterian sense of ritual; in the introduction to *The Symbolist Movement*, Symons wrote that literature 'becomes itself a kind of religion, with all the duties and responsibilities of the sacred ritual'. A few years later T. S. Eliot, as an undergraduate at Harvard, was to find Symons's book extremely fruitful:

> I myself owe Mr Symons a great debt. But for having read his book I should not, in the year 1908, have heard of Laforgue and Rimbaud; I should probably not have begun to read Verlaine, and but for reading Verlaine, I should not have heard of Corbière. So the Symons book is one of those which have affected the course of my life.[10]

Yeats and Symons were associated in a group of poets calling themselves the Rhymers' Club that met during the nineties; in Yeats's words, the Club 'for some years was to meet every night in an upper room with a sanded floor in an ancient eating-house in Fleet Street called the Cheshire Cheese'. The Rhymers, as their name denoted, aimed at the unpretentious pursuit of pure song, purged of Victorian rhetoric or moralising, and their habit of meeting regularly in such surroundings was an attempt to combine French literary café life with Johnsonian conviviality. These poets were later to be mythologised by Yeats as the 'tragic generation': two of the Rhymers, Ernest Dowson and Lionel Johnson, were to die in their thirties, and another, John Davidson, committed suicide in 1909 at the age of forty-three. Symons, although he lived to be nearly eighty, was afflicted by madness in his later years. The Rhymers did not have the temper of literary revolutionaries, but they aimed to break with the recent past in a way that has been memorably described by Yeats:

> The revolt against Victorianism meant to the young poet a revolt against irrelevant descriptions of nature, the scientific and moral discursiveness of *In Memoriam* – 'When he should have been broken-hearted,' said Verlaine, 'he had many reminiscences' – the political eloquence of Swinburne, the psychological curiosity of Browning, and the poetical diction of everybody. Poets said to one another over their black coffee – a recently imported fashion – 'We must purify poetry of all that is not poetry', and by poetry they meant poetry as it had been written by Catullus, a great name at that time, by the Jacobean writers, by Verlaine, by Baudelaire. Poetry was a tradition like religion and liable to corruption, and it seemed that they could best restore it by writing lyrics technically perfect, their emotion pitched high, and as Pater offered instead of moral earnestness life lived as 'a pure gem-like flame' all accepted him for master.[11]

As I have remarked, the brief concentrated lyric could serve as the literary crystallisation of a Paterian sensation; the most obvious stylistic influences at work in such poetry were the Elizabethan lyric and the short poems of Verlaine. Even now, so long after they wrote, it is not easy to get the poets of the nineties in critical focus. It is tempting to mythologise them as men, as Yeats did, and to regard their verses as infinitely poignant human records; alternatively, one can dismiss them as *poseurs* of patently limited talent, whose literary achievement is minuscule, when it is not wholly unnotice-able. Looked at as objectively as possible, the poets of the nineties do have certain definable qualities in their favour. They were at their best extremely skilful craftsmen, who could bring off subtle and striking rhythmic effects, and who were surprisingly successful in importing a Verlainian music into their poems. And by following the example of Baude-laire they were able to enlarge the subject-matter of poetry, even though Baudelaire was systematically misunderstood in the nineties as a romantically decadent celebrant of 'sin' rather than as the tormented Catholic moralist that he was later to appear to T. S. Eliot. At all events, the sensibility of the nineties was inclined to write about prostitutes, or other sources of casual amour: 'the chance romances of the streets, the Juliet of a night', in Symons's words. However much the poets may have romanticised these matters, by touching on them at all they were acknowledging an element in the social reality of Victorian London that had not, so far, received much literary recognition. Despite the narrowness of their poetic means, poets such as Dowson and Symons broadened the spectrum of poetic material in a way that anticipates Eliot, and which shows the influence not merely of French poetry, but of French fiction. Where they were weakest was in the resources of their diction. Dowson's well-worn (and hard-wearing) anthology favourite, 'Non sum qualis eram bonae sub regno Cynarae', illustrates these considerations:

> Last night, ah, yesternight, betwixt her lips and mine
> There fell thy shadow, Cynara! thy breath was shed
> Upon my soul between the kisses and the wine;
> And I was desolate and sick of an old passion,
>   Yea, I was desolate and bowed my head:
> I have been faithful to thee, Cynara! in my fashion.

> All night upon mine heart I felt her warm heart beat,
> Night-long within mine arms in love and sleep she lay;
> Surely the kisses of her bought red mouth were sweet;
> But I was desolate and sick of an old passion,
>   When I awoke and found the dawn was gray:
> I have been faithful to thee, Cynara! in my fashion . . .

It is evident that Dowson's Swinburnian or Pre-Raphaelite diction is strained to breaking-point in his attempt to convey a novelistic complexity of the erotic life. But I would argue that the poem's achievement is that it can take the strain: Dowson's intentions are reinforced by a remarkable verbal energy that underlies the seemingly debilitated surface of the poem, and by his virtuoso manipulation of rhythm.

Symons treats of a similar theme, more succinctly and equally musically, in 'Leves Amores II', a poem which conveys an intensely 'realistic' experience with all the immediacy demanded by twentieth-century poetics:

> The little bedroom papered red,
> The gas's faint malodorous light,
> And one beside me in the bed,
> Who chatters, chatters, half the night.
>
> I drowse and listen, drowse again,
> And still, although I would not hear,
> Her stream of chatter, like the rain,
> Is falling, falling on my ear.
>
> The bed-clothes stifle me, I ache,
> With weariness, my eyelids prick;
> I hate, until I long to break,
> That clock for its tyrannic tick.

Symons was an intensely visual poet, who often anticipates the effects demanded by the Imagists of *c.* 1912; as, for instance, in 'At Dieppe: After Sunset', written in 1890:

> The sea lies quieted beneath
> The after-sunset flush
> That leaves upon the heaped grey clouds
> The grape's faint purple blush.
>
> Pale, from a little space in heaven
> Of delicate ivory,
> The sickle-moon and one gold star
> Look down upon the sea.

Symons was a passionate frequenter of the music-halls of London and Paris, and he constantly celebrates them in his verse. His interest in ballet-girls was not merely amorous; he was a great exponent of the *fin de siècle* interest in the dance as a momentary fusion of art and ritual, a pure expressive image lifted out of discourse and the flux of everyday life. This topic has been discussed by Frank Kermode in *Romantic Image* and pursued in detail in 'Poet and Dancer before Diaghilev', an essay which combines theatrical and literary history (included in Kermode's *Puzzles and Epiphanies*, 1962).

Another of the Rhymers, Lionel Johnson, has left an unflattering comment both on Symons's proto-Imagist methods and his propensity for sordid subjects:

> [Symons] is a slave to impressionism, whether the impression be precious or not. A London fog, the blurred, tawny lamplights, the red omnibus, the dreary rain, the depressing mud, the glaring gin-shop, the slatternly shivering women: three dexterous stanzas telling you that and nothing more. And in nearly every poem, one line or phrase of absolutely pure and fine imagination. If he would wash and be clean, he might be of the elect.[12]

Johnson was a poet of more austere temperament than Dowson or Symons; his indulgence was alcohol rather than harlots. Like his contemporaries Johnson was a disciple of Pater, but he followed the implications of *Marius the Epicurean* to their logical conclusion and joined the Roman Catholic Church. Catholicism was very much in the air in the nineties: Dowson also became a Catholic, of an intensely aesthetic, wistful kind, though he does not seem to have shared Johnson's attachment to reading the Fathers of the Church and otherwise speculating on doctrinal niceties (graphically described by Yeats in the *Autobiographies*). Aubrey Beardsley was converted to Catholicism towards the end of his short life, and Oscar Wilde became a Catholic on his death-bed. Another convert was the poet John Gray, not one of the Rhymers, who was a close friend of Wilde and who was falsely alleged to be the original of Dorian Gray: he in-

terestingly broke the *fin de siècle* pattern of the 'tragic
generation' by becoming a priest and not dying young. Gray
ended his days in 1934 at the age of sixty-eight as a well-loved
parish priest in Edinburgh. The temper of this aesthetic
Catholicism is well illustrated in two poems on the same
theme by Dowson and Johnson, which also serve to contrast
the temperaments of the two poets:

'Benedictio Domini'

Without, the sullen noises of the street!
   The voice of London, inarticulate,
Hoarse and blaspheming, surges in to meet
   The silent blessing of the Immaculate.

Dark is the church, and dim the worshippers,
   Hushed with bowed heads as though by some old
     spell.
While through the incense-laden air there stirs
   The admonition of a silver bell.

Dark is the church, save where the altar stands,
   Dressed like a bride, illustrious with light,
Where one old priest exalts with tremulous hands
   The one true solace of man's fallen plight.

Strange silence here: without, the sounding street
   Heralds the world's swift passage to the fire:
O Benediction, perfect and complete!
   When shall men cease to suffer and desire?
                        Dowson

'The Church of a Dream'

Sadly the dead leaves rustle in the whistling wind,
Around the weather-worn, gray church, low down the
   vale:
The Saints in golden vesture shake before the gale;
The glorious windows shake, where still they dwell en-
   shrined;

Old Saints by long dead, shrivelled hands, long since de-
  signed:
There still, although the world autumnal be, and pale,
Still in their golden vesture the old saints prevail;
Along with Christ, desolate else, left by mankind.

Only one ancient Priest offers the Sacrifice,
Murmuring holy Latin immemorial:
Swaying with tremulous hands the old censer full of
  spice,
In gray, sweet incense clouds; blue, sweet clouds mysti-
  cal:
To him, in place of men, for he is old, suffice
Melancholy remembrances and vesperal.

Johnson

Both poems convey a Paterian feeling for liturgy, but where
Dowson is fervid and aspiring, Johnson is cold and melancholy. Johnson was, if anything, a more accomplished verbal
artist than Dowson or Symons, but compared with theirs, his
poetry, which dwells on religious topics or fragments of Celtic
legend (although born a Welshman, Johnson transformed
himself into an honorary but patriotic Irishman), is somewhat
stiff and lacking in human interest. He is seen at his best in
such accomplished anthology pieces as 'By the Statue of King
Charles at Charing Cross' and 'The Dark Angel'.
   In attacking Symons for his taste for low urban subjects,
Johnson was drawing attention to another poetic preoccupation of the *fin de siècle*: if a tormented eroticism was one way
of extending the range of poetry, a fascination with the
multifarious life of the modern city was another. London was
not, of course, a completely untouched poetic subject;
Tennyson momentarily caught the anomic quality of urban
life in a superb image in *In Memoriam*:

He is not here; but far away
  The noise of life begins again,
  And ghastly thro' the drizzling rain
On the bald street breaks the blank day.

Wordsworth treated London positively in 'Sonnet Written on Westminster Bridge' and negatively in the middle books of the *Prelude*; and there are dark visions of London life in Blake and the Augustan satirists. Yet the great exemplar for the *fin de siècle* poets was Baudelaire, whose poems about Paris had shown the intense but sombre poetic possibilities of the huge modern metropolis. A more romantic source of urban imagery was Whistler and other painters; Wilde wrote in 'The Decay of Lying':

Where, if not from the Impressionists, do we get those wonderful brown fogs that come creeping down our streets, blurring the gas-lamps and changing the houses into monstrous shadows? To whom, if not to them and their master, do we owe the lovely silver mists that brood over our river, and turn to faint forms of fading grace curved bridge and swaying barge?[13]

He had already shown a similar response in his poem, 'Impression du Matin', published in 1881:

The Thames nocturne of blue and gold
  Changed to a Harmony in grey:
  A barge with ochre-coloured hay
Dropt from the wharf: and chill and cold

The yellow fog came creeping down
  The bridges, till the houses' walls
  Seemed changed to shadows and St Paul's
Loomed like a bubble o'er the town.

Among the Rhymers there were similarly romantic treatments of the urban scene; Richard Le Gallienne's 'A Ballad of London' indulges in the characteristic *fin de siècle* preference for the artificial over the natural:

Ah, London! London! our delight,
Great flower that opens but at night,
Great City of the midnight sun,
Whose day begins when day is done.

> Lamp after lamp against the sky
> Opens a sudden beaming eye,
> Leaping alight on either hand
> The iron lilies of the Strand . . .

Symons wrote copiously about London – his third book of
poems, published in 1894, is appropriately called *London
Nights* – and his treatment ranges between the romantic and
the intensely realistic; he is usually most effective when he is
most purely descriptive:

> The grey and misty night,
> Slim trees that hold the night among
> Their branches, and, along
> The vague Embankment, light on light.

One of the most striking of the poets associated with the
Rhymers was John Davidson, a melancholy Scotsman of
philosophical inclinations – he was one of the first people in
England to be interested in Nietzsche – whose treatment of
urban themes was realistic to the point of grimness. Perhaps
Davidson's best-known poem is 'Thirty Bob a Week', the
monologue of an impoverished clerk hopelessly struggling to
keep up appearances and make ends meet:

> For like a mole I journey in the dark,
>   A-travelling along the underground
> From my Pillar'd Halls and broad Suburbean Park,
>   To come the daily dull official round;
> And home again at night with my pipe all alight,
>   A-scheming how to count ten bob a pound.

T. S. Eliot wrote interestingly about his admiration for this
poem:

> I am sure that I found inspiration in the content of the
> poem, and in the complete fitness of content and idiom:
> for I also had a good many dingy urban images to reveal.
> Davidson had a great theme, and also found an idiom

which elicited the greatness of the theme, which endowed
this thirty-bob-a-week clerk with a dignity that would not
have appeared if a more conventional poetic diction had
been employed. The personage that Davidson created in
this poem has haunted me all my life, and the poem is to
me a great poem for ever.[14]

Davidson coldly appraised the newer aspects of the spreading
metropolis in 'A Northern Suburb':

> In gaudy yellow brick and red,
>   With rooting pipes, like creepers rank,
> The shoddy terraces o'erspread
>   Meadow, and garth, and daisied bank.
>
> With shelves for rooms the houses crowd,
>   Like draughty cupboards in a row –
> Ice-chests when wintry winds are loud,
>   Ovens when summer breezes blow.

In such poems as these Davidson suggests a poetic equivalent
to the fiction of George Gissing. In a late poem, written not
long before he died, Davidson turned to the fairly well-worn
subject of the Thames and treated it in a way that is both
realistic and richly textured:

> As gray and dank as dust and ashes slaked
> With wash of urban tides the morning lowered;
> But over Chelsea Bridge the sagging sky
> Had colour in it – blots of faintest bronze,
> The stains of daybreak. Westward slabs of light
> From vapour disentangled, sparsely glazed
> The panelled firmament; but vapour held
> The morning captive in the smoky east.
> At lowest ebb the tide on either bank
> Laid bare the fat mud of the Thames, all pinched
> And scalloped thick with dwarfish surges. Cranes,
> Derricks and chimney-stalks of the Surrey-side,
> Inverted shadows, in the motionless,
> Dull, leaden mirror of the channel hung.

The poets associated with the Rhymers were not the only ones who expressed a *fine de siècle* sensibility. I have already referred to John Gray, the author of *Silverpoints* (1893), a slender volume designed with infinite preciousness by the artist Charles Ricketts; Gray's poetry was of a matching preciousness – Lionel Johnson dismissed him as a 'sometimes beautiful oddity' – although some of it has a curious distinction; like Symons, Gray was very familiar with the French symbolists, and translated some of their verse, usually in a more restrained and laconic fashion than Symons.[15] Another Catholic, Francis Thompson, continues to be well-known, at least on the strength of his 'Hound of Heaven': Yeats remarked of him in relation to the Rhymers, 'Francis Thompson came once but never joined'. Thompson's life of indignity and suffering makes him a signal embodiment of the late nineteenth-century myth of the *poète maudit*, and his Catholicism was more existential and less Paterian or aesthetic than that of his contemporaries. In literary respects, too, his perspective was somewhat different from theirs; his models were the Metaphysicals, particularly Crashaw, and Shelley, whom he saw, curiously as fulfilling their promise. The influence of these poets is evident in 'The Hound of Heaven', which remains a vigorous if over-forceful record of spiritual adventure. In 'In No Strange Land' Thompson writes more calmly of mystical experience:

> O world invisible, we view thee,
> O world intangible, we touch thee,
> O world unknowable, we know thee,
> Inapprehensible, we clutch thee!

> Does the fish soar to find the ocean,
> The eagle plunge to find the air –
> That we ask of the stars in motion
> If they have rumour of thee there?

Another poet chiefly remembered as the author of a famous anthology piece is W. H. Henley; the poem is, of course, 'Invictus':

Out of the night that covers me,
  Black as the Pit from pole to pole,
I thank whatever gods may be
For my unconquerable soul.

The rhetoric now seems a little stagey and unconvincing, though the poem's defiant spirit reflects Henley's own lifelong struggle against physical disability. His most interesting work is the early sequence of poems called 'In Hospital', which dates from the 1870s; its exact descriptive realism gives it a surprisingly modern flavour. Henley also experimented with *vers libre*, and in his 'London Voluntaries' he treated a familiar topic, although in a more rhapsodic spirit than most of the Rhymers would have thought appropriate. Although his verse reflected something of the *fin de siècle*, in his role as publicist, critic and editor Henley was decidedly out of sympathy with anything that smacked of aestheticism or decadence. He favoured a robust, extravert attitude in literary matters, and in politics he was a vehement imperialist. Henley was a friend of R. L. Stevenson, with whom he collaborated in several works, and as editor of the *Scots Observer*, the *National Observer* and the *New Review* he sponsored such new arrivals on the literary scene as Kipling and Wells. The nineties was a great period for literary magazines: the *Yellow Book*, which ran from 1894 to 1897, is generally regarded as the quintessential expression of the *fin de siècle* spirit, although this was only true, if at all, of the first four numbers, of which Aubrey Beardsley was art editor; after the débâcle of Wilde in 1894, Beardsley was removed from his post, and the *Yellow Book*, although unchanged in appearance, became a sober middle-of-the-road publication. The spirit of the nineties was better captured in the *Savoy*, which was edited by Arthur Symons, and although it ran for only a few months during 1896, it was described by Holbrook Jackson as 'the most ambitious and, if not the most comprehensive, the most satisfying achievement of *fin de siècle* journalism in this country',[16] Beardsley's drawings were prominent in the *Savoy*, which also published one of his occasional ventures into literature, the consciously decadent romance, *Under the Hill*. A prominent contributor to the early *Yellow Book* was Max Beerbohm; his love of witty paradox and his preference for the artificial as against the natural – his essay, 'The Pervasion of Rouge', is characteristic – made him thoroughly *fin de siècle*, but he always wrote in a spirit of ironical, mocking detachment, and his essays have lasted better than the work of his more fervid contemporaries. The wealth of literary periodicals in the nineties meant that the short story as a literary form was encouraged, and excellent work was done in this medium by Kipling and Wells and James. Closer to the *fin de siècle* spirit were English disciples of Maupassant like Hubert Crackanthorpe and Ella D'Arcy.

Considered as a literary period the 1890s was rich and various, and much of its best work was written outside the ambience of the *fin de siècle* mood. A comprehensive survey of the period would certainly acknowledge, for instance, in poetry, Kipling's *Barrack-room Ballads*, Housman's *A Shropshire Lad* and Alice Meynell's *Poems*, as well as the poets I have discussed. In fiction, the major achievements of the nineties include Gissing's *New Grub Street*, Stevenson's *Weir of Hermiston*, George Moore's *Esther Waters*, James's *Spoils of Poynton* and *The Awkward Age*, and Hardy's *Tess of the D'Urbervilles* and *Jude the Obscure*. The last-named of these does, in fact, embody a good deal of the *fin de siècle* state of mind, notably in the presentation of the neurasthenic 'new woman', Sue Bridehead, and in the grotesque child, 'Father Time'. H. G. Wells's *The Time Machine* is a highly distinguished piece of fiction which, as I have argued elsewhere,[17] is pervaded by *fin de siècle* feelings, little as one would normally associate them with Wells. And the picture would need to be completed by some consideration of Shaw's achievement in *Plays: Pleasant and Unpleasant*.

Yet to concentrate on what I have tried to isolate, however imperfectly, as the *fin de siècle* mentality is to stress what from Pater onward was known as the 'modern', and to emphasise those elements in late nineteenth-century literary theory and practice that were to be picked up by the Modern Movement in the early twentieth. In one sense the activity exemplified by the Rhymers did not last beyond the end of the century. As Yeats put it:

Then in 1900 everybody got down off his stilts; henceforth
nobody drank absinthe with his black coffee; nobody went
mad; nobody committed suicide; nobody joined the Catholic church; or if they did I have forgotten.[18]

(Yeats, in his habitual mythologising, *had* forgotten: Symons
went mad and Davidson committed suicide.) And yet, in a
deeper sense, the continuities between Pater and Joyce, and
between Symons or Davidson and Eliot, are apparent. Yeats
himself, who has appeared in this essay as a commentator
rather than a creative participant, is the supreme example of
a great writer of our century who was nurtured in the nineties, and who transcended the *fin de siècle* spirit without
abandoning it.

1970

3 R.L.S.

When Robert Louis Stevenson died in Samoa at the age of forty-four, in 1894, Henry James wrote: 'He lighted up one whole side of the globe, and was in himself a whole province of one's imagination. We are smaller fry and meaner people without him.' The mutual regard of these two writers, which involved genuine literary admiration as well as personal friendship, may be surprising to the modern reader, who thinks of James as the great luminary of the 'serious' novel, while Stevenson is remembered, if at all, simply as a writer of superior children's books. And yet James was by no means alone in his veneration for Stevenson; there were many similar expressions of desolation at the news of his death, and a widespread opinion that a major literary talent had been prematurely extinguished. In the last few years there has been a slow but noticeable growth of interest in the 'minor' writers of the late nineteenth century, and it would be surprising if Stevenson, once so much admired, had not been selected for a fresh assessment. He is fortunate in having found so perceptive a critic as Mr Kiely to unfold his essential qualities, and to make a case for the mature Stevenson as a serious novelist.*

One element in Stevenson's appeal was, undoubtedly, the irresistibly charming personality that filters through all his earlier writings, and particularly the essays and travel books. It constantly manifests itself in *From Scotland to Silverado*, a newly edited collection of three of Stevenson's travel books, *The Amateur Emigrant*, *Across the Plains* and *The Silverado Squatters* (which restores a substantial amount of material suppressed in earlier editions), together with some previously uncollected essays.† The book describes Stevenson's trip from

* *Robert Louis Stevenson and the Fiction of Adventure* by Robert Kiely.
† *From Scotland to Silverado* by Robert Louis Stevenson, edited by James D. Hart.

Glasgow to New York in 1879, which he made in an emigrant
ship, followed by a train journey across the United States to
California. In Monterey he was reunited with Fanny
Osbourne, with whom he had fallen in love in Europe, and
they were married in May 1880. The last section is about the
rugged but happy summer they spent living at the site of a
deserted silver mine in northern California. Stevenson's
charm is always present, ingratiating and at times a little too
insistently self-regarding: Mr Kiely rightly compares Stevenson's literary *persona* to a precocious and highly intelligent
schoolboy, very much aware of the impression he is creating.
Nevertheless, the touch of the born novelist is unmistakable
in his account of the voyage. Conditions were exceedingly
squalid, but the emigrants kept their spirits up and Stevenson
was a fascinated recorder of the odds and ends of drama and
human eccentricity that life at sea manifested. He is equally
vivid about the transcontinental rail journey, which was still
very much an adventure in those days and nearly as uncomfortable as the voyage across the Atlantic.

Yet, enjoyable though his travel writings are, it is, ultimately the novelist in Stevenson who most engages our interest – above all, the author of *The Master of Ballantrae* and
the unfinished *Weir of Hermiston*. The popular opinion
which, from a recollection of childhood reading, sees Stevenson primarily as the author of *Treasure Island* and *Kid-
napped* is not, of course, wrong. These books are works of
genius in their own kind, and remind us of Stevenson's profound and lifelong commitment to the fiction of adventure.
But he was at the same time an extremely conscious and conscientious artist, and it was this aspect of his craft that Henry
James so respected; Walter Allen has neatly remarked that
Stevenson 'successfully married Flaubert to Dumas'. One of
the most fascinating parts of Mr Kiely's book is the chapter in
which he outlines Stevenson's fictional aesthetic; in the
course of doing so he throws out hints that seem to me very
relevant to recent developments in the novel. Stevenson
combined a quasi-symbolist belief in the self-contained separateness of art, with the conviction that 'life' would always be
larger and more various than art, and that the novel could
never, as James had suggested, hope to compete with life:

'Life is monstrous, infinite, illogical, abrupt, and poignant; a work of art, in comparison, is neat, finite, self-contained, rational, flowing and emasculate.' At the same time, art could successfully improve on life by offering vivid images of possibilities that were unattainable in fact; in other words (disapprovingly modern words), by being frankly escapist. Stevenson also claimed, however, that adventure fiction achieves an ultimate universality by reproducing archetypal forms of action: 'Thus novels begin to touch not the fine dilettanti but the gross mass of mankind, when they leave off to speak of parlours . . . and begin to deal with fighting, sailoring, adventure, death or child-birth. . . . These aged things have on them the dew of man's morning. . . .' Stevenson is implying a view of fiction that is at odds, not only with James, but with virtually all later critics, apart, perhaps, from Chesterton and C. S. Lewis, both of whom were vehement defenders of fictional romance. Mr Kiely suggestively remarks that for Stevenson – who once wrote 'It is a better thing to travel hopefully than to arrive' – 'process becomes its own goal'. Here, and in Stevenson's conviction that the heroes of adventure stories should not be too fully realised since too much personality might affect our involvement with the action, we are close to the characteristic procedures of TV serials, magazine fiction or the comic strip. Certain tenuous but genuine lines of descent can be traced, since Stevenson leads directly to John Buchan, who points the way to the adventures of that deracinated Scotsman, James Bond. And with the current vogue of pop culture, which means that serious novels are adopting, by a kind of feedback effect, the techniques of the comic strip, Stevenson's principles of fiction might prove useful in taking bearings on works that the hallowed post-Jamesian categories can do nothing with. Mr Kiely is certainly aware of the revolutionary implication of the Stevensonian aesthetic of adventure, but is a little timid about making full critical use of it. If he praises *The Master of Ballantrae* and *Weir* it is because they offer more than simple adventure: a real depth and complexity of feeling, psychological interest and, for the first time in Stevenson's fiction, a mature sexual awareness.

If Mr Kiely doesn't follow up all the implications of his

treatment, he is, nevertheless, a highly professional critic, whose lucid and tactful performance is a model of how these things should be done. He has all the appropriate tools and knows how and when to use them; thus he will move easily from the analysis of imagery to the use of biographical material, and thence to, say, glancing at mythic patterns in the manner of Frye or Fiedler. Where he is, I think, a little weak is in not giving sufficient weight to Stevenson's Scottishness. The truth about Scotland is that it is not an inferior northern appendage to England, though the English often regard it as such, but a separate country, which is different from England in much more than landscape; its history, romantic, bloody and uniformly tragic, is more reminiscent of an East European nation. It was this exotic quality that Stevenson distilled so finely, particularly in the late novels that he wrote out of an imagination brooding on his native land from the other side of the globe; the rainy moorland and the grey stones of Edinburgh were never more real to him than in the sun of the South Seas.

Mr Kiely is right to play down Stevenson's obvious debt to Scott, but there are other antecedents he might have allowed for. He remarks:

> In *Jekyll and Hyde* ... Stevenson probes the Calvinist tradition of personified evil largely for Gothic effect. Much as he came to despise the moral rigidity of his religious heritage, he remained throughout his life enchanted by its atmosphere – the damp chapels and bleak kirkyards, the dour believers, the darkness and devilry.

This is undoubtedly true; but Mr Kiely does not tell us whether Stevenson knew, or was influenced by, that small masterpiece of Calvinist Gothic, James Hogg's *Confessions of a Justified Sinner*. The interest in evil and in duality that Stevenson gave famous expression to in *Jekyll and Hyde* is more fully and seriously developed in *The Master of Ballantrae*, which Henry James described as 'a pure hard crystal, my boy, a work of ineffable and exquisite art'. At the risk of descending into a parochial modernism, one must say that there are elements about it that are very much of our own times. The technique is of an assured sophistication, and involves us with that familiar topic in recent novel-criticism, the problem of the unreliable narrator. Our knowledge of the Master and his younger brother Henry is mostly derived from the narrative of the old servant Mackellar, and, as Mr Kiely puts it, his 'effort to describe Ballantrae is like an inadequate attempt to catalogue a new species'. In the relationship between the energetic and Satanic Master and his brother, dull and decent at first, but increasingly corrupted, we have an embodiment of the *Doppelgänger* theme that anticipates many of the characteristic concerns of twentieth-century literature. Mr Kiely's treatment of the novel is generally illuminating, but I think he makes a crucial misreading of it in one respect. He suggests that Ballantrae fits into a line of literary descent deriving from Milton's Satan, and including such nineteenth-century representatives as Manfred, Rochester and Heathcliff, whose vices are in large measure balanced by the positiveness of their energy. Mr Kiely is dismissive about Ballantrae's sins, implying that they consist in little more than drinking, wenching, flirting with his brother's wife, and constantly extorting money from him. But he misses the point that the blackest mark against the Master is that he is a traitor to the Jacobite cause; and treachery, for which Dante placed sinners in the lowest circle of Hell, is hardly to be regarded so lightly. It seems to me that in some ways Mr Kiely reduces *The Master of Ballantrae* by giving insufficient weight to the Master's absolute evil, which is something more than merely Gothic or melodramatic. If the pattern is a little less clear than Mr Kiely implies, then that is surely to Stevenson's advantage; this remarkable novel shows its author's long allegiance to the fiction of adventure, and is yet subtler, richer and harder to define. As Mr Kiely remarks, it shows a curious progress from the historical and epical to the individual until the two brothers, at the end of the novel, are buried in the same grave. With *Weir of Hermiston*, which is a fragment merely, we have moved entirely beyond adventure, and the wonderful, Rembrandtesque figure of the Justice-Clerk, Adam Weir, illustrates the power of realising character that Stevenson came to possess by the end of his life. 1967

4 *New Grub Street*

I

Most novels deal with leisure rather than with work, with the margins of life, where the human personality is free to expand and enter into interesting relationships, rather than with the quotidian toil which, for the greater part of humanity, both defines and limits existence. Even novels that are overtly about industrial life present the factory or the mine as a menacing shape in the background influencing the lives of the characters, but do not dwell for long on the actual industrial processes. This is natural, even inevitable; many forms of work – or at least the more mechanical forms that Hannah Arendt describes as 'labour' in distinction to 'work' – are basically dehumanising, and the novelist is bound to be interested in people when they are most fully and articulately human, even if, at the same time, they may be crushed by adversity. *New Grub Street* is one of the few exceptions, and this fact should, I think, be recognised initially, before one passes on to make the more familiar point that it is the most explicit fictional study of literary life ever written in English. Granted, the 'work' involved – the writing of novels – is, in the eyes of most people, at the furthest possible extreme from mere 'labour', and might even be considered so delightful and rewarding an activity as scarcely to deserve the name of work at all. Such an assumption is likely to be supported by those works of popular fiction where the 'novelist' who appears as a character is a glamorised tweedy figure, with infinite time at his disposal and subject to little apparent necessity to spend long hours at his desk or typewriter.

Gissing presents a very different picture, of a society where literature has become a commodity, and where the writing of fiction does not differ radically from any other form of commercial or industrial production: 'After all, there came a day when Edwin Reardon found himself regularly at work once more, ticking off his stipulated quantum of manuscript each four-and-twenty hours.' The splendid freedom of creativity has become, quite literally, a mechanical process. Gissing relentlessly involves the reader in Edwin Reardon's attempts to write as a professional whilst desperately preserving some vestige of literary integrity, culminating in the brutal forcing of his exhausted imagination as he tries to meet the demands of the three-volume novel convention. In one sense, *New Grub Street* is a remarkably self-contained book: a reader quite ignorant of Gissing's life and the literary climate of the 1880s will learn enough from the novel to be able both to enjoy the story and grasp its larger implications; indeed, *New Grub Street* is far more directly informative in a social-historical way than most Victorian novels, and contains a mass of material about such things as the cost of living among the shabby-genteel population of London in the eighties. And yet the reader who is fairly sure that Edwin Reardon is a direct autobiographical portrait of Gissing himself might still find it illuminating to learn, from Gissing's letters and other biographical sources, just how faithful the rendering is, and how exactly the mode of composition described in *New Grub Street* corresponded to Gissing's own practice. Thus, Edwin Reardon is shown as habitually writing about 4,000 words a day when engaged on a novel. Gissing himself wrote *New Grub Street* in exactly two months in the autumn of 1890, and since it is a book of over 220,000 words, a simple calculation shows that it must have been written at a daily rate not far short of Edwin Reardon's. The principal difference, however, between Gissing's work and that of his character is that whereas Reardon, who is not at heart a novelist at all, suffers disastrously from this cruel rate of composition and produces work of increasingly little merit, in *New Grub Street* Gissing drew on a unique source of strength in writing so immediately out of his personal predicament, and the result was a singular if not flawless masterpiece. In the words of Mrs Q. D. Leavis:

But when he took as the subject of a novel his most vital interest – the problem of how to live as a man of letters, the

literary world being what it is, without sacrificing your
integrity of purpose – he produced his one permanent contribution to the English novel. I think it can be shown to
be a major contribution. The subject was both inside and
outside him.[1]

When he began work on *New Grub Street* Gissing was
approaching his thirty-third birthday. He had already published eight novels, which had achieved for him the kind of
modest, limited reputation that must be very trying for the
aspiring novelist, falling as it does between the clear catastrophe of total literary failure and the clear success of wide
and unequivocal critical recognition. After ten years of such
disappointment and genteel poverty Gissing was approaching
a personal crisis, and it is his encounter with it that gives *New
Grub Street* so much of its peculiar distinction, and which
helps to explain the barely restrained bitterness with which it
treats literary life. Nevertheless, it would be too simple to regard Gissing as a mere victim of circumstances, whose fate
was entirely out of his own control. There is ample biographical evidence that he had a marked self-destructive
streak that led him often to embrace tribulations that might
have been avoided, and to exaggerate the nature of those that
he had undergone. In 1880 the philosopher Frederic Harrison had read the young Gissing's first novel, *Workers in the
Dawn*, with considerable enthusiasm; as a result, Gissing became a protégé of Harrison's. He was introduced to John
Morley, then editor of the *Pall Mall Gazette*, who professed
admiration for his work and pressed him to write for the
paper. Gissing contributed a couple of articles but was disinclined to write more. Here is an account of the refusal by
Frederick Harrison's son, Austin, to whom Gissing had been
made tutor:

We implored him to write again. But Gissing refused. He
hated editors; he was no journalist, he said; he could not
degrade himself by such 'trash'. In truth, at any time after
1882 Gissing could have obtained a place as critic or writer
on some journal, which could have enabled him to write at
leisure. But he would never hear of such a thing. My father

begged him to accept some post, but Gissing declined to 'serve'. Gissing positively chose to live in strife.[2]

In addition to tutoring Harrison's two sons, Gissing was found other pupils, but he was determined to earn a living solely by writing novels, and in 1884 he courteously declined Harrison's offer of more pupils, since he wished to devote his whole time to fiction. The payment he could expect was meagre, since his reputation was scarcely established, but, Austin Harrison insisted, 'if he remained poor it was largely because he chose to'. Integrity and perversity were inextricably interwoven in Gissing's make-up, and his life seems to have been dominated by the myth of the artist who *must* subject himself to intense suffering if he is to produce work of any value. Austin Harrison's final summary of his character emphasises this aspect:

> He deliberately regarded himself as a sort of social outlaw, making a virtue of self-indulgence and self-concentration, fostering the hunger of querulous self-pity. He gloried in the vanity of self-compassion. In literature he thought of poverty in avoirdupois. He revelled in the gloom of London's misery. Every fibre of him betrayed the artist, and because he was an artist he was also an aristocrat. His delight in poverty, in misery, and in vice was purely literary and consciously egotistical.

Even though this outline may seem unsympathetic to Gissing, one must admit that it gives a good impression of the characteristic atmosphere of much of his fiction. It also helps to place him in a larger cultural context, for the collocation of 'outlaw' and 'artist' and 'aristocrat' is familiar in late nineteenth-century life and letters, and has been usefully discussed by Frank Kermode in *Romantic Image*.

At the beginning of his adult life Gissing had been an 'outlaw' in a painfully literal sense, when his brilliant academic career at Owen's College, Manchester, was cut short when he was discovered in an act of theft. He was tried, convicted and briefly imprisoned, and Gissing felt that his whole life had been branded by this experience. He had stolen in order to obtain money to help a young prostitute, Helen Harrison,

whom he subsequently married; he endured several years of
totally miserable married life with her before she finally
drank herself to death. Gissing felt that life without a partner
was impossible, but he was convinced that his lack of financial
prospects made it impossible for him to marry an educated,
middle-class girl, and early in 1891, whilst *New Grub Street*
was in the press, Gissing married another working-class girl,
Edith Underwood, a match which was to prove no less disastrous for a man of his sensitive and fastidious temperament
than his first marriage. Here, more than anywhere, one sees
evidence of Gissing's self-destructive tendencies, for there is
no evidence that he was passionately in love with Edith, and
in *New Grub Street* Gissing had described with great lucidity
the unhappy situation of Alfred Yule, a man of letters married to an ignorant wife who is quite unable to share his interests and aspirations. And Mrs Yule was at least a woman of
placid and amenable temperament, which, by all accounts,
the second Mrs Gissing was not. Jacob Korg, Gissing's biographer, remarks that Gissing must have been aware of the
likely consequences of his second marriage, but adds:

> It is difficult to escape the obvious conclusion that he
> married Edith in spite of his foreknowledge because a part
> of him wanted to suffer those consequences. Apparently,
> the marriage was another of those acts of self-mortification
> that Gissing committed from time to time with the sub-
> conscious motive of putting himself at a disadvantage.[3]

It was, then, at a crucial period in his life that Gissing embarked on *New Grub Street*, a book which seems to have
been regarded during the frenzied process of composition as
merely one more piece of competent routine fiction, and
whose outstanding quality he was slow to realise. Whilst cor-
recting the proofs in February 1891 he wrote to his brother:
'I am astonished to find how well it reads. There are savage
truths in it.' When the novel appeared it was generally admired both by his family and by his German friend Eduard
Bertz, to whom he wrote:

> Well now, it is unnecessary for me to say how your remarks
> on *New Grub Street* rejoice me. As all my acquaintances

agree in loud praise of the book, I suppose it is not bad. I
wrote it in utter prostration of spirit; no book of mine was
regarded so hopelessly in the production. This experience
encourages me; if I could write tolerably *then*, I am pretty
sure to be able to produce under any circumstances likely
to befall me.[4]

Gissing's last encouraging assumption was plausible but
false: it was precisely the fact that it had been wrung out of
'utter prostration of spirit' that gave *New Grub Street* its
unique character. With a few reservations, the critics shared
the favourable opinion of *New Grub Street* expressed by his
intimates, and within a month the novel went into a second
impression, being the first of his books to achieve this distinction. Nevertheless, this general approval, though encouraging, was not marked enough to bring Gissing's reputation to
the decisive take-off point that he had hoped for, and the
book's sales could have no effect on his financial position,
since he had sold it outright to Smith, Elder & Co. for £150.

II

The pressure of Gissing's predicament is everywhere apparent in *New Grub Street*. Nevertheless, it would be a mistake
to see the novel as exclusively concerned with the unhappy
situation of Edwin Reardon. He forms part of a complex of
personal and literary relationships; almost as important is
Jasper Milvain, the thrusting and ambitious young journalist, who represents the new-style, exploitative view of the
literary profession, as opposed to Reardon's gentle, old-
fashioned integrity. We meet Jasper on the first page of the
novel and again on the last, and his rise to fame and wealth is
set against the decline of Reardon to failure and final disaster.
Gissing presents a society in miniature, a microcosm of the
literary world as he had experienced it, whose significance is
symbolised by the novel's title. He explained it in a letter to
Bertz:

Grub Street actually existed in London some hundred and
fifty years ago. In Pope and his contemporaries the name

has become synonymous for wretched-authordom. In Hogarth's 'Distressed Author' there is 'Grub Street' somewhere inscribed. Poverty and meanness of spirit being naturally associated, the street came to denote an abode, not merely of poor, but of insignificant, writers.[5]

The Grub Street of the 1880s was still homogeneous enough to include within its confines types who today would have little point of contact. In addition to Reardon, who at heart is a classical scholar but who is determined to make a respectable name and living by writing novels, we have the ageing, embittered critic Alfred Yule and his clever daughter, Marian, who earns a living by ghost-writing and devilling for her father. Nowadays, since the rise of English as a university subject, both of them would be more at home as academics; Alfred Yule's conversation provides some choice examples of the shop-talk of Eng. Lit. professionals. On the other hand, Jasper Milvain – who thinks of marrying Marian, until he sets his sights higher – would probably be destined for a job in advertising or public relations. Grouped around these central figures are the lesser occupants of the picture, like Reardon's pathetic friend, Biffen, an exponent of what he calls 'an absolute realism in the sphere of the ignobly decent', toiling with Flaubertian concentration at a novel called *Mr Bailey, Grocer*; or Whelpdale, a failed writer who shows considerable ingenuity at exploiting the commercial fringes of literature: he dabbles in the lowest forms of the new popular journalism, runs a fiction-writing course, and launches a literary agency.

In Gissing's novel all natural human relationships are affected by the claims of 'literature', which forms a thin disguise for basic economic pressures, since literature is itself no more than a commodity. Jasper Milvain, who is the sole support of his family, successfully sets his two sisters to work at writing children's stories (a better alternative, as he reasonably argues, than taking employment as governesses, which was the only other possibility for middle-class girls at that period). The relationship between Alfred Yule and Marian has dwindled to one entirely defined by the literary hack work she does for him, until she receives a legacy, when Alfred sub-

jects her to intolerable pressures to use it to finance a new
literary magazine which he will edit. Above all, the relationship between Edwin Reardon and his wife Amy is eroded by
his lack of literary success. Gissing presents his vision of
literature as a commodity in a powerful passage in chapter viii.
Marian Yule is in the British Museum Reading Room:

> One day at the end of the month she sat with books open
> before her, but by no effort could fix her attention upon
> them. It was gloomy, and one could scarcely see to read; a
> taste of fog grew perceptible in the warm, headachy air.
> Such profound discouragement possessed her that she
> could not even maintain the pretence of study; heedless
> whether anyone observed her, she let her hands fall and
> her head droop. She kept asking herself what was the use
> and purpose of such a life as she was condemned to lead.
> When already there was more good literature in the world
> than any mortal could cope with in his lifetime, here was
> she exhausting herself in the manufacture of printed stuff
> which no one ever pretended to be more than a commodity
> for the day's market. What unspeakable folly! To write –
> was not that the joy and the privilege of one who had an
> urgent message for the world? Her father, she knew well,
> had no such message; he had abandoned all thought of
> original production, and only wrote about writing. She
> herself would throw away her pen with joy but for the
> need of earning money. And all these people about her,
> what aim had they save to make new books out of those
> already existing, that yet newer books might in turn be
> made out of them? This huge library, growing into un-
> wieldiness, threatening to become a trackless desert of
> print – how intolerably it weighed upon the spirit!

Marian's reflection about 'the manufacture of printed stuff' is
subsequently echoed when Reardon is shown as 'ticking off
his quantum of manuscript each four-and-twenty hours':
writing is, in such conditions, reduced to a purely mechanical
process. In Marian's dismal conception of the endless super-
fetation of works of unnecessary literature, Gissing catches
something of Pope's vision of the original Grub Street in the

Dunciad. He develops her reverie in a paragraph which has, for Gissing, an unusual intensity of metaphoric life:

> The fog grew thicker; she looked up at the windows beneath the dome and saw that they were a dusky yellow. Then her eye discerned an official walking along the upper gallery, and in pursuance of her grotesque humour, her mocking misery, she likened him to a black, lost soul, doomed to wander in an eternity of vain research along endless shelves. Or again, the readers who sat here at these radiating lines of desks, what were they but helpless flies caught in a huge web, its nucleus the great circle of the Catalogue? Darker, darker. From the towering wall of volumes seemed to emanate visible motes, intensifying the obscurity; in a moment the book-lined circumference of the room would be but a featureless prison-limit.

The image of the reading-room as a great spider's web is very apt, and so is its transformation, in the final phrase, into a panopticon or circular prison. It is in passages such as this, as well as in many incidental felicities of characterisation, that we see Gissing's basic debt to Dickens. Gissing is sometimes spoken of in literary histories as an English disciple of the Continental Naturalists, and particularly as one whose immersion in grim realism owed much to Zola. In point of fact, although Gissing came inceasingly to admire Zola in the latter part of his life, during the 1880s, when his fiction was at its most unrelentingly naturalistic, he shared the customary English distaste for Zola as a morally subversive writer. It is more appropriate to see him as a novelist whose realism, particularly his awareness of the darker side of London life, derives very largely from Dickens, though without the Dickensian exuberance and pervading fantasy.

In such a world, where literature has become a commodity and its production a mechanical business, one may either accept the prevalent standards and try to succeed by them, which is the role freely adopted by Jasper Milvain, or one can vainly struggle against them in the interests of a nobler ideal of literature, as does Edwin Reardon. But Edwin's struggle is undermined, not merely by his weak and faltering temperament, but by a radical scepticism about values of any kind, which, as an up-to-date positivist of the eighties, he is unable to repress:

> 'And yet,' he continued, 'of course it isn't only for the sake of reputation that one tries to do uncommon work. There's the shrinking from conscious insincerity of workmanship – which most of the writers nowadays seem never to feel. "It's good enough for the market"; that satisfies them. And perhaps they are justified. I can't pretend that I rule my life by absolute ideals; I admit that everything is relative. There is no such thing as goodness or badness, in the absolute sense, of course. Perhaps I am absurdly inconsistent when – though knowing my work can't be first-rate – I strive to make it as good as possible. I don't say this in irony, Amy; I really mean it. It may very well be that I am just as foolish as the people I ridicule for moral and religious superstition.'

This was not the spirit that inspired Pope or Dr Johnson, and it is scarcely surprising that Reardon is constantly unable to overcome the obstacles of his environment. Yet he is sufficiently distanced and integrated into the fictional pattern to be more than a mere vehicle for Gissing's own self-pity and special pleading.

In his relations with his wife, Reardon illustrates Gissing's lifelong contention that girls of middle-class background could not make suitable wives for poor and struggling writers, since they were used to high material standards and could not bring themselves to sacrifice them. Amy married Reardon in the hope and expectation that he was on the verge of a distinguished career as a novelist, and she becomes less and less sympathetic with his failure. Following the passage quoted above, there is a painful scene in which Reardon tells his wife that they are living above their means and that they must move to a cheaper flat; she receives this news with cold incomprehension. The scene is curiously reminiscent of the exchanges between Lydgate and Rosamond in *Middlemarch*, when the conflict between Lydgate's lack of means and his wife's extravagant habits finally explodes. This theme of the inevitable conflict between masculine aspiration and feminine materialism was common in the fiction of the final decades of the nineteenth century and the early years of the twentieth. The pitfalls of marriage for the ambitious male are dwelt on by Hardy in *Jude the Obscure* and by Wells in *Love and Mr Lewisham* and *Tono-Bungay*. The ideal of masculine exclusiveness and self-sufficiency as a viable alternative to marriage was frequently manifested, and was expressed in scenes evoking the cosy male companionship of the club or smoking-room, such as we find, for instance, in Kipling or Conan Doyle. Their humble equivalent in *New Grub Street* is in the evenings that Reardon and Biffen spend together discussing the metrics of Greek poetry.

Set against Reardon and Biffen, who try to preserve their integrity and resist the pressures of the environment, are Amy and Milvain, who accept the fact that literature is a commodity, and the literary world a system, whose workings must be mastered by the would-be author. Amy realises this very thoroughly, and early in the novel she coldly and shrewdly tells Reardon: 'Art must be practised as a trade, at all events in our time. This is the age of trade. Of course if one refuses to be of one's time, and yet hasn't the means to live independently, what can result but break-down and wretchedness?' Gissing is very fair-minded, even sympathetic, towards Amy and Jasper. For most of the novel Amy, a clearly intelligent and attractive girl, is treated ironically but not unkindly; Gissing makes it apparent that she could have made a good wife for a successful novelist, and her inability to share Edwin's ideals and sacrifice herself with him is as much a hall-mark of her class and upbringing as a personal fault. Nevertheless, in a rather shocking fashion, Gissing seems to withdraw all sympathy from Amy towards the end of the novel, and to regard her with open dislike; and this at a point – after she has experienced the death, within a day or so, of her husband and her only child – when even a wholly disagreeable character might be entitled to a modicum of tenderness. It is as if the death of Reardon, his fictional *persona*, had aroused in Gissing something of the self-pity and bitterness that, for most of the novel, are successfully kept in check.

C

The conclusion of the novel is heavily ironical, with Jasper
and Amy, who speak the same language and understand the
world in the same way, joined in marriage and 'dreamy bliss'.
Mrs Leavis has remarked that 'when any nineteenth-century
novelist names a character Jasper I think we may safely conclude that that character is intended to be the villain'. Nevertheless, Jasper Milvain is not presented as emphatically villain-
ous. If he is ruthlessly calculating in his careerism, he also has
an attractive energy, a Stendhalian quality which is rare in
Gissing's work. He is seen in this light by Marian Yule, who
loves him; she thinks of Jasper as a 'man who aimed with
frank energy at the joys of life. . . . She did not ask for high
intellect or great attainments; but vivacity, courage, determination to succeed were delightful to her senses.' In the event,
Jasper's determination to succeed causes him to jilt Marian,
and shows him at his least agreeable. Yet, for the most part,
Jasper's moral faults, like Amy's, are seen as arising from his
deliberate decision to accept the prevalent system of values.
In this context, the close and necessary relationship between
Jasper and Edwin becomes intelligible. If Edwin's poverty
and wretchedness serve as a constant warning to Jasper of the
results of a 'pure' dedication to literature, then conversely,
Jasper's brutal careerism and incessant pursuit of the main
chance repel Edwin from any idea of writing for the market,
since, it seems, to do so will inevitably turn one into a Milvain. On his part, Jasper respects the values that he is unable
to pursue, and has a real admiration for Edwin's fiction,
whilst lamenting Edwin's inability or refusal to operate the
system in such a way as to ensure the maximum advantage for
his reputation. Early in the novel Jasper points this out to
Marian:

'There's a friend of mine who writes novels,' Jasper pursued. 'His books are not works of genius, but they are glar-
ingly distinct from the ordinary circulating novel. Well,
after one or two attempts, he made half a success; that is to
say, the publishers brought out a second edition of the
book in a few months. There was his opportunity. But he
couldn't use it; he had no friends, because he had no
money. A book of half that merit if written by a man in

the position of Warbury when he started would have established the reputaton of a lifetime. His influential friends
would have referred to it in leaders, in magazine articles,
in speeches, in sermons. It would have run through numerous editions, and the author would have had nothing to
do but to write another book and demand his price. But
the novel I'm speaking of was practically forgotten a year
after its appearance; it was whelmed beneath the flood of
next season's literature.'

The ironic counterpointing of the two men's careers is
brought to its culmination when, after Edwin's death, Milvain writes a respectful article called 'The Novels of Edwin
Reardon', which arouses a grateful response from the wid-
owed Amy; she is by now well off, as she has received a convenient legacy, and the nuptials of Jasper and Amy follow
with smooth inevitability.

If the system is the ultimate villain of *New Grub Street*,
rather than the individuals who live by its demands, the
novel certainly cannot be seen as striking any very severe
blow against the system. For Gissing is writing a novel of resentment rather than of protest. Although no one knew better the evils of industrial capitalism and the wretchedness of
the poor, Gissing was the reverse of a reformer. His resentment was fed by his conviction that nothing could be done
about the evils of modern society, and that all attempts at
political reform were folly, or worse. In his combination of a
profound immersion in misery, together with an engrained
conservatism, he has some affinity with Dostoevsky, even
though his range is infinitely narrower. Gissing's social attitudes are made clear in *Demos* (1886), where he writes movingly about the plight of the London poor, and at the same
time makes a violent onslaught on the socialist movement.
And yet there is a strong streak of primitive Marxism implicit
in *New Grub Street*, with its insistence that so-called intellectual values are merely a concealment for economic realities, that money underlies most forms of social and cultural
attainment, and that literature has become reified into a
market commodity. (One sees much the same attitudes apparent in George Orwell's *Keep the Aspidistra Flying* (1936), a

novel which reads rather like a pastiche of *New Grub Street* transplanted to the London of the early 1930s.)

There are no hints for reform or improvement in *New Grub Street*, and it is implied that the cultural scene so bitterly anatomised is changing rapidly for the worse, and that there must once have been a period when things were better. In this area there is very little conclusive evidence, and one must be cautious about accepting Gissing's implicit valuations. The 1880s were certainly a time when the commercial possibilities of the printed word were being vigorously exploited, and there are many references to this in his novel, particularly to the rise of cheap sensational magazines, and to Whelpdale's manifold other activities. Twentieth-century cultural criticism has been possessed with myths of catastrophe, and *New Grub Street* lends itself with dangerous ease to such readings, with its suggestion that there had once been the possibility of a decent standard of literary endeavour, but that now the world has fallen into the hands of the Milvains and the Whelpdales. Raymond Williams, in *The Long Revolution*, provides material to offset any easy assumption of a sudden disastrous decline in standards, as opposed to a long, slow and exceedingly complex process of cultural change. If Gissing, writing about the 1880s, formulated the complaint that literature had been turned into a commodity, then it is salutary to remember that Defoe, a long time before, had described writing as a 'very considerable Branch of the English Commerce'. Even in specific practices, what seemed objectionable in the 1880s had been equally prevalent fifty years before. Thus, the puffing of books, which Jasper Milvain claimed to be essential for a soundly established reputation, had been a great feature of literary life in the 1830s as Royal A. Gettman has shown in his invaluable study of the Bentley papers, *A Victorian Publisher* (1961). And Edwin Reardon's struggles to spin out his story to fill the space required by the three-volume novel seem to have been anticipated much earlier in the century.

New Grub Street is an absorbing volume for the social historian, but it also has its dangers, since Gissing was consumed by his own highly personal myth of catastrophe, which effectively coloured his view of reality. In this novel he has out-

lined for us a *romancier maudit* who has affinities with the
poète maudit of much late nineteenth-century literature,
though Gissing's mythopoeic tendencies are controlled and
balanced by his infinitely scrupulous narrative realism (also,
in a different way, so characteristic of its time), and his infallible patience before the surface of life. This balance, or
tension, between opposites gives *New Grub Street* some of its
essential quality. Although Edwin Reardon seems very much
like an example of the modern over-sensitive, exacerbated
consciousness, he is not presented in stark isolation, as such
figures tend to be in twentieth-century fiction. He is very
much part of a social context, which is defined in considerable detail, and the interest arises from his feeble attempts to
assert his independence from its demands. Again, there is the
skilfully handled tension between the rising Milvain and the
falling Reardon. One should also mention the blend of sympathy and judgement with which we are invited to regard
Milvain and – at least until the last part of the novel – Amy
Reardon. Finally, and least specifically, there is the reconciliation of opposites in the pervasive but unobtrusive irony
with which Gissing conducts his narrative, and which occasionally becomes memorable in such phrases as 'They had
had three children; all were happily buried'. (If, like Gissing,
one believes that life is both intolerable and irredeemable,
one will have frequent recourse to some form of defensive
irony.) Gissing has several qualities in common with the great
Victorian novelists: the ability to fill a broad canvas, skill in
characterisation, and in the evocation of atmosphere. But he
lacks their energy and inventiveness, and there are various
longueurs in *New Grub Street* that clearly arise from the
desperate processes of its composition, so vividly described in
the novel itself. If *New Grub Street* cannot claim a place in
the very front rank of English fiction, it certainly deserves a
prominent and permanent place in the second rank.

III

I have referred in passing to Edwin Reardon's bitter struggles
with the three-volume novel form, or three-decker; indeed,
the three-decker assumes the role of a major though silent

character in *New Grub Street*, and I should like, finally, to devote some space to this phenomenon, which is both an important element in the content of *New Grub Street* and the formal vehicle by which Gissing's novel came into the world. During the eighteenth century novels had been published in any number of volumes, but early in the nineteenth the three-volume variety became dominant, and was to remain so for seventy years. Professor Gettmann has described it thus: 'In the simplest physical terms the three-decker may be described as a work of prose fiction in three post-octavo volumes, with a list price of 31s. 6d.' Price and format remained stable for a remarkably long time, at least for as long as the circulating libraries found this kind of book a profitable commodity. It is true that the three-decker was never totally dominant: novels in one or two volumes continued to appear, although the libraries did not care for them, and a novelist like Dickens could reach a wide audience through serialisation in monthly parts. Nevertheless, for several decades the three-decker was pre-eminent, and the circulating libraries maintained pressure on publishers to ensure that most novels came out in that form (since subscribers could take out only one volume at a time, a reader who wanted all three volumes at once had to take out three subscriptions). Publishers in turn put pressure on their authors by offering much higher payment for the three-decker than for novels in one or two volumes.

The dimensions of the three-decker were clearly defined and limited: each volume had to consist of about three hundred pages, with something over twenty lines to the page. Sometimes these specifications could be extraordinarily detailed, as Mr Gettman points out: 'In a letter written in 1883 George Bentley informed an author that a novel consisted of 920 pages with twenty-one and a half lines on each page and nine and a half words in each line.' In point of fact, the composition of the three-decker was not always so minutely laid down as this, and books could be stretched to fit the three-volume format in ways suggested by Gissing's description of Edwin Reardon at work:

He wrote a very small hand; sixty written slips of the kind habitually used would represent – thanks to the astonishing system which prevails in such matters: large type, wide spacing, frequency of blank pages – passable three-hundred-page volume. On an average he could write four such slips a day; so here we have fifteen days for the volume, and forty-five for the completed book.

Reardon's resentment at the mechanical demands of the three-decker forms a prominent motif in *New Grub Street*:

The second volume ought to have been much easier work than the first; it proved far harder. Messieurs and mes-dames the critics are wont to point out the weakness of second volumes; they are generally right, simply because a story which would have made a tolerable book (the common run of stories) refuses to fill three books.

In his desperation to fill out the space, Reardon – like many real-life novelists – resorts to the most patent forms of padding:

Description of locality, deliberate analyis of character or motive, demanded far too great an effort for his present condition. He kept as much as possible to dialogue; the space is filled so much more quickly, and at a pinch one can make people talk about the paltriest incidents of life.

New Grub Street itself is undoubtedly marred by an excess of thinly spun conversation, as Gissing himself realised, for when the book was translated into French in 1898 he made radical cuts in the conversational material.

At times Reardon vows he will have no more to do with the accursed three-decker, and takes heart from a suggestion that 'numbers of authors were abandoning that procrustean system'. But in an important conversation with Milvain in chapter xv, Reardon makes clear the precise nature of his dependence on the library-supported three-decker; publishers, assured of a steady sale to the libraries, could take the risk of paying their authors a fairly substantial sum in outright purchase of copyright:

'For anyone in my position,' said Reardon, 'how is it possible to abandon the three volumes? It is a question of payment. An author of moderate repute may live on a yearly three-volume novel – I mean the man who is obliged to sell his book out and out, and who gets from one to two hundred pounds for it. But he would have to produce four one-volume novels to obtain the same income; and I doubt whether he could get so many published within twelve months. And here comes in the benefit of the libraries; from the commercial point of view the libraries are indispensable. Do you suppose the public would support the present number of novelists if each book had to be purchased? A sudden change to that system would throw three-fourths of the novelists out of work.'

The curiously Luddite note in the last sentence is significant. In the eighties it was evidently possible for the not very successful novelist to scratch a modest living, just like, say, a not very successful barrister. It was the system of outright purchase that made this possible. This system is often spoken of as unfair to authors, and so it is in principle, particularly if a book sells very well and the author reaps no benefit at all from its success. But it did at least mean that a man of mediocre reputation could still live as a professional novelist, even if in a straitened fashion. Since the general switch to the royalty system, an author's rewards have been related to his book's sales, and only unusually successful writers can hope to make a living exclusively from novels. Arnold Bennett recalls that his first novel, written when he was a full-time journalist, made the net sum of precisely one guinea when it appeared in 1898.

The change in the system, which was discussed in *New Grub Street*, in fact came about in the middle-nineties, when the circulating libraries, which for so long had buttressed the three-decker, turned abruptly against it, and informed publishers that they would no longer be ordering it. Publishers had been following up the traditional three-volume edition of a novel at 31s. 6d. with a cheap one-volume edition at 6s. and this had badly undermined the libraries' dependence on the former. In retaliation they wrecked the three-decker altogether: in 1894, 184 three-volume novels appeared; in 1897, only four. The change was abrupt and decisive: novels became shorter and cheaper, and outright purchase gave way to the royalty system. The way of life so memorably described in *New Grub Street* would no longer be possible.

1968

5 The Correspondence of Gissing and Wells

The volumes of letters which, during the last few years, have been appearing from the Wells archive at the University of Illinois have, alas, been getting steadily less interesting. The first of them, the Wells–James correspondence, formed a *locus classicus* in the criticism of fiction, and documented one of the oddest literary friendships of all time. The Wells–Bennett letters, which came out in 1960, were more ordinary; nevertheless, they provided a useful picture of the Edwardian literary scene under the increasing dominance of the two friendly rivals. With Wells and Gissing,* however, we have a relationship of much shorter extent, lasting only from 1896 to Gissing's death in 1903, and one in which there was, fundamentally, rather little common ground between the two participants. During the final years of his life Gissing was plagued by ill-health, by marital difficulties and, above all, by his increasing sense of failure; Wells had had his own share of the first two of these, but success came quickly, and whilst Gissing declined further into flatness and despair, the trajectory of Wells's reputation soared ever higher. Wells remained loyal to Gissing, however, and was with him just before his death at Saint-Jean-Pied-de-Port. Gissing seems not to have minded his friend's success; if anything, he was rather gratified by Wells's increasing wealth and fame, as though they provided some assurance that the literary life need not inevitably bring penury and neglect. 'A literary man able to declare that he has hundreds laid aside! It is too wonderful for envy,' he remarked in a letter to Wells in 1899; and in the quasi-autobiographical reverie, *The Private Papers of Henry Ryecroft*, Wells appears as 'N', the admired epitome of de-

* *George Gissing and H. G. Wells*, edited by Royal A. Gettmann.

served literary success. Yet though there was a certain piquancy in the relationship between the two writers, their correspondence contains remarkably little in the way of genuine literary interest. Many of the communications are frankly trivial, being concerned merely with travelling arrangements, minor social engagements and so on. There is a preponderance of letters by Gissing, and their air of gloom is, at times, almost insupportable; they are full of carefully written complaints about bad health, bad weather, bad food and the incompetence of publishers. The few letters by Wells are, in comparison, refreshingly brisk and lively. This material will undoubtedly be useful when proper biographies of Gissing and Wells come to be written, but one can't pretend that the collection will be of outstanding value to the student of late nineteenth-century fiction or particularly absorbing for the general reader.

In his introduction, Mr Gettmann does his best to justify and explain what is to follow, but with a certain amount of understandable evasiveness. He overstates the parallels between the careers of Gissing and Wells. Though some of their experiences, objectively described, may have been similar, the temperaments concerned, and what they made of their experiences, were vastly different. Mr Gettmann goes on to make some apt critical comments on Gissing, in whom he is obviously more interested; he remarks of Gissing's prose:

On many of his pages one does not sense the pressure of a state of mind or of emotion behind the sentences, because Gissing was unable to immerse himself in alien attitudes and feelings. The result is a kind of neutral, formal style which makes the dialogue stiff and not quite credible. . . . Passages which rise above clarity and competence – and they are more numerous than is commonly supposed – are likely to be those which express the thrust of Gissing's private concerns. . . .

One can readily think of examples to illustrate Mr Gettmann's final observation; as, for instance, in *The Year of Jubilee*, where the frightful Mrs Peachey, and the pathos of the scene in which Arthur Peachey finally takes his little son

away from her, obviously derive from the horror of Gissing's
second marriage. Much the same point is implicit in Mrs
Leavis's claim, made in *Scrutiny* in 1938, that *New Grub
Street* is the one work of Gissing's with a title to greatness,
since in it he was most deeply and intimately involved with
his subject; though Mr Gettmann doesn't appear to recognise the outstanding quality of this novel. But if his comments on Gissing are at least adequate, and sometimes perceptive, his remarks on Wells are rather conventional and
perfunctory. Thus, he says of Wells's books: 'His gusto and
inventiveness made them vastly entertaining, but his first
purpose was to broach ideas, with aesthetic effects incidental.'
This may have been increasingly true of Wells after 1900,
and was entirely so by the time *Boon* appeared in 1915; but
in the nineties, when so much of Wells's best fiction was
written, he was less directly concerned with ideas and more
conscious of aesthetic effects than Mr Gettmann implies.

Editorially, Mr Gettmann has done a very competent job.
In the Appendices he reprints a number of critical pieces by
Wells about Gissing that are in many ways more interesting
than the letters that form the bulk of the book; these include
two reviews of novels from the *Saturday Review* published in
1895–6, a critical study of Gissing from the *Contemporary
Review* of 1897, and a memorial article that appeared in the
National Review of 1904, after Gissing's death. This section
might well have included the article by Wells called 'The
Truth about Gissing', which was published in Middleton
Murry's magazine *Rhythm* in 1912. In this piece Wells reviews Frank Swinnerton's study of Gissing and Morley
Roberts's *The Private Life of Henry Maitland*; Wells praises
Swinnerton, but most of his review is a savage attack on the
inadequacy of Roberts's fictionalised portrait of Gissing. His
vindication of Gissing is moving and has an immediacy that is
lacking in the more formal *National Review* memoir. I regret
Mr Gettmann's omission of this article, and I am also inclined to regret that he doesn't tell the reader a little more
about the context of Wells's friendship with Gissing. There
are indications that, before it began, Wells had been temperamentally adverse to Gissing's brand of fictional realism.
The two men first met at a dinner in November 1896; Wells

in his contribution to a symposium in the *Ludgate Monthly* the previous September had remarked: 'I believe there are inducements for a funny novelist – an antidote to the earlier teachings of Mr George Gissing', while in his comic novel, *The Wheels of Chance,* published at about the same time, Wells describes his hero, Hoopdriver, in these terms:

> Like I know not how many of those who do the fetching and carrying of Life – a great number of them certainly – his real life was absolutely uninteresting, and if he had faced it as realistically as such people do in Mr Gissing's novels, he would probably have come by way of drink to suicide in the course of a year. But that was just what he had the natural wisdom not to do. (chapter x)

As their friendship developed, Wells seems to have formed a genuine though not altogether uncritical admiration for Gissing's fiction. In fact, I would suggest that Gissing's influence caused a certain deflection in Wells's career as a writer – though these letters don't, unfortunately, provide any direct backing for this assumption. But a story such as 'Miss Winchelsea's Heart', which arose out of Wells's holiday in Rome with Gissing in the spring of 1898, is, with its flat, played-down irony, closer to Gissing's characteristic manner than to Wells's. *Love and Mr Lewisham* provides a more interesting case. In general, Wells's earliest attempts at realistic fiction were in the direction of comedy, as in *The Wheels of Chance* and a number of his short stories. His more serious apprehensions of reality, as I have argued elsewhere, found expression in the scientific romances. And Wells's Edwardian works which have survived best, *Kipps* and *Mr Polly,* are also in this comic vein. But *Love and Mr Lewisham,* which appeared in 1900, is distinguished from these by its relatively sombre tone. It is pre-eminently a story of the nineties in that its hero, the pathetic, aspiring young science student, has to surrender the possibility of advancement and a successful career in favour of marriage and domesticity. This theme – the defeat of masculine self-advancement by love and marriage – was strangely common in the nineties. Gissing, for evident reasons, was preoccupied with it; but one can discover it equally in *Jude the Obscure* and in Bennett's first novel, *A Man from the North*, as well as in short stories by such writers as Ella D'Arcy and Hubert Crackanthorpe. Writing to Bennett in 1900, Wells remarked on the (accidental) similarities between *A Man from the North* and *Love and Mr Lewisham*, though he added that Bennett's book was closer in spirit to Gissing than his own. This is true, for Lewisham, despite his defeats, is still a more ebullient figure than one of Gissing's depressed victims of circumstance. But Wells continues, significantly: 'I am reminded by that, that Gissing some years ago when I was telling him the idea of *Lewisham* told me that he also had contemplated the same story.' Wells's novel ends with the ironical and stoical acceptance of defeat; whereas his later comedies such as *Kipps* and *Mr Polly* leave their heroes in some kind of idyllic seclusion.

Yet Wells's temporary affinities with Gissing are not merely thematic. He is at his most Gissingesque in *Love and Mr Lewisham* when stressing the oppressiveness of the London scene, the grey, muddy streets which young George Lewisham walked night after night during his courtship of Ethel. With the growth of huge modern cities like London and Paris there came a crucial development in nineteenth-century sensibility, which reflected the brutal life of the poor in the contemporary megalopolis: one finds it, for example, in the later Dickens, in Baudelaire and, most subjectively, in James Thomson's *City of Dreadful Night*. More than any of his contemporaries in fiction, Gissing inherited this sensibility, and his fiction is at its most powerful when fully expressing it. In *New Grub Street*, one's perpetual awareness of the filthy streets, smoke-blackened buildings and cheap eating-places of the London of the eighties is a large element in the total effect of the work. But one can find characteristic passages in Gissing's other novels:

> Manor Park Cemetery lies in the remote East End, and gives sleeping-places to the inhabitants of a vast district. There Jane's parents lay, not in a grave to themselves, but buried amidst the nameless dead, in that part of the ground reserved for those who can purchase no more than a portion in the foss which is filled when its occupants

reach statutable distance from the surface. The regions around were then being built upon for the first time; the familiar streets of pale, damp brick were stretching here and there, continuing London, much like the spreading of a disease. Epping Forest is near at hand, and nearer the dreary expanse of Wanstead Flats.

Not grief, but chill desolation makes this cemetery its abode. A country churchyard touches the tenderest memories, and softens the heart with the longing for the eternal rest. The cemeteries of wealthy London abound in dear and great associations, or at worst preach homilies which connect themselves with human dignity and pride. Here on the waste limits of that dread East, to wander among tombs is to go hand in hand with the stark and eyeless burden of mortality; the spirit fails beneath the cold burden of ignoble destiny. Here lie those who were born for toil; who, when toil has worn them to the utmost, have but to yield their useless breath and pass into oblivion. For them is no day, only the brief twilight of a winter sky between the former and the latter night.

That passage occurs in chapter XVI of *Demos* (1886), while the following extract is from *In the Year of Jubilee* (1894):

It was one of those cold, dry clouded evenings of autumn, when London streets affect the imagination with a peculiar suggestiveness. New-lit lamps, sickly yellow under the dying day, stretch in immense vistas, unobscured by fog, but exhibit no detail of the track they will presently illumine; one by one the shop-fronts grow radiant on deepening gloom, and show in silhouette the figures numberless that are hurrying past. By accentuating a pause between the life of daytime and that which will begin after dark, this grey hour excites to an unwonted perception of the city's vastness and of its multifarious labours; melancholy, yet not dismal, the brooding twilight seems to betoken Nature's compassion for myriad mortals exiled from her beauty and her solace. (pt V, chapter IV)

One might object to the touches of over-writing and rhetorical exaggeration, but the essential spirit of these passages is, it seems to me, not very far removed from that of Baudelaire's 'Le Crépuscule du soir'. This mode of feeling was largely alien to Wells, but he came close to it in *Love and Mr Lewisham*. To some extent, of course, he was simply re-enacting memories of his own grim acquaintance with the London streets as an impoverished student of the Normal School of Science at Kensington; but his presentation seems to owe a good deal to Gissing's treatment of similar material.

The association of these two writers in Mr Gettmann's book, disappointing though its contents may be, does provide an opportunity to remember that they were, in their different ways, the last direct heirs of Dickens in serious English fiction. This statement perhaps needs amplification: Dickens, like Shakespeare, is a writer of such towering and uncontainable stature that it is impossible to set a limit to his ultimate influence. But the Dickensian elements in recent fiction are, I think, oblique and at one or more removes. A convenient example is Anthony Powell's *The Music of Time*, parts of which have a Dickensian flavour, though this is derived, I think, from the Dickensian elements in Proust rather than directly. Gissing, however, was saturated in Dickens, and in 1897 he wrote a good book about him (though without much enthusiasm, to judge from his correspondence). This study emphasised the darker, more sombre elements in Dickens, to an extent which dismayed a cheerful critic like Chesterton. And in Gissing's own fiction we get much of the local flavour of *Bleak House* or *Little Dorrit*, though without the genius or the intricate symbolism. We find this quality in *Love and Mr Lewisham*, too, though for the most part Wells, in his comedies, is closer to the early Dickens, with his effortless creation of exaggerated but plausible characters, and the cheeky high spirits of his heroes: as Henry James was to exclaim, 'You must at moments make dear old Dickens turn – for envy of the eye and the ear and the nose and the mouth of you – in his grave.'

Though radically different in temperament and attitude, Gissing and Wells did share a common debt to Dickens, early or late; and they were both uninterested in the achievements of the Continental Naturalists. The Wells–Bennett letters show how vigorously Wells resisted his friend's attempt to make him read and follow French novelists; while Gissing, though he spent the last years of his life in France, retained a strong prejudice against French *mœurs*; 'Morally, they are very low in the scale of nations', he observed in 1902. It is this insularity, which looked back to Dickens, rather than across the Channel to Flaubert, Zola or Maupassant, that distinguished the realism of Gissing or Wells from that of such contemporaries as George Moore, Hubert Crackanthorpe (whose early death cut short what might have become a major talent) or Arnold Bennett. The limitations of the insular approach, and indeed of Gissing's own gifts, are apparent if we compare *Demos*, as a novel about industrialism and working-class life, with Zola's *Germinal*, published the year before. In a sense Zola's sensationalism and brutality are as unsatisfactory as Gissing's evasiveness; but his novel has infinitely greater power and authority. It ends with the total victory of the system, whereas *Demos* concludes with the physical destruction of the factories that have been polluting a green English valley. The fantasy of an escape into pastoral seclusion was an abiding element in Gissing's nature, which received its final, full expression in *Henry Ryecroft*. And the ultimate haven of the Potwell Inn points to something comparable in Wells, though of a less dominating kind. At its best, in *New Grub Street* or *The History of Mr Polly*, the native realism of Gissing and the Dickensian humour of Wells could rival anything produced by the disciples of the Naturalists. But they represented the end of a line. The future lay with those who had learnt from Continental models. About the time that Gissing died, Joyce began work on the first draft of *Portrait of the Artist*: the greatest realistic novel of the twentieth century in English is *Ulysses*, not *Angel Pavement*.

1962

6 *Tono-Bungay*

I

In 1908 H. G. Wells was forty-two. It was only thirteen years
since he had published his first book, but in that time he had
written so much, and with such energy and fluency, that he
had established himself with the Edwardian reading public as
the simultaneous master of half a dozen different fields of
literary activity. There was the brilliant succession of scientific romances that had begun with *The Time Machine* in
1895 and of which *The War in the Air* (1908) was the most
recent example. *Love and Mr Lewisham* (1900) had shown
that Wells could write a novel of pathetic realism in the vein
of George Gissing; and the comic realism of *Kipps* (1905) had
captivated a large number of readers. Apart from fiction,
Wells's endlessly fertile mind had produced three volumes of
sociological speculation and prophecy: *Anticipations* (1901),
Mankind in the Making (1903) and *New Worlds for Old*
(1908), as well as a personal statement of his intellectual position, *First and Last Things* (1908). In *A Modern Utopia*
(1905) Wells gave imaginative guise to his speculations, and
this work had proved instantly and immensely popular.
Wells's fame was not confined merely to a wide and fairly un-
demanding public; he was held in great esteem by his fellow-
writers, though they may have felt that he was squandering
his prodigious gifts. Henry James, then in his sixties and
deeply out of sympathy with most Edwardian literary manifestations, was fascinated by Wells and his books (the quarrel
that followed the publication of Wells's *Boon* in 1915 was still
several years ahead); for James, Wells's vigour and inventiveness compensated for his lack of aesthetic concentration. In
1905 he wrote to Wells, after reading *A Modern Utopia* and
Kipps in succession: 'Let me tell you . . . that they have left
me prostrate with admiration, and that you are, for me, more

than ever, the most interesting "literary man" of your generation – in fact, the only interesting one.'[1]

Wells was certainly aware of the dangers in disseminating his gifts in so many different directions, and he had long dreamt of writing a large-scale novel, of Victorian capaciousness, that could incorporate the various strands of his literary and intellectual interests: science fiction, realism, comedy, sociological analysis. He embarked on this book in 1903, but had constantly to put it aside in order to work on more immediate projects, and it was not completed until 1908. Wells considered a number of titles for this novel, which he regarded as offering a 'view of the contemporary social and political system in Great Britain', suggesting in different ways its range and themes; 'A Picture of the World', 'One Man's View of England', 'The End of an Age' and 'Waste'.[2] Finally, however, Wells decided on the cryptic but memorable Tono-Bungay, the name of the patent medicine which brings fame and fortune to Edward Ponderevo, and which functions symbolically as the false nostrum offered to a sick society.

After completion Tono-Bungay was serialised by Ford Madox Ford (then still known as Ford Madox Hueffer) in the English Review, starting with the first issue in December 1908: Ford founded this review in order to print the finest available work by both established and new writers, and in large measure he succeeded; during the short period of his editorship the English Review was one of the most distinguished literary magazines in the English-speaking world. Tono-Bungay was a prized contribution, and in a letter to Wells of November 1908 Ford remarked: ' "Tono-Bungay" really is a great book. It has all the qualities of the traditional classical English novel and it is much better handled than any of the British classical novels.'[3] (Shortly afterwards Wells and Ford were in bitter disagreement about the terms and conditions of the serialisation.) Ford's high opinion of Tono-Bungay was echoed by the young D. H. Lawrence, who had enthusiastically followed the serial version, and who in March 1909 urged his friend Blanche Jennings: 'At any rate, you must, must read Tono-Bungay. It is the best novel Wells has written – it is the best novel I have read for – oh, how long?'

Two months later Lawrence exhorted her again: 'read, *read Tono-Bungay*, it is a great book'.[4]

The novel was well received when it appeared in book form in February 1909, though Wells felt that public response underestimated the extent to which he had tried to write a novel in the grand Victorian manner, and to make a serious contribution to the art of fiction. 'I shall never come as near to a deliberate attempt upon The Novel again as I did in *Tono-Bungay*,' he wrote in his *Experiment in Autobiography*. In fact, *Tono-Bungay* represented something of a watershed in his attitude to the art of fiction. When he began his career in the mid-nineties Wells regarded himself as primarily a novelist, and although he fell short of the self-conscious and total dedication of James, Conrad and Ford, he took the business of writing fiction very seriously, as the astringent novel-reviews that he contributed to the *Saturday Review* make plain. In the 1900s Wells was drawn more and more to debate and exposition, and the discussion of ideas in a disembodied form rather than their imaginative enactment. Nevertheless, he tried to preserve his allegiance to the art of the novel, and *Tono-Bungay* was almost his last and certainly his most extended tribute to it. In 1909 Wells also published *Ann Veronica*, which has its lively moments but is now fairly dated; and this was followed in 1910 by *The History of Mr Polly*, a slighter but more perfect work than *Tono-Bungay*, a distillation of Wells's comic genius in a flawless pastoral, which, in effect, marks his farewell to the novel as a form with its own artistic laws and necessities.

The tenor of Wells's changing attitude to fiction can be seen in his essay, 'The Contemporary Novel', first published in book form in 1914.[5] Here we see Wells continuing to take the novel seriously; his critical intelligence is still apparent and he offers some penetrating observations about various of his contemporaries. He makes a reasonable plea for the kind of novel which is discursive and inclusive, even at the sacrifice of aesthetic concentration, as *Tono-Bungay* had been, and he pays a generous, indeed provocative, tribute to Sterne, whom he sees as the master of that kind of fiction:

the master to whom we of the English persuasion, we of the

discursive school, must for ever recur is he, whom I will maintain against all comers to be the subtlest and greatest *artist* – I lay stress upon that word artist – that Great Britain has ever produced in all that is essentially the novel, Laurence Sterne.

But as Wells develops his arguments it becomes apparent that he is advancing an instrumentalist concept of the novel: 'So far as I can see, it is the only medium through which we can discuss the great majority of the problems which are being raised in such bristling multitude by our contemporary social development.' Wells was not advocating a revolutionary break with the past or present of the novel, merely, as he believed, trying to extend its scope and its relevance to the problems of the modern world. But the emphasis on *discussion* is significant, for almost all of Wells's fiction after 1910 is marred by an excessive reliance on discussion and description, as against realisation and enactment; as F. R. Leavis has observed, 'there is an elementary distinction to be made between the *discussion* of problems and ideas, and what we find in the great novelists'. In 'The Contemporary Novel', Wells argued for a greater breadth and flexibility in definitions of 'the novel', complaining that 'the novel has been treated as though its form was as well-defined as the sonnet'. One can sympathise with the spirit of this complaint whilst believing that Wells's particular insistence on the fictional discussion and interplay of ideas was likely to lead one away from the novel form altogether – no matter how generously conceived of – towards some such medium as the Platonic dialogue. In his autobiography Wells conceded as much:

By 1919, in *The Undying Fire*, I was at last fully aware of what I was doing and I took a new line. I realised I had been trying to revive the Dialogue in a narrative form. I was not so much expanding the novel as getting right out of it.

When he wrote *Tono-Bungay* Wells was still safely within the confines of the novel form, even though in a different part of the territory from that usually cultivated by James or

Conrad. As we shall see, his novel has some grave imperfec-
tions; but it is, for the most part effectively, a novel of ideas
which functions by transmuting problems and questions into
imaginative entities, rather than by subduing everything to
the brisk interchanges of 'discussion', no matter how frank
and fluent.

II

Tono-Bungay has two central characters: the engineer,
George Ponderevo, who narrates the story in the first person,
and his uncle, Edward Ponderevo, whose career we follow,
through George's eyes, from modest beginnings as a chemist
in a sleepy Sussex town, onward and upward through the
ranks of late-Victorian and Edwardian society, as a patent-
medicine tycoon, and then as a multi-millionaire financier,
until his final rapid and shocking collapse. In the first chapter
George Ponderevo dismisses the idea of the formally planned
and selective novel with much the same impatience that
Wells was to show in 'The Contemporary Novel':

> I warn you this book is going to be something of an
> agglomeration. I want to trace my social trajectory (and my
> uncle's) as the main line of my story, but as this is my first
> novel and almost certainly my last, I want to get in too all
> sorts of things that struck me, things that amused me and
> impressions I got – even although they don't minister
> directly to my narrative at all. (1 i 1)

This all-embracing approach was summed up by Wells in
'The Contemporary Novel' with the ringing phrase: 'Before
we have done, we will have all life within the scope of the
novel.'

In the context of *Tono-Bungay* it enabled him to incorporate many of the disparate elements to be found in his earlier
books. The superb opening section, in which George describes his childhood spent in the servants' quarters of the
great country house at Bladesover where his mother was
housekeeper, has a Dickensian vitality and reminds us that
Wells was, indeed, one of the last direct heirs of Dickens. The

accounts of George's days as a science student in London and his courtship of Marion recapitulate and amplify parts of *Love and Mr Lewisham*. And the subsequent lengthy reflections on George's unhappy marriage and later love-affairs recall Wells's growing interest in marital problems, and his conviction that there was a necessary tension between masculine aspiration and female demands: this preoccupation was already apparent in *Love and Mr Lewisham* and was enlarged upon in a fantasy, *The Sea Lady* (1902); it was to be further developed in a number of inferior later novels, such as *Marriage* (1912), *The Passionate Friends* (1913) and *The Research Magnificent* (1915).

In George's characterisation of his Uncle Teddy we find a splendid expression of Wells's comic vein: Teddy has the uneducated naïvety and perkiness of *Kipps*, but also possesses a rich fantasy life, unlimited ambitions, profound (though self-deceiving) unscrupulousness and a truly Napoleonic will. There is a necessary ambiguity in George's attitude to his uncle; he has a great affection for him, but he sees Edward's rise and fall as an emblem of the waste and pointlessness that are endemic in 'the most unpremeditated, subtle, successful and aimless plutocracy that ever encumbered the destinies of mankind' (III ii 7). In attempting to anatomise this society, Wells continues, in fictional form, the series of sociological analyses and speculations that had begun with *Anticipations*. Finally, the aeronautic experiments to which George devotes himself with monastic austerity when he has turned in disgust from his uncle's commercial empire-building are very much in the line of Wells's earlier studies in science fiction; in particular, they recall a short story, 'The Argonauts of the Air', which he had published as early as 1895. (He was always strangely tentative and conservative in his attitude to the possibility of human flight; George Ponderevo's experiments are shown as attempts upon a still largely unsolved problem, whereas the Wright brothers had already flown in 1903, and Blériot was to fly the Channel in 1909, the year of *Tono-Bungay*'s publication.)

Confronted with this remarkable multiplicity of constituents, later critics have tended to be less assured of the 'greatness' of *Tono-Bungay* than contemporary admirers like Ford

and Lawrence, and more aware of the novel's seemingly epi-
sodic nature and lack of unified structure. In this respect,
Walter Allen's opinion in *The English Novel*, that '*Tono-
Bungay* is a novel of excellent interludes in an embarrassing
muddle', can be taken as representative. Recently, however,
two critical examinations of the novel have suggested that it
is more highly ordered and less improvised and muddled than
Mr Allen and other readers have assumed. In an essay, 'The
Structure of H. G. Wells's *Tono-Bungay*', published in *English Fiction in Transition* in 1961 (IV 2), Kenneth B. Newell
points out the persistence of certain images in the novel,
which exemplify the underlying theme of the transformation
of reality into illusion. First, there is the rocket-like rise and
fall of Edward Ponderevo, a movement which is outlined in
the titles of the three final books: 'The Rise of Tono-
Bungay', 'The Great Days of Tono-Bungay', 'The Aftermath
of Tono-Bungay'. In one sense, of course, this recalls the medieval conception of tragedy as essentially the rise and fall of a
great man, often symbolised by the Wheel of Fortune. But, as
Mr Newell shows, not only does the rocket metaphor recur in
the novel, it is objectified in George Ponderevo's experiments
with flight, culminating in the dramatic airship escape of
George and Edward from England: one can point to such
chapter headings as 'Soaring' (III iii), 'The Stick of the Rocket'
(IV i) and 'Love among the Wreckage' (IV ii). The second set
of images to which Mr Newell draws attention is that of the
growth, maturity and decay of an unhealthy organism; the
organism being not merely Edward Ponderevo and his enterprise, but the whole society which supported him and on
which he battened. The persistence of image-patterns is not
necessarily a criterion of merit, but Mr Newell's discussion
does indicate that there is a considerable degree of unity in
Tono-Bungay and points the way to a fresh assessment.

   To a great extent this has now been provided by David
Lodge in a brilliant essay, '*Tono-Bungay* and the Condition
of England', which forms part of his book, *Language of Fiction* (1966). His aim is to re-establish *Tono-Bungay* in the way
that Wells and its first readers saw it, as a novel of considerable artistic seriousness, with, in particular, a sensitive (if not
always faultless) use of language. Mr Lodge also contends that

Tono-Bungay needs to be read as an example of a particular literary genre, known to the Victorians as the 'Condition of England novel', which uses fiction to explore the health of the nation as a whole, by concentrating on the lives of a number of figures in representative social contexts. *Sybil* and *Hard Times* are two celebrated examples; a similar concern was expressed in discursive form by Carlyle in *Past and Present*. Mr Lodge writes that:

> the main vehicle of Wells's social analysis of the condition of England in *Tono-Bungay* is not the story or the characters, but the descriptive commentary which, in most novels, we regard as the frame. I refer to the descriptions of landscape and townscape, or architecture and domestic interiors, and the narrator's reflection on them, which occupy so prominent a place in the novel.

He goes on to point out that Wells's England 'is simply the central character of the novel, as England is the central character of Shakespeare's history plays'.

Mr Lodge, like Mr Newell, analyses *Tono-Bungay* in terms of its dominant patterns of imagery and metaphor, though he takes his analysis a good deal further, and his conclusion is similar: *Tono-Bungay* is permeated by a sense of negative change, of dissolution, of decay.

> It is the language of the novel which brings it into a unified whole, setting up verbal echoes which establish connections between the many disparate subjects of George's discourse, and giving that discourse a consistent and individual tone of voice. To summarise: George sees life in terms of society, and society as an *organism* or *system* which is often spatially conceived in terms of architecture or topography, and which is involved in a process of *change* and *growth* characterised by negative qualities of *confusion, disorder, disarrangement, disturbance, degeneration, dissolution, disproportion, muddle* and *waste*, and more concretely, by *cancer, disease, decay, festering, swelling*, and *rot*. The spectacle is *huge, immense, stupendous* – hence all the more *strange* and *sinister*. These words, or

words with associated meanings, recur in the most heightened passages of the novel, and suggest that Wells used
language with more discrimination and a firmer sense of
artistic purpose and design than critics have usually given
him credit for.

Mr Lodge makes out a good case for the metaphorical unity
and verbal acuteness of *Tono-Bungay*, and there need be
nothing inherently improbable in finding that Wells's imagination, when under pressure, could produce this close interplay and reiteration of thematic elements; he had, after all,
done as much in his earliest fiction, particularly *The Time
Machine*. But Mr Lodge perhaps concedes something to
Wells's critics when he observes that this sensitivity of language occurs only in the most heightened passages; elsewhere
in the book, as Norman Nicholson has pointed out, Wells
was quite capable of writing a sentence such as: ' "Look here,
Marion," I said abruptly, "what would you marry on?" ' (II ii
5).

 Mr Lodge's discussion of *Tono-Bungay* is essential to any
comprehensive understanding of the novel; I shall, however,
defer consideration of it in order to pursue the implications
of his suggestion that Wells's real subject was the condition of
England itself, rather than the predicament of the individual characters.

III

Such an interpretation, we may assume, would not have
struck Wells as unwelcome. Indeed, he put forward a very
similar view of *Tono-Bungay* in his autobiography. After saying that it represented his most 'deliberate attempt' on the
novel, he added:

> Even *Tono-Bungay* was not much of a concession to Henry
> James and his concept of an intensified rendering of feel-
> ing and characterisation as the proper business of the
> novelist. It was an indisputable Novel, but it was extensive
> rather than intensive. That is to say it presented characters
> only as part of a *scene*. It was planned as a social panorama
> in the vein of Balzac.

In no way is *Tono-Bungay* closer to the major Victorian novels – and correspondingly less like the characteristic offerings of twentieth-century fiction – than in this insistence on the panoramic view, on placing the characters in an elaborate set of contexts in class, community and nation, rather than stressing their isolation in the manner of more recent novels. Raymond Williams, in his essay 'Realism and the Contemporary Novel', has some valuable remarks on this nineteenth-century interrelation of individual and community:

> When I think of the realist tradition in fiction, I think of the kind of novel which creates and judges the quality of a whole way of life in terms of the qualities of persons. The balance involved in this achievement is perhaps the most important thing about it. It looks at first sight so general a thing, the sort of thing most novels do. It is what *War and Peace* does; what *Middlemarch* does; what *The Rainbow* does. Yet the distinction of this kind is that it offers a valuing of a whole way of life, a society that is larger than any of the individuals composing it, and at the same time valuing creations of human beings who, while belonging to and affected by and helping to define this way of life, are also, in their own terms, absolute ends in themselves. Neither element, neither the society nor the individual, is there as a priority. The society is not a background against which the personal relationships are studied, nor are the individuals merely illustrations of aspects of the way of life. Every aspect of personal life is radically affected by the quality of the general life, yet the general life is seen at its most important in completely personal terms.[6]

Tono-Bungay was not, perhaps, the kind of novel that Mr Williams had in mind when he made this formulation; nevertheless, what he has to say seems to me very useful in helping to ascertain the degree of success and failure in Wells's novel.

Certainly, in *Tono-Bungay* Wells showed himself to be deeply concerned with English society as a whole, which he saw as passing through a major collective crisis. The opening chapter of the novel is dominated by the magnificent descrip-

tion of Bladesover, the great Kentish mansion, standing
secure in its own extensive parkland, with a dependent
village, church and cottages near by. For the young George
Ponderevo, growing up in the servants' quarters, Bladesover
and the way of life which it had enshrined for centuries
seemed an absolute and immutable part of the very nature of
things. Bladesover, which Wells renders with considerable
sympathy, is an emblem of the deep-seated English attachment to feudal ways of thought and behaviour:

> The great house, the church, the village, and the labourers
> and the servants in their stations and degrees, seemed to
> me, I say, to be a closed and complete social system. About
> us were other villages and great estates, and from house to
> house, interlacing, correlated, the Gentry, the fine Olym-
> pians, came and went. The country towns seemed mere
> collections of shops, marketing places for the tenantry,
> centres for such education as they needed, as entirely de-
> pendent on the gentry as the village and scarcely less
> directly so. I thought this was the order of the whole world.
> I thought London was only a greater country town where
> the gentlefolk kept town-houses and did their greater shop-
> ping under the magnificent shadow of the finest of all fine
> gentlewomen, the Queen. It seemed to be in the divine
> order. That all this fine appearance was already sapped,
> that there were forces at work which might presently carry
> all this elaborate social system in which my mother in-
> structed me so carefully that I might understand my
> 'place', to Limbo, had scarcely dawned upon me even by
> the time that Tono-Bungay was fairly launched upon the
> world.
>   There are many people in England today upon whom it
> has not yet dawned. There are times when I doubt
> whether any but a very inconsiderable minority of English
> people realise how extensively this ostensible order has
> even now passed away. The great houses stand in the parks
> still, the cottages cluster respectfully on their borders,
> touching their eaves with their creepers, the English coun-
> tryside – you can range through Kent northward and see –
> persists obstinately in looking what it was. It is like an

early day in a fine October. The hand of change rests on it all, unfelt, unseen; resting for a while, as it were half reluctantly, before it grips and ends the thing for ever. One frost and the whole face of things will be bare, links snap, patience end, our fine foliage of pretence lie glowing in the mire. (I i 3)

This last image, of the fine October day and the impending frost, gives an effective concrete manifestation to Wells's sense of a traditional order poised on the verge of dissolution. The account of Bladesover and what it stands for is a superb product of the sociological imagination. In many ways, it sets the key for the whole novel: when young George goes to London as a student he sees the metropolis as an expansion of the great country house and its familiar way of life. And the architectural motif is pursued in the ascending career of Edward Ponderevo: we follow his moves from a flat in Bloomsbury to successively larger houses in the London suburbs of Beckenham and Chislehurst; then to the beautiful old mansion of Lady Grove, parts of which date back to the thirteenth century. This does not satisfy Edward for long, and he devotes his final years to the building of the aptly named Crest Hill, which stands on a Surrey hill-top, 'four-square to the winds of Heaven', as Edward says. This colossal structure embodies every conceivable refinement of Edwardian opulence: the visible sign of the way in which modern plutocracy has overthrown the kind of civilisation symbolised by Bladesover. It is still unfinished at Edward's financial collapse, and George contemplates the vast deserted mass of building, a fitting symbol of the waste and futility which had supported the Ponderevos' wealth and was expressed throughout the whole social order:

It struck me suddenly as the compactest image and sample of all that passes for Progress, of all the advertisement-inflated spending, the aimless building up and pulling down, the enterprise and promise of my age. (IV i 2)

The architectural theme is brought to its consummation in Edward Ponderevo's delirious ramblings on his death-bed:

'What is this great place, these cloud-capped towers, these airy pinnacles? ... Ilion. Sky-y-pointing ... Ilion House, the residence of one of our great merchant princes...' (IV i 7). This echoes George's original remarks about Crest Hill: 'I know not what delirium of pinnacles and terraces and arcades and corridors glittered at last upon the uplands of his mind...' (III ii 10).

Wells was by no means alone in his preoccupation with the condition of England, for it weighed heavily on most sensitive Edwardian writers. Kipling was constantly brooding on the gloomy future of an England that he felt was failing its imperial responsibilities, and in *Puck of Pook's Hill* (1906) he made an imaginative exploration of the English past in the guise of a children's book. In 1909 the Liberal politician and journalist C. F. G. Masterman published *The Condition of England*, a penetrating survey of the whole of Edwardian society, ranging from the fatuous excesses of the grossly affluent to the bitter lives of the very poor. Masterman quotes from *Tono-Bungay* and pays high tribute to the value of its sociological witness; both books cover similar ground and spring from much the same impulse. Nor was Wells alone in his use of an architectural image to focus his feelings about the condition of England. In 1910 E. M. Forster published *Howards End*, which uses the eponymous Hertfordshire country house – a very much more modest affair than Bladesover – to symbolise the continuity of English tradition. Like *Tono-Bungay*, *Howards End* contains many discursive reflections on the past, present and future of England: the extended rhapsody on the southern counties in chapter XIX is perhaps the most prominent example. But in general, Forster's novel lacks the panoramic vision of *Tono-Bungay*, and is concerned with large social issues only by implication; where Wells is preoccupied with the break-up of the feudal patterns which have dominated England for so long, Forster is more directly involved with his characters as personalities; for him, the most immediate problem is to achieve a harmony and mutual understanding between the sensitive Liberal and the activist Tory sections of the middle class, and the new, emergent forces of the lower orders (that Forster understood the latter only imperfectly is evident if we compare the very

external and unsure portrayal of Leonard Bast with Wells's
deeply sympathetic presentation of essentially the same type
in a Kipps or a Mr Polly).

In both books, however, there is a similar sense of fore-
boding, a feeling that the crumbling certainties of Edwardian
England cannot endure much longer. And with the outbreak
of war in 1914 catastrophe finally came. Thereafter the
literary manifestations of the 'Condition of England' question were more urgent and poignant, dwelling more persist-
ently on what had, in fact, been lost. One can point to Lawrence's war-time letters, and *Lady Chatterley's Lover*, and to
Ford's *Parade's End*; while in the early work of W. H. Auden
we find a more resilient interest, backed by romantic Marxism, in the crack-up of English culture. In *The Orators*
Auden exactly echoes Wells's diagnosis in *Tono-Bungay* of a
diseased society: 'What do you think about England, this
country of ours where nobody is well?'

I V

Mr Lodge's demonstration that *Tono-Bungay* is a 'Condition
of England' book is essential to our understanding of it, and
so too is his careful tracing of the web of metaphor and
imagery which unifies the story. I shall paraphrase one or two
of his more outstanding points, and refer the interested
reader to the rest of his analysis. He quotes the following
crucial passage from book II, as a key example of the way in
which Wells responds to the unplanned growth of early
twentieth-century London:

The railway termini on the north side of London have
been kept as remote as Eastry had kept the railway-station
from Wimblehurst; they stop on the very outskirts of the
estates, but from the south, the South Eastern railway had
butted its great stupid rusty iron head of Charing Cross
station – that great head that came smashing down in 1905
– clean across the river between Somerset House and White-
hall. The south side had no protecting estates. Factory
chimneys smoke right over against Westminster with an air
of carelessly not having permission, and the whole effect of

industrial London and of all London east of Temple Bar and of the huge dingy immensity of London port, is to me of something disproportionately large, something morbidly expanded, without plan or intention, dark and sinister toward the clean clear social assurance of the West End. And south of this central London, south-east, south-west, far west, north-west, all round the northern hills, are similar disproportionate growths, endless streets of undistinguished houses, undistinguished industries, shabby families, second-rate shops, inexplicable people who in a once fashionable phrase do not 'exist'. All these aspects have suggested to my mind at times, do suggest to this day, the unorganised, abundant substance of some tumorous growth-process, a process which indeed bursts all the outlines of the affected carcass and protrudes such masses as ignoble comfortable Croydon, as tragic impoverished West Ham. To this day I ask myself will those masses ever become structural, will they indeed shape into anything new whatever, or is that cancerous image their true and ultimate diagnosis? (ii i 1)

Ponderevo – or Wells – has already made an identification of London with the country-house order; it is, in fact, merely Bladesover and its surroundings on an infinitely larger scale. In this paragraph Wells brilliantly identifies the architectural-topographical on the one hand, and the pathological on the other; the linking concept and word is *growth*, which lets us see urban sprawl in terms of a malignant, indeed cancerous, growth; and this, in turn, symbolises the aimless acquisitiveness of the social order. (And, as Mr Lodge points out, this picture of London is still very recognisable after nearly sixty years; much of the diagnosis of English society in *Tono-Bungay* remains valid, not least in Wells's ascription of many social ills to the effects of feudalism in decay.)

Mr Lodge is particularly illuminating about one of the most puzzling episodes of *Tono-Bungay*. In chapter iv of book iii, Edward Ponderevo's fortunes are beginning to collapse and George makes a dash by sea to Mordet Island, off the African coast, where there is a large deposit of an exceedingly valuable radio-active substance called quap; he hopes to bring back enough of it to rescue the Ponderevo enterprises, but the attempt fails. Critics have been inclined to regard this section as an improvisation or afterthought on Wells's part; an exciting enough narrative interlude, but having very little to do with the main outlines of the story. Mr Lodge, however, shows that the quap has a powerful metaphorical force, which unifies the novel's principal thematic elements. Quap is of enormous commercial value, but its radio-active nature makes it a very embodiment of decomposition and decay. The seamen who are trying to remove it from Mordet Island become diseased and broken in morale. Then, on the home-ward voyage, the radio-activity of the quap causes the ship's timbers to decompose, and ship and cargo are lost. The whole of the 'quap' episode is saturated with a sense of decay and dissolution; in George's contemptuous reference to the brig in which he is sailing to Africa we have a significant recurrence of the architectural motif:

These brigs and schooners and brigantines that still stand out from every little port are relics of an age of petty trade, as rotten and obsolescent as a Georgian house that has sunken into a slum. (III iv 3)

The quap is described in terms which deliberately echo George's account of the tumorous growth of London:

But there is something – the only word that comes near it is *cancerous* – and that is not very near, about the whole of quap, something that creeps and lives as a disease lives by destroying; an elemental stirring and disarrangement, incalculably maleficent and strange.

In the following paragraph the metaphorical implications of the quap are made unambiguously clear:

This is no imaginative comparison of mine. To my mind radio-activity is a real disease of matter. Moreover, it is a contagious disease. It spreads. You bring those debased and crumbling atoms near others and those too presently catch the trick of swinging themselves out of coherent existence. It is in matter exactly what the decay of our old culture is

D

in society, a loss of traditions and distinctions and assured reactions. (III iv 5)

Under the influence of the quap George murders a native; the incident is starkly described, and left without elaboration. It seems to me possible that in this scene Wells was being more than merely sensational; it looks forward to characteristic modes of experience of the later decades of this century, when violence was to become inextricably part of the texture of human life in many societies:

> The terrorist Chan in Malraux's *La Condition Humaine* utters one of the most terrifying sentences written in the mid-twentieth century: 'A man who has never killed is a virgin.' This sentence means that killing is cognition, just as, according to the Old Testament, the sexual act is cognition; it also means that the experience of killing cannot be communicated, just as the experience of the sexual act cannot be conveyed. But this sentence means also that the act of killing changes the person who has performed it; from then on he is a different man living in a different world.[7]

The interpretation of the quap episode is one of the most valuable things in Mr Lodge's essay. I do not think, though, that his demonstration of its metaphorical significance need necessarily exclude the possibility that this section of *Tono-Bungay* was a brilliant improvisation. Considered simply as a narrative it has a very different force and movement from the rest of the novel, and the African descriptions inevitably seem rather second-hand after the strongly realised English landscapes and townscapes (I shall refer subsequently to its apparent debt and allusions to Conrad). But there need be nothing surprising in the idea that an artist can, in the process of composition, eagerly grasp and enlarge upon the thematic relevance of something which, in terms of his original conception, was an afterthought.

In the final pages of *Tono-Bungay* Wells offers a last comprehensive, recapitulatory vision of the state of England: 'Again and again in this book I have written of England as a

feudal scheme overtaken by fatty degeneration and the acci-
dents of hypertrophy.' After the Ponderevo financial bubble
has burst, George abandons aeronautics and turns to marine
design; the novel ends with an elaborate set-piece in which he
sails down the Thames on a new destroyer he has built, passing through the heart of London, with the whole course of
English history visible in the buildings along its banks. In the
unplanned chaos and congestion of the docks, Wells once
more asserts the pathological motifs that have dominated the
previous descriptions of London:

> Each day one feels that the pressure of commerce grew,
> grew insensibly monstrous, and first this man made a wharf
> and then that erected a crane, and this company set to
> work and then that, and so they jostled together to make
> this unassimilable enormity of traffic. Through it we
> dodged and drove, eager for the high seas. (IV iii 2)

The destroyer's rapid movement towards the open sea is a
radical symbol of disengagement, a leaving behind of the
whole hopeless confusion of Edwardian England. George, as
Mr Lodge remarks, has retreated into a kind of scientific
mysticism, an austere retreat from the untidiness and inherent decay of organic life. There is undoubtedly a sense of
verbal strain, of rhetorical overemphasis, in parts of this conclusion, though the total effect seems to me impressive, a fit
summation of Tono-Bungay's panoramic concern with England. The destroyer itself is, perhaps deliberately, an ambigu-
ous symbol: a pre-eminently destructive object, it nevertheless seems to George an embodiment of the purity of scientific
achievement. (There is a disparaging reference to 'turgid de-
generate Kiplingese' on the last page of the novel; but it is
worth pointing out that Wells, despite his scientific training,
is always much vaguer, more merely rhetorical in his writing
about machines than Kipling.)
In a last reflection George Ponderevo looks back on his
story in a spirit that is beyond mere disillusionment:

> It is a note of crumbling and confusion, of change and
> seemingly aimless swelling, of a bubbling up and medley

of futile loves and sorrows. But through the confusion sounds another note. Through the confusion something drives, something that is at once human achievement and the most inhuman of all existing things. Something comes out of it . . . I have figured it in my last section of the symbol of my destroyer, stark and swift, irrelevant to most human interests. Sometimes I call this reality Science, sometimes I call it Truth. (IV iii 3)

The positives that George is groping for here remind one of the demands of *avant-garde* artistic circles in the years 1910 to 1914, for an art which would be austere, geometrical, mechanical, and above all 'irrelevant to most human interests'. This demand was manifested in various ways in Cubism, Futurism, Vorticism; it was given a theoretical statement in the aesthetics of T. E. Hulme. Impatience with the merely organic and what Nietzsche called the 'human, all too human' was part of the mental climate of the years in which Wells wrote *Tono-Bungay*; the outbreak of war in 1914 was to bring in unprecedented ways 'something that is at once human achievement and the most inhuman of all existing things'.

v

Mr Lodge's analysis of the panoramic aspect of *Tono-Bungay*, of Wells's concern with the pathology of English society, has given a definitive answer to some of the most pressing questions that the novel raises. But it leaves others unanswered, and these come to seem, by contrast, all the more urgent. He is, I think, making a rather misleading analogy when he tells us that 'England' is the central character of *Tono-Bungay*, just as it is in Shakespeare's history plays. Mr Lodge dwells heavily on the panoramic side of the novel, the descriptive passages rather than the dramatic interplay of characters, the 'frame' rather than the 'picture'; and we have seen how fruitful his examination is. But if this were the only important element in *Tono-Bungay* it would be difficult to distinguish it in kind from a purely discursive survey like Masterman's *The Condition of England*, which makes no pretence to a fic-

tional dimension. In Shakespeare's histories the concern with
England emerges, as it were, cumulatively and by implication, from the unfolding of the dramatic action; it does not
try to replace that action.

In his *Experiment in Autobiography* Wells admitted that
his real interest in *Tono-Bungay* was *extensive* rather than
intensive; the scene as a whole interested him more than the
characters. And one may now recall Raymond Williams's
formulation that the traditional realistic novel depended for
its success on a proper balance of – or tensions between – the
social and the personal. I think we must conclude that Wells
did not fully achieve such a balance in *Tono-Bungay*: the
panoramic vision is not always a function of the action but
sometimes seems superimposed on it. There is a significant
paragraph at the opening of book II, chapter iv:

> As I look back on those days in which we built up the great
> Tono-Bungay property out of human hope and a credit for
> bottles and rent and printing, I see my life as it were
> arranged in two parallel columns of unequal width, a
> wider, more diffused, eventful and various one which con-
> tinually broadens out, the business side of my life, and a
> narrow, darker and darkling one shot ever and again with
> a gleam of happiness, my home life with Marion.

So far, we have been concerned with the wider column, the
record of George's public activities and interests. The narrower one, the account of his private life, takes up a substantial part of the story; and there can be no denying that
much of it is a failure. There are moments of credible poignancy in George's relationships with Marion and Beatrice,
but these are constantly betrayed by the slushy, adolescent
language and imagery in which George chooses to express his
erotic aspirations and disappointments: 'to see one's married
life open before one, the life that seemed in its dawn a glory,
a garden of roses, a place of deep sweet mysteries and heart
throbs and wonderful silences . . .' (II iv 5). As Walter Allen
has justly remarked: 'Wells was incapable of being anything
but sentimentally vulgar on the subject of sexual love.'
He was not helped by employing first-person narrative

throughout. Not, of course, that one need accept Henry
James's partisan objections to the 'terrible fluidity of self-
revelation'; the confessional, digressive narrative that stems
from Wells's master, Laurence Sterne, is, or can be, a perfectly valid fictional vehicle, capable of a high degree of art;
this much has been amply demonstrated by Wayne C. Booth
in his *The Rhetoric of Fiction* (1961). Nevertheless, first-
person narrative is not a good medium for the conveying of
strong erotic feelings: a sense of strain and embarrassment
almost inevitably develops and alienates the reader. Wells
falls into this trap time and again in *Tono-Bungay*, quite
apart from the fact that George Ponderevo's sexual attitudes
have a remarkable crudeness and immaturity. It has been
often remarked that Ponderevo's ideas and responses to experience are close to Wells's own: this is not always a problem, but certain of Wells's hypergamous obsessions about
well-born women obtrude heavily in the account of George's
affair with Beatrice Normandy. (The early scene in which the
ten-year-old-Beatrice appears sitting on a wall, before the
adoring gaze of young George (1 i 8), is closely repeated in
The History of Mr Polly, when the beautiful schoolgirl
Christabel appears to Mr Polly in much the same situation.)
    Walter Allen has, in fact, claimed that George's sensibility
is 'too crude for the criticism even of the economic system to
have much weight'. Whilst admitting the crudity, I would
disagree with this opinion, since, as we have seen, the socio-
economic criticism is conveyed by the cumulative interplay
of metaphor and language rather than by the fineness of
George's feelings. It is, however, true that although Wells
hoped, by his use of the confessional form, to show us a good
deal of George in both his public and private aspects, he
seems – after the admirable childhood scenes – hardly to exist
as a properly established character, but rather as a *voice*, insistently, sometimes naggingly, commenting, haranguing,
disputing; we are already moving ominously close to Wells's
later conception of the novel as dialogue rather than drama.
And it is very much Wells's voice that we hear: the confessional has been partly transformed into the ventriloquial.
    Wells has much greater success with the characters of
George's Uncle Teddy – 'the pinchbeck Napoleon of com-

merce', in Walter Allen's phrase – and Aunt Susan. On the whole, Wells does not attempt to present fully rounded, autonomous characters in the manner of, say, George Eliot. Uncle Teddy is a great creation, however, in Wells's own inspired vein of caricature, which owes everything to Dickens. He is far more energetic than a Lewisham, a Kipps or a Polly, and it is this that distinguishes him from them. Indeed, there is an almost Stendhalian quality about his energy which makes us readily forgive Teddy's moral shabbiness and duplicity.

E. M. Forster made some interesting comments on Wells's characterisation in *Aspects of the Novel*:

> With the possible exceptions of Kipps and the aunt in *Tono-Bungay*, all Wells's characters are flat as a photograph. But the photographs are agitated with such vigour that we forget their complexities lie on the surface and would disappear if it was scratched or curled up. A Wells character cannot indeed be summed up in a single phrase; he is tethered much more to observation, he does not create types. Nevertheless his people seldom pulsate by their own strength. It is the deft and powerful hands of their maker that shake them and trick the reader into a sense of depth. Good but imperfect novelists, like Wells and Dickens, are very clever at transmitting force.

This is penetrating, but certain qualifications need to be made. Forster's distinction between 'flat' and 'rounded' characters is a useful tool for dealing with some kinds of fiction, or for emphasising differences between characters within a single novel; but it is of very little value in satisfactorily explaining Dickens. Forster evidently senses as much in the preceding paragraph, when he remarks of Dickens, 'there may be more in flatness than the severer critics admit': if, in fact, one regards Dickens, not as a striking but somehow second-rate talent (as it was not unusual to regard him in the 1920s, when Forster wrote), but as one of the great creative geniuses of our literature, then one will feel the need of a more adequate critical terminology. At best, the 'flat' versus

'rounded' distinction will be descriptive rather than evalua-
tive. And if this is true of Dickens, then it will also be true, to
an appropriate degree, of Dickens's disciple, Wells.

One can, however, agree with Forster that there is an evident difference between Uncle Teddy and Aunt Susan: the
one is a violently animated caricature of a small tradesman of
Napoleonic will and aspirations; the other is a genuinely
rounded, autonomous-seeming, fictional character. The aunt,
with her cool ironic mind, unpretentious elegance, high
spirits and penetrating wit, is one of Wells's most engaging
creations. It is all the more regrettable, therefore, that he
should have done so little with her, apart from occasionally
letting her make shrewdly detached comments on the Ponderevos' rising fortunes. Even at the end, when Teddy is
ruined and Susan loyally stands by him, one feels that Wells
is throwing away dramatic opportunities that other novelists
would have used triumphantly. This reflects the novel's imbalance: Wells's determination to concentrate on the panoramic, the extensive, led him to neglect the intensive, and to
do a serious injustice to his characters.

There are many fine things in *Tono-Bungay*, quite apart
from its overriding social analysis. All the early chapters, for
instance, have a splendid vitality and humour. And Teddy
and Susan keep our interest and sympathy to the end, no
matter how weary we may become of the priggish, disembodied voice of George. The novel is, I think, impressive
but flawed; and the flaw lies precisely in Wells's over-concen-
tration on the extensive and public side of his story, and his
failure properly to relate the individual lives to the social
action. At times he comes close to achieving this: as when he
shows how Edward is as much a victim as a manipulator of
the Edwardian economic order. But the inert mass of
George's 'private' story remains an unassimilated element in
the novel.

The unique value of *Tono-Bungay* however, lies in the
breadth of its panoramic vision, where the sociological imagination works through metaphor and symbol to achieve a
memorable analysis – and indictment – of a whole social
order. And as I have remarked, some of this analysis is still
relevant to the England of our own time. The imbalance in

the novel means that it falls short of the greatness that Ford and Lawrence claimed for it; but if it does not, as Ford asserted, possess 'all the qualities of the traditional classical English novel', it has a good many of them. Certainly, it is one of the last examples we have of the panoramic novel, of a kind familiar to the Victorians, before the emphasis of modern fiction switched from society as a whole, or even individuals-in-society, to the study of individuals in isolated separateness.

APPENDIX: WELLS AND CONRAD

There are a number of apparent allusions to Conrad in *Tono-Bungay* which can be conveniently discussed under a separate heading. Wells and Conrad had been on friendly terms for several years; in fact, since the mid-nineties, when Wells was one of the first English reviewers to recognise the quality of Conrad's early fiction. In 1907 Conrad had affectionately dedicated *The Secret Agent* to Wells; but there is no surviving correspondence between the two men after this date, and all the evidence points to a growing estrangement. At this time, Wells was reacting sharply against the novel of aesthetic concentration, of which he regarded James and Conrad as the most eminent practitioners. In *Boon* (1915), a piece of literary boat-burning which provoked Wells's final quarrel with James, Conrad is referred to disparagingly: 'Conrad he could not endure. I do him no wrong in mentioning that; it is the way with most of us. . . .' a few pages later there is a contemptuous dismissal of 'the florid mental gestures of a Conrad'.[8]

Many readers may have felt that the 'quap' episode of *Tono-Bungay*, whatever its other qualities, has a somewhat Conradian air. This element is, I think, introduced into the story at the first appearance of Gordon-Nasmyth:

He talked very well. He talked of the Dutch East Indies and of the Congo, of Portuguese East Africa and Paraguay, of Malays and rich Chinese merchants, Dyaks and negroes and the spread of the Mahometan world in Africa today. And all this time he was trying to judge if we were good

enough to trust with his adventure. Our cosy inner office
became a little place, and all our businesses cold and life-
less exploits beside his glimpses of strange minglings of
men, of slayings unavenged and curious customs, of trade
where no writs run, and the dark treacheries of eastern
ports and uncharted channels. (III i 4)

One or two items in this list suggest that Wells may have
been thinking of the Scottish traveller, writer and politician,
R. B. Cunninghame Graham, particularly the mention of
Paraguay, a country Cunninghame Graham knew well and
had written about. But the general tenor of the paragraph is
highly reminiscent of Conrad; or, to be more precise, of the
way in which Conrad was regarded by the reading public in
1908. Conrad had utilised the setting of the Dutch East Indies
in his early novels, *Almayer's Folly* and *An Outcast of the
Islands*, while the Congo is the scene of *Heart of Darkness*
(1902). And it is of this last work that one is reminded in
parts of *Tono-Bungay*, particularly in the voyage down the
African coast of the brig, *Maud Mary*; in certain paragraphs
Wells seems to have been writing with half-remembered passages of *Heart of Darkness* in mind, as the following compari-
sons may indicate:

The edge of a colossal jungle, so dark-green as to be almost
black, fringed with white surf, ran straight, like a ruled
line, far, far away along a blue sea, whose glitter was
blurred by a creeping mist. The sun was fierce, the land
seemed to glisten and drip with steam. (*Heart of Darkness*)[9]

But so it was I made my voyage to Africa, and came at last
into a world of steamy fogs and a hot smell of vegetable
decay, and into sound and sight of surf and distant inter-
mittent glimpses of the coast.

(*Tono-Bungay*, III iv 3)

There is also a general resemblance between the final pages
of *Tono-Bungay*, with their portentous historical reflections,
as the destroyer moves down the Thames and out into the

estuary, and the opening pages of *Heart of Darkness*. The 'quap' episode may also incorporate a recollection of the attempted expedition to the guano island in chapter 14 of *Lord Jim*.

But the most curious and significant link between Wells and Conrad is to be found in the captain of the *Maud Mary*. He is described in these terms:

> The captain was a most extraordinary creature, under the impression we were after copper ore; he was a Roumanian Jew, with twitching excitable features, who had made his way to a certificate after some preliminary naval experiences in the Black Sea. (III iv 2)

The captain is a naturalised Englishman, who nevertheless spends much of his time denouncing everything English. His personal characteristics are very marked; he has learnt English from a book and he tends to pronounce the final 'e' in words like 'there' and 'here'; he has a beard and is much given to violent gesticulation:

> He had all those violent adjuncts to speech we Western Europeans have abandoned, shruggings of the shoulders, waving of the arms, thrusting out of the face, wonderful grimaces and twiddlings of the hands under your nose until you wanted to hit them away. (III iv 3)

Turning to Wells's *Experiment in Autobiography* we find a remarkably similar description:

> He was rather short and round-shouldered with his head as it were sunken into his body. He had a dark retreating face with a very carefully trimmed and pointed beard, a trouble-wrinkled forehead and very troubled dark eyes, and the gestures of his hands and arms were from the shoulders and very Oriental indeed.... He had learnt to read English long before he spoke it and he had formed wrong sound impressions of many familiar words; he had for example acquired an incurable tendency to pronounce the last *e* in these and those. He would say, '*Wat* shall we do with *thesa* things?'[10]

This, of course, is Joseph Conrad as Wells recollected him: and the resemblances of the captain of the *Maud Mary* to Conrad are too close and numerous to be anything other than deliberate. In another passage the captain asserts the virtues of the East European aristocracy, as against the bourgeois materialism of the English, thus recalling another predilection of Conrad's. It is hardly possible that Conrad should have remained unaware of this caricature, which is not merely ludicrous but malicious (the captain is cowardly and financially corrupt); and, given his notorious sensitivity, it is certain that he would have been outraged by it. There appears to be no surviving documentary evidence on the point, but it is reasonable to assume that this portrayal played its part in the estrangement of Conrad and Wells.

1966

7 Wells, Fiction and Politics

As an eager and impoverished science student in the 1880s, H. G. Wells had declared himself a socialist, even though he was not at all sure what being a socialist meant. Nor, indeed, were most other English socialists, beyond a general agreement on the undesirability of the profit motive. In his semi-autobiographical novel, *Love and Mr Lewisham*, Wells conveyed the hopeful atmosphere of those days, which he referred to again in his *Experiment in Autobiography*:

> Wearing our red ties to give zest to our frayed and shabby costumes we went great distances through the gas-lit winter streets of London and by the sulphurous Underground Railway, to hear and criticise and cheer and believe in William Morris, the Webbs, Bernard Shaw, Hubert Bland, Graham Wallas and all the rest of them, who were to lead us to that millennial world.

Yet though the young Wells responded enthusiastically to the ideas that he heard expounded on these occasions, his iconoclastic and critical intelligence was never able to swallow them whole. But it was at such meetings that Wells first became interested in the possibility of a 'millennial world', a topic which was to dominate his later literary career. 'World' was a favourite word of Wells's – it occurs in the titles of many of his books – and it was a major part of his achievement that he was able from the beginning to think in the all-embracing, global terms that have only lately become a common part of our intellectual intercourse.

In his early days as a creative writer Wells entertained global visions that were apocalyptic rather than millennial. He established his reputation in the 1890s as a writer of scientific romances which were both brilliantly entertaining nar-

ratives and oblique, mythic reflections of the dilemmas and
perturbations of the time. In the first of them, *The Time
Machine* (1895), Wells looked far into the future, to the year
802,701, when the elements of the late nineteenth-century
class struggle have become incorporated into the evolutionary
development of mankind. Humanity has divided itself into
the Eloi, who are frail, aesthetic, childlike creatures, and the
Morlocks, who are stunted and brutish, living in underground machine-shops, and who feed upon the Eloi, whom
they breed like cattle. The vivid but repulsive presentation
of the Morlocks is the first appearance in Wells's writing of a
recurring element: the conviction that the proletariat were
inherently barbarous and hateful. Towards the end of *The
Time Machine* the time-traveller moves forward many mil-
lions of years to witness the extinction of all life upon a dying
planet. In *The War of the Worlds* (1898) Wells showed, with
great imaginative relish, the destruction of late-Victorian
bourgeois society by Martian invaders. There is a similarly
apocalyptic note in the short stories that Wells published in
the nineties; in one of the finest of them, 'The Star', he describes the global havoc that ensues when a star passes close to
the earth and plunges into the sun. On a smaller scale, *When
the Sleeper Awakes* (1899) is a projection into the future of
the urban brutality and chaos, the accumulative monopoly
capitalism, and the violent class-struggles of late-Victorian
England or America. It also reflects Wells's interest in the
Nietzschean concept of the *Übermensch* that was becoming
fashionable in England in the nineties, and which he had already touched on in the most horrifying of all his scientific
romances, *The Island of Dr Moreau* (1896). A version of the
Superman, though sociologically cut down to size and dedicated to useful work as the member of a ruling elite, occurs
throughout Wells's fiction and speculative writings in the
twentieth century.

In the scientific romances, which I have discussed in detail
in *The Early H. G. Wells* (Manchester and Toronto, 1961),
we see some of the major facets of Wells's imagination: in
particular, his ability to think and feel in large-scale spatial
and temporal terms, and his intense curiosity about the
future state of the world. There is also a fascination with

images of destruction, and particularly of fire (V. S. Pritchett has remarked on the way in which fires occur in practically all Wells's novels). In these novels and stories we see Wells contemplating his environment, speculating on the possibilities that could descend upon it, and imaginatively transforming it. But the author's will is not exercised upon his material: Wells is content to reflect on the world as it is and might become, without attempting to make projections about what it should become. The tone throughout is cool and detached, and this detachment was an important element in the early development of Wells's literary *persona*. In the opening paragraph of *The War of the Worlds* the Martians observe the futile and pretentious activity of late-Victorian society with the cool gaze of a scientific observer looking at a specimen under a microscope. It was rather in this spirit that Wells himself dwelt on the future discomfort – or even disappearance – of humanity. In his early fiction Wells is admittedly concerned with humanity in the mass rather than with individuals, although Griffin, the Invisible Man, is presented as an interestingly realised character. In his first serious attempt at a realistic novel, *Love and Mr Lewisham* (1900), the detachment is preserved, in a way that partly adheres to the canons of 'scientific' naturalism, but which is also combined, a little uneasily, with an affectionate and even sentimental regard for the hero, who so clearly represents the genteel failure that Wells himself, minus his particular genius and drive, might so easily have become. Wells's own social origins provide further reasons for his stance of observant detachment: springing from the insecure lowest stratum of English middle-class life, he hated and feared the workers – his socialism was always elitist rather than populist – but at the same time he did not have the advantages of a conventional upper-middle-class background and education like most English men of letters. There was no class he could readily identify with, though after 1900 his striking literary success meant that he could enter the English Establishment on his own terms. In fact, Wells's need to discover a class or group that he could identify with seems to have expressed itself in the frequently updated versions of a ruling elite that recur throughout his writings. They are variously described

as scientists, teachers, trained administrators, practical ideal-
ists and clear-headed ideas-men with the ability to take de-
cisions. They first occur as the *samurai* of *A Modern Utopia*
(1905), and in later versions they appear as the progressive
businessmen of *The World of William Clissold*, and the air-
men of *The Shape of Things to Come*. But in all versions
they possess essentially the same attributes: they are highly
intelligent men and women who have risen by their own
abilities (meritocrats, to use a later terminology), they are
courageous, energetic and far-sighted. In short, they are versions of what Wells was himself, being free from the inherited
privileges and mental limitations of the upper and upper-
middle classes, and equally removed from what Wells regarded as the mental poverty and bloody-mindedness of the
working class. In his later life, Wells was constantly trying to
detect the possible elements of such an elite in the world
around him, and he claimed to have discovered it variously in
the Russian Communist Party and Franklin Roosevelt's
Brain Trust.

During the opening phase of his literary career he remained in an ill-defined way a socialist, but there is little
trace of direct political conviction in his writings of the 1890s.
If anything, the combination of a keen but detached interest
in disaster, and a vigorous stylistic energy, would suggest a
conservative rather than a radical cast of mind. Even where
Wells writes realistically about the common lot of suffering
humanity – as in *Love and Mr Lewisham* – he is more concerned with the pathetic or dramatic possibilities of his
material than with protesting against the intolerable. With a
writer of more ordinary gifts or less expansive temperament
this limited but effective literary approach might have continued indefinitely. But although Wells was a fiction writer
of genius, he was, in his own estimation of himself, a great
many other things too. By about 1900 other aspects of his personality had begun to emerge: notably those of the journalist
and the sociological speculator and even the preacher. During
the next ten years the artist in Wells existed in uneasy tension with these other *personae*, and in the end was defeated;
in a famous letter to Henry James, written in 1915, Wells
remarked: 'I had rather be called a journalist than an artist –

that is the essence of it.' With these new aspects of his literary personality a sense of direction appears in Wells's writing: he projects images of the future that are not merely exciting or terrifying, but which contain hopefully constructive suggestions about improving the human condition. Wells, who began as a bold and inventive drafter of anti-Utopias, now turned to positive Utopias. The cool pessimism of the nineties was displaced by a reasoned faith in the possibility (and in some moods, the certainty) of human betterment. The reasons for this shift of attitude on Wells's part at the end of the decade are not at all clear, but it seems likely that his restless speculative intellect did not find enough outlet in the production of 'pure' fiction, and was increasingly impelled to take over from the contemplative imagination. Again, the attainment of an increasing degree of personal success and even prosperity from his writing might have given Wells a greater sense of security, and correspondingly less motive to subject the existing social order to ingenious forms of symbolic destruction. For whatever reason, Wells became more systematic and discursive in his descriptions of the future, and the first result of this new approach was *Anticipations*, published in 1901, which Samuel Hynes has described in *The Edwardian Turn of Mind* (Princeton, 1968) in these words:

> Coming as it did just after the turn of a new century, it appealed to a natural popular curiosity about what this twentieth century was going to be like. Wells offered a vivid, simplified, credible image of the future, based apparently on the firm authority of scientific principles, but thoughtfully sparing readers the dull details of science – the evidence, the logic, and the proofs. The tone of the book is the confident, categorical tone of a classroom lecturer, enlivened with imagined scenes of future wars in the style of Wells's romances.

The confident tone is very persuasive, but the book is essentially a compilation of bold guesses about the future. Wells was more right about technological than political developments; he foresaw trench warfare and tanks, but was remarkably cautious about flying, saying no more than that a successful aeroplane may well have flown by 1950! However, Wells shrewdly foresaw that the improvement of methods of transportation would mean that the future city would consist of scattered low-density dwellings (like present-day Los Angeles), rather than the dense roofed-in metropolis that he had described in *When the Sleeper Wakes*.

Beatrice Webb was very impressed with *Anticipations*, while regretting Wells's lack of detailed knowledge of social organisation, and invited him to join the Fabians. Wells accepted; he was very willing to regard the Fabian Society as an elite dedicated to the socialist reconstruction of society. But the mutual admiration did not last long; Wells found himself temperamentally at odds with the Webbs, however much he might have agreed in a purely intellectual way with their approach. The Webbs were diligent and conscientious and essentially bureaucratic; they had no sympathy with Wells's speculative, high-flying imaginative cast of mind. Relations soon deteriorated, although Wells remained in the Fabian Society for several years and tried to reshape it in accordance with his own ideas. When faced with a dedicated practitioner of 'pure' literature like Henry James, Wells impatiently preferred to regard himself as a journalist; but on the other hand, when faced with a statistically-minded sociologist like Beatrice Webb, he could not disguise the fact that he was, in essence, an imaginative writer of idiosyncratic temperament, however much he too tried to be a sociologist. In the end Wells broke with the Webbs, and in 1911 he pilloried them in *The New Machiavelli* as Alitiora and Oscar Bailey: there is a long and absorbing account of the whole tragi-comic episode in Mr Hynes's book.

In 1905 Wells published *A Modern Utopia*, his first attempt to combine speculation about the future with a fairly coherent fictional framework. The book was immensely popular and influential: Henry James was delighted by it, whilst Beatrice Webb at least approved to the extent of assuming that the *samurai* showed how far Wells had absorbed her ideas. Wells took a good deal of trouble over the form of *A Modern Utopia*, saying that he aimed at a 'sort of shot-silk texture between philosophical discussion on the one hand and imaginative narration on the other'. At the beginning of the book the narrator and his companion, a rather gloomy and difficult person who is referred to as the 'botanist', are on a walking tour in the Alps: as a result of some cosmic conjuring-trick they are transported to the corresponding spot on another planet, which is physically identical with our own, but where life and its environment have been utterly changed for the better by advanced technology and improved social organisation. A recent critic, David Lodge, has precisely summed up the limitations of *A Modern Utopia* as they appear to the present-day reader:

Time has been cruel to *A Modern Utopia*. It would be difficult to arouse any enthusiasm for this vision of the good life today. Most of the things against which the current wave of youthful protest is directed in the Western World are to be found hopefully foreshadowed in Wells' Utopia: an examination-selected meritocracy, mixed economy, paternalistic state welfare, bureaucratic control over personal freedom, privilege based on productivity but controlled by fiscal means, minority participation in government, academic monopoly over culture, and a generally low-keyed, rather conformist contentment regarded as the desirable norm in behaviour. Wells' Utopia is a class society in which the classes are distinguished not by breeding or by cash, but by intelligence and vocational aptitude, with a decent middle-class standard of living available to all. In a sense it was a generous attempt on Wells' part to imagine a social structure which would make available to everyone the kind of success and happiness he had personally achieved in the teeth of great disadvantages. (*The Novelist at the Crossroads*, 1971)

There are, perhaps, elements of Fabian thinking in *A Modern Utopia*, but as Samuel Hynes has remarked, 'the Webbs worked for precise and particular reforms within the existing social fabric, whereas *A Modern Utopia* abandons the present for a spacious, self-indulgent daydream'. All Utopias are, in one sense, daydreams; but to say as much is not to dismiss their utility; as Karl Mannheim as shown in *Ideology and Utopia*, one function of 'utopian' thinking is to present the less forunate members of a society with images of transcendence, with goals which can be striven for politically. Yet Mr Hynes is right in underlining the hierarchical and undemocratic nature of Wells's ideal society: below the 'voluntary nobility' of the *samurai*, the dedicated, ascetic elite who actually run the country, there exist four fixed classes. Mr Hynes describes them in these words:

> The Poetic, based on creative imagination; the Kinetic, based on unimaginative intelligence; the Dull, based on lack of intelligence; and the Base, a class containing all those who lack moral sense. Wells' profoundly anti-demo-cratic turn of mind reveals itself here not only in the *fact* of this class division, but also in the very language he used – the Dull and the Base classes.

A Modern Utopia sets out most of the elements that were to become an abiding part of Wells's political thinking. As well as the elitist conception of administration, it demon-strates his conviction that the application of really rational, and particularly scientific, thinking to social problems would inevitably cause them to disappear. Always, for Wells the scientific spirit was the embodiment of true wisdom: only at the end of his life, after Hiroshima, did he have any doubts about this axiom, and by then the only alternative was flat despair. Wells was more interested in organisation than in ideology, and his lifelong quarrel with Marxism arose from the Marxists' refusal actively to plan for the utopian society and to project what Wells called a 'competent receiver' for the new social forms (the Marxist reliance on the working class as the prime agent of revolutionary change was an even more fundamental reason for his opposition).

Wells had little real interest in how the necessary changes in society would come about: sometimes, in his more imag-inatively excited moods, he would envisage a traditional form of violent insurrection; occasionally, as in his novel *In the Days of the Comet* (1906), social change would follow on an accidental transformation of the physical environment; but usually it would come with the inevitable onward march of evolution. In the twenties, Wells imagined a new society being established by what he called the Open Conspiracy, in which the social forms of the new order would be established alongside those of the old, gradually making the latter obsolete. All of this was very removed from the meticulous, middle-range planning that the Fabians favoured. At the same time, Wells had no grasp of the Marxist contention that the forms of consciousness are dependent on the patterns of ownership of the forces of production; and still less of the later and subtler applications of this approach in terms of the sociology of knowledge. Wells was happy to remain the quintessential bourgeois that Lenin described him as being. For Wells, the ideal society was some form of managerial capitalism, with a sizeable degree of state intervention; large-scale planning and a strong emphasis on science and technology. This is precisely the state of affairs that exists in most of the Western world at the present time, and although it has made the lot of the populace physically easier than ever before, it has not radically diminished discontent. The long-term response to *A Modern Utopia* is Marcuse's *One-Dimensional Man*.

The truth is that Wells was not genuinely interested in politics in the strict sense, which concerns the reconcilement of legitimate but opposed claims, with balancing the needs of society with those of the individual, and with coping with all the obstacles to progress that arise from material shortages or human perversity. Wells's Utopia is apolitical or post-political: it assumes that all opposed claims have been brought into harmony, and concentrates on describing the technologically efficient and mildly hedonistic society that has come into being. (There is, admittedly, an aesthetic rebel against the utopian order in *A Modern Utopia*, but he is treated as an amiable fool.) To some extent, this partial vision is inherent in the literary form Wells adopted. In his realistic fiction he understood very well the gritty recalcitrance and unpredictability of human beings. There is a significant passage in the opening chapter of *A Modern Utopia* in which the narrator reflects on the artistic limitations of the utopian mode; it shows Wells's sense of the tension between the artist and the prophet, and indicates the way in which a literary form can have political implications:

There must always be a certain effect of hardness and thinness about Utopian speculations. Their common fault is to be comprehensively jejune. That which is the blood and warmth and reality of life is largely absent; there are no individualities, but only a generalised people. In almost every Utopia – except, perhaps, Morris's *News from Nowhere* – one sees handsome but characterless buildings, symmetrical and perfect cultivations, and a multitude of people, healthy, happy, beautifully dressed, but without any personal distinction whatever.... It is a disadvantage that has to be accepted. Whatever institution has existed or exists, however irrational, however preposterous, has by virtue of its contact with individualities, an effect of realness and rightness no untried thing may share. It has ripened, it has been christened with blood, it has been stained and mellowed by handling, it has been rounded and dented to the softened contours that we associate with life; it has been salted, maybe, in a brine of tears. But the thing that is merely proposed, the thing that is merely suggested, however rational, however necessary, seems strange and inhuman in its clear, hard, uncompromising lines, its unqualified angles and surfaces.

This is an eloquent statement of the way in which traditional literature, and particularly the novel as opposed to the utopian blueprint, speaks to the conservative rather than the innovating aspects of the human imagination. One recalls Hyacinth Robinson's shattering realisation, in Henry James's *The Princess Casamassima*, that the bloody history of civilisation is interwoven with much magnificence. For several more years after *A Modern Utopia* appeared, Wells was to write true novels that would embody both the confusions and the 'blood and warmth and reality' of life itself. The characteristically Wellsian *persona* of the little man who is a victim of external circumstances in the conventional naturalistic manner, but who ebulliently and comically refuses to surrender to fate, is splendidly visible in *Kipps* (1905) and *The History of Mr Polly* (1910): in both books the hero, after many vicissitudes and humiliations, ends up in semi-pastoral seclusion from the cruel demands of an unjust and inefficient social order, which is left to continue its progress undeflected. *Mr Polly* is a pure gem of Dickensian comedy and Wells's finest achievement in the realistic mode, just as *The Time Machine* is his finest achievement in the field of fantasy. But it is a small-scale creation, and rather less interesting than Wells's major attempt at a substantial panoramic novel in the Victorian manner, *Tono-Bungay* (1909). This is an imperfect but immensely vital book, which combines the existing strands of Wells's literary interests: science fiction; social comedy; the 'discussion' of human problems. Among other things, it is an incisive anatomy of late-Victorian and Edwardian society, with a remarkable degree of imaginative unity. There are detailed studies of *Tono-Bungay* by David Lodge in his *Language of Fiction* (New York and London, 1966) and by the present writer in his introduction to the Riverside edition of the novel (Boston, 1966).

The difficulty of combining the collective vision of utopian fiction with the interest in individual character of the true novel continued to preoccupy Wells, and in one of his later utopian books, *Men Like Gods* (1923), he made a vigorous attempt to provide interesting characters. But in *A Modern Utopia* the stress, as Wells was uncomfortably aware, was very much on the collective, and the problems of the individual are rather airily dismissed. This, at least, is the impression one gets in the treatment of the 'botanist', whom the narrator chides for complaining bitterly about the unhappy love-affair he is involved in back on earth, instead of appreciating the marvels that surround him. Love, as Wells was well aware, is not easily reconciled with dreams of a tidy utopian order. Wells's imagination was deeply divided on this point, and the other side of the picture is seen in his realistic novels of the next few years. To point the contrast, I should like to refer, not to the relatively successful and well-known novels I have just mentioned, but to *The New Machiavelli* (1911), which was Wells's one systematic attempt to write a political novel in the narrow sense – that is to say, in the manner established by Trollope's Palliser sequence – and which shows quite clearly the vulnerability of large schemes for collective improvement when faced with the irrational desires of the individual. Considered in purely literary terms, *The New*

Machiavelli is not a particularly good novel, and the comparison with Trollope's political novels can only be damaging to Wells. But it has some merits, both as a story and as a source of insights into the embittered political climate of England at the end of Edward's reign. For Wells, it marked the close of his Fabian phase, and it has an interesting antithetical relationship with *A Modern Utopia*. Samuel Hynes, as I have remarked, described the earlier book as 'a spacious, self-indulgent day dream', and he uses a similar phrase about *The New Machiavelli* in his succinct summary of the novel:

> The novel is in fact a fictionalised account of Wells' Edwardian political life, improved and elevated, as one improves an unsatisfactory conversation after the fact; it is, as so many of Wells' topical novels are, a kind of daydream version of actuality. It has for its hero one of Wells' alter egos, a poor boy called Richard Remington, out of a Kentish town, who enters Parliament as a Liberal, revolutionises British politics with a campaign for the Endowment of Motherhood (the slogan that sweeps the nation is 'Love and Fine Thinking'!), switches parties, and finally throws his career away to go off with the woman he loves.

All of Wells's novels, one should add, have elements of fantasy or daydream, and their heroes are recognisable versions of their author at different stages of his life. Nevertheless, in the best of his realistic fiction the fantasy is subject to a genuine imaginative transformation. This is not so in *The New Machiavelli*, and for that reason Wells's dominant preoccupations loom much more palpably through the narrative. The book has some effective moments. The waspish caricature of the Webbs, with which Wells closed his account with the Fabians, is entertainingly done. And there is a vivid episode at a dinner party, where a fire breaks out in an upper part of the house, while the conversation round the table imperturbably continues, reflecting on the crimes committed by the representatives of the so-called civilised Western nations during the Boxer Rising in Peking. Whilst efforts are going on upstairs to put out the fire, one of the diners remarks on the flimsiness of civilisation: 'a mere thin net of habits and associations'. Here Wells momentarily anticipates the symbolic insight of Shaw's *Heartbreak House*.

In most of the book, though, Wells – or his hero – is not concerned with apocalyptic possibilities, but with the perennial problem of the large-scale ordering and transformation of society. Remington, having associated first with the socialists, both in their working-class and Fabian variety, and then with the Liberals, finds both groups insufferably small-minded and lacking in vision. Although a Liberal M.P., he turns to the Conservatives and the upholders of the imperialist ideal, in the hope that here, at last, he might find the largeness of thought that he had always desired. Remington describes the attraction for him of the imperialist movement, whilst admitting the evils that have so far been associated with it:

But a big child is permitted big mischief, and my mind was now continually returning to the persuasion that after all in some development of the idea of Imperial patriotism might be found that wide, rough, politically acceptable expression of a constructive dream capable of sustaining a great educational and philosophical movement such as no formula of Liberalism supplied. The fact that it readily took vulgar forms only witnessed to its strong popular appeal. Mixed in with the noisiness and humbug of the movement there appeared a real regard for social efficiency, a real spirit of animation and enterprise.

This is Remington talking, and not Wells, but the emphases are very familiar: ideology is far less important than largeness of vision and energy and efficiency. After this passage, Remington refers approvingly to the Boy Scout movement, which he seems to see as something like a *samurai* League of Youth. But in the end, all Remington's vision and attempts at a large-scale transformation of society come to nothing. His love for Isabel Rivers proves too strong: he leaves his wife and parliamentary career, and settles in Italy with his mistress, where he devotes himself to writing his autobiography, like Machiavelli in an earlier exile. In *The New Machiavelli* the intractable realities of individual human life triumph

over utopian aspirations: it is as though the unhappy
botanist of *A Modern Utopia*, having been scoldingly hushed
up by the narrator of that book, is finally permitted to show
that he too has a case, and an embarrassingly strong one.

During the Edwardian decade Wells was active both as a
straightforward novelist and a would-be sociological analyst
and speculator. Although he was aware of the opposition between the two roles, he contrived with some success to keep
them in balance. During those years his involvement with the
Fabians took him closer to practical politics than ever again
(except for a brief and unfruitful flirtation with the Labour
Party in the early twenties). Mr Hynes is undoubtedly right
to regret the waste of an imaginative writer's time and effort
that this activity meant for Wells. Nevertheless, it is a tribute
to his energy and powers of concentration that he was still
able to produce works of considerable literary quality, like
Kipps, *The War in the Air*, *Tono-Bungay* and *The History of
Mr Polly*. From the beginning Wells had taken the art of fiction with a good deal of seriousness, and in these novels the
creative imagination is allowed to go on its autonomous way.
But after 1910 the impulse to discuss and explain takes over
from the desire to contemplate and explore. In 1915 comes
the symbolic rift with his old friend, Henry James, and his
rejection of the title of 'artist'. For thirty more years Wells
continued to write works which read more or less like novels,
but are essentially arguments or tracts. Not all of them are
devoid of interest: coming from such a mind, it would be
surprising if they were, and occasionally there are flickers of
the old Wellsian imagination. For most of this time Wells
had nothing new to say, and although he wrote copiously he
was doing no more than enlarge on and refurbish the arguments that had taken possession of his mind during the first
decade of this century. As George Orwell showed in his sharp
but just essay, 'Wells, Hitler and the World State', written
during the Second World War, Wells was quite unable to
grasp the true meaning of modern totalitarianism. Orwell remarked that many of Wells's ideas had been embodied in
Nazi Germany: 'The order, the planning, the State en-
couragement of science, the steel, the concrete, the aero-
planes, are all there, but in the service of ideas appropriate to

the Stone Age.' In his later redraftings of the ordered future Wells became increasingly wilful and mechanical, and less and less inclined to heed the warning that the artist in him had inserted in the first chaper of *A Modern Utopia*, that all such projections are liable to founder on a basic sense of unreality. Only in the *Experiment in Autobiography* (1934), the most impressive work of Wells's later years, does he rise again to his full stature as a writer, in a remarkable work which combines the narrative gifts and interest in people of the novelist with the large-scale, expository interest in ideas of the teacher and prophet.

1971

8 John Gray

John Gray was once regarded as an archetypal young man of the 1890s. He was a friend of Oscar Wilde's, and was indeed rumoured to be the original of Wilde's Dorian Gray, though he denied it. He was a frequenter of some rather hot-house literary and theatrical *salons*, and his two books of poems, *Silverpoints* (1893) and *Spiritual Poems* (1896), both designed by Charles Ricketts, were slender monuments of *fin de siècle* preciosity in book production. Ada Leverson remarked of *Silverpoints*: 'I remember looking at the poems of John Gray (then considered the incomparable poet of the age), when I saw the tiniest rivulet of text meandering through the very largest meadow of margin. I suggested to Oscar Wilde that he should go a step further than these minor poets; that he should publish a book *all* margin; full of beautiful unwritten thoughts. . . .' Gray was not, perhaps, considered quite so 'incomparable' a poet as Ada Leverson suggested: Lionel Johnson dismissed him as 'a sometimes beautiful oddity' and Yeats does not mention him in the *Autobiographies*. He remains a rather shadowy figure in the annals of the period.

Like Lionel Johnson, Ernest Dowson and Aubrey Beardsley, Gray was a convert to Catholicism; and his beliefs were reflected in *Spiritual Poems*, 'chiefly done out of several languages'. But Gray was significantly unlike many of his contemporaries in refusing to complete the pattern by dying young. In 1898 he made a radical break with the London fashionable world and literary scene, leaving it for good to become a student for the Catholic priesthood at the Scots College in Rome – where his stay was happier than that of his predecessor of a few years before, Frederick William Rolfe. In 1901 Gray was ordained, and the one-time decadent poet and young man about town was transformed into a curate working with complete dedication in one of the toughest slum parishes in Edinburgh: a metamorphosis more extraordinary than anything invented by the writers of that paradox-haunted age. Gray spent the rest of his life in Edinburgh as a well-loved parish priest, and in 1930 he was made a canon of the diocese of St Andrews and Edinburgh. He died in 1934 at the age of sixty-eight.

Gray's break with his early life was dramatically sharp, but he did not entirely reject it. Visitors to his presbytery in Edinburgh were impressed with its *fin de siècle* décor, and he seems to have preserved affectionate memories of his friends of the nineties, though he would rarely talk about them: every year he said a special mass on the anniversary of Verlaine's death. And in becoming a priest Gray did not feel any need to abandon completely his literary activities, though for many years he wrote only a few hymns and devotional verses. But towards the end of his life he published two more books of poems – mostly secular in content – *The Long Road* (1926) and *Poems (1931)*, followed in 1932 by a novel, *Park*. As a writer, and particularly as a poet, Gray, in his long if not highly productive literary career, showed an interesting blend of continuity and innovation. Several of the poems in *Silverpoints* can be dismissed as no more than elegant and decorative exercises in the customary idioms of the nineties, though all are marked with an unusual degree of verbal fastidiousness. A poem such as 'Les Demoiselles de Sauve', to take a typical example, is like a skilful attempt at a verbal equivalent of a Beardsley drawing. But some of Gray's early poems show an unexpected degree of originality, as for instance 'Song of the Seedling', which attempts an empathetic penetration into vegetable life:

> Rain drops patter above my head –
>   Drip, drip, drip.
> To moisten the mould where my roots are fed –
>   Sip, sip, sip.
> No thought have I of the legged thing,
>   Of the worm no fear,
>   When the goal is near;
> Every moment my life has run,
> The livelong day I've not ceased to sing;
>   I must reach the sun, the sun.

This offers curious anticipations of some poems on similar themes by the late Theodore Roethke.

One of the oddest, and most successful, poems in *Silverpoints* is called simply 'Poem'. Its way of shedding a sinister and bizarre light on an ordinary scene may recall that Gray was an early admirer – and translator – of Rimbaud and other French symbolists:

> Geranium, houseleek, laid in oblong beds
> On the trim grass. The daisies' leprous stain
> Is fresh. Each night the daisies burst again,
> Though every day the gardener crops their heads.
>
> A wistful child, in foul unwholesome shreds,
> Recalls some legend of a daisy chain
> That makes a pretty necklace. She would fain
> Make one, and wear it, if she had some threads.
>
> Sun, leprous flowers, foul child. The asphalt burns.
> The garrulous sparrows perch on metal Burns.
> Sing! Sing! they say, and flutter with their wings.
> He does not sing, he only wonders why
> He is sitting there. The sparrows sing. And I
> Yield to the strait allure of simple things.

In this sonnet one sees, I think, some of Gray's typical qualities as a poet: a laconic precision of language, an unusual, carefully manipulated verse movement, and a certain oddity of phrasing – as in 'the daisies' leprous stain' – which is Gray's most obviously ninety-ish trait.

In Gray's later poetry these qualities are substantially unchanged, though he had in the meantime become aware of the changes in poetic attitude associated with Pound and Eliot. There is a slightly strident air of modernity, for instance, in the final stanzas of 'Audi Alteram Partem', from *Poems (1931)*:

> Unwinding its concentric crawl,
> a needle scrapes your epiderm,
> methodically as the firm's
> unnumbered patents foolproof all.

Pay the price. Prolong the search
for, right or wrong, what pleases us.
Listen, the patriarch of Uz
Is singing in the Temple church.

The last two lines seem to contain a distinct echo from Eliot's
'Sweeney among the Nightingales'. And one sees in the
rhyme of 'us/Uz', recalling the 'burns/Burns' of 'Poem', that
Gray preserved a taste for *rime riche* over a period of nearly
forty years. Gray's essential gifts are very apparent in another
late poem, 'Evening'. Its terse but suggestive understatements
and deliberate bareness combine effectively with a wavering
but beautifully controlled movement (though I find the
descent into conventional 'poetic' imagery in the final stanza
rather a disappointment):

We are just barbarians.
Our camp is vast.
The present camp and the past
show little variance.

For today we do
Whatever we did
in times bysped
and the years ago.

All over the ground
is bewildering;
scarcely a thing
where it should be found.

Children and hens,
wherever they group,
all mixed up;
not without offence.

A true to the life
picture of us
ourselves, incongruous;
neither at peace nor strife.

Opposite each door
blue feathers stand,
or sway to the wind
just as ever before.

Once call it night,
all disarray
has melted away
with the melting light.

Hens aroost,
children abed,
we break our bread
as we ever used.

Hardly stopping he goes
silently for hours
picking flowers
of stars reflected in the snow.

During the nineties Gray contributed a few short stories to
the periodicals of the time; an interesting story called 'The
Person in Question', a treatment of the *Doppelgänger* theme
with a certain flavour of *Dorian Gray* about it, was first published a few years ago in a limited edition. But it was not
until he wrote *Park* in the last years of his life that Gray fully
displayed his remarkable talent as a prose writer: *Park*, it
seems to me, is Gray's most sustained imaginative achievement, and a work that deserves a niche in the history of
modern English fiction. Subtitled 'a fantastic story', *Park* is a
curiously timeless work; though in one sense it looks back to a
utopian romance like William Morris's *News from Nowhere*, and has clear affinities with H. G. Wells's *Time
Machine* and other fantastic tales of the nineties, it is also
reminiscent of the more sophisticated forms of present-day
science fiction. This timeless quality is particularly evident in
the style, on which much of the novel's claim to distinction
must rest, a dry, mannered and deliberately understated
mode of narration which recalls the laconic precision of the
best of Gray's verse.

The eponymous hero of the book, the Revd. Mungo Park,

is a Catholic priest of sixty who undisguisedly seems to embody many of Gray's own attributes. He is a professor of moral theology in a seminary who is spending a holiday on a solitary walking tour in the Cotswolds. On the road from Burford to Oxford he undergoes some kind of alarming experience whose nature is not revealed; but we are abruptly shown its effect on Park in the opening Paragraph:

> Mungo Park walked on in the belief, absurd as he knew it to be, that he had died. There are catastrophes (so he assured himself) where the victim need not add to his perplexity the pain of suspending his judgment. And this hypothesis was some relief to him here and now – if, as in his anguish he thought, it *is* here & *is* now. He dismissed as impertinent his own critical question: when did it happen and where and how?

Park discovers that he is not dead, but he is in a transformed England which affords him many surprises, and quite a few puzzles. The original inhabitants have all disappeared, and the country is now run by a theocracy of Catholic Negroes – an aristocratic and highly cultivated race. Park is well treated by them – after an initial unfortunate incident when he is peppered in the legs with gunshot by an irresponsible gamekeeper – but they regard him with a good deal of wariness, as he cannot give what they would regard as a satisfactory account of his origins. At first Park has to communicate with the Wapami, as this new ruling race is called, in Latin, but eventually he is able to learn something of their language; his principal frustration stems from his inability to practise his priestly office. The Wapami do, indeed, suspect that he is a priest, like many of themselves, but since he is unable to produce any tangible proof of his ordination he is not permitted to function. A principal cause of difficulty between Park and his hosts is that they employ a different system of arithmetical notation from the decimal method, so that they do not accept that Park is telling the truth, or even talking sense, when he insists that he is fifty-nine years old. Eventually, since they cannot account for him, nor he for himself, he is given the status of one officially 'dead', which means that he

E

has freedom of movement though subject to certain legal disabilities; Park is now known as Drak. and has a companion
among the Wapami called Dlar (formerly Dom Egid Reni
of Reni), who is also legally a 'dead man', since he was once
condemned to death for an unnamed offence and then re-
prieved.

Park makes a variety of discoveries about this new world,
like the original Mungo Park, the late eighteenth-century
Scot who also made explorations among Negroes, though
those were savages whilst the Wapami are an eminently civilised race. The Wapami are organised as a feudal society leading a generally pastoral existence, though (as in *News from
Nowhere*) there seems to be a certain amount of technological
organisation behind the scenes. Motor-cars do not exist –
Dlar, who is a keen student of the vanished English civilisation, questions Park about the internal combustion engine –
and horses are the normal means of transit over short dis-
tances; but at the same time railway trains exist and are regarded as quite normal for longer journeys. Most remarkably,
Park discovers that sizeable remnants of the once dominant
white race continue to live a highly organised troglodytic
existence in vast caverns and tunnels beneath the surface of
the earth. They are described in these terms (Gray eschews
the use of quotation marks in writing dialogue, perhaps a result of his dedication to economy of effect):

When the wine had been tasted, Ini'in said: It is certain
that the underground tunnels and caverns are in part more
ancient than our coming to this island. They are excavated
& strengthened with consummate engineering art; & are
still the wonder of our greatest men. It is even supposed by
some that these works were carried out by people of whom
no other record has remained.
   People almost mythical.
   Yes. For if, it is said, you place them anywhere in history as
we teach it, you are faced by an intolerable paradox:
mechanical construction & genius we cannot overpraise,
with moral degeneration the most complete. The palace of
Vulcan inhabited by rats; Vulcan & the rats contemporary,
if not identical.

Well?

Why, to make a short ending of a long story, when their troubles came upon them, they took refuge underground and are there to this day.

Contented? asked Drak.

I think so, said Dlar and Ini'in at once.

This passage gives some idea of the eloquent terseness of style that characterises *Park*; but it also provides a useful point of departure for placing the story in its literary perspective. It contains immediate echoes of the fantastic fiction of the 1880s and 1890s. The division of the story between the Wapami on the earth and the vanquished white race living beneath recalls Wells's *The Time Machine*, though Gray does not attempt the unmitigated horror of Wells's story. Again, the notion of a cataclysm that has overthrown traditional society, replacing it with a utopian or pastoral order, is manifest in such works as *News from Nowhere* or Richard Jefferies's *After London*. And the theme of a race living permanently below the ground has come into greater prominence in the science fiction of our own day, reflecting a preoccupation with nuclear war, as, for instance, in James Blish's *A Case of Conscience* where it is the threat, which did not materialise, of war which has driven city populations underground, where they have lost the desire to emerge (this, too, is a novel which has a Catholic priest as its hero). Gray was original, however, in reversing the customary racial paradigm and making the black races superior to the white. Gray's sister wrote of him that he 'was deeply interested in the black man (he was a keen anthropologist) and used to say, although he was a white man he was black inside, and foretold in a general way that the black man would rule'.

Like all good writers of fantasy, Gray sustains his imaginative world by preserving an air of absolute matter-of-factness; we are given plausible-sounding details of the vocabulary and grammar of Bapama (the Wapami language), and occasional footnotes remind us of the difference between Wapami numeration and our own. If the story seems obscure in places on a first reading, it is because Gray presents his narrative solely through the dramatised consciousness of Mungo

Park, and events are presented as they impinge upon his sensibility, not in the order which would best form a coherent objective picture of what is happening. Gray displays a Jamesian austerity in suppressing overt authorial comment, but through the eyes of Park he occasionally offers some haunting, strongly visual descriptive passages, as in the account of Ini'in's garden, which is an imagist poem in prose:

> They passed into an enclosed quadrangle as beautiful as a bowling green, though the elements of its beauty were simpler: a sheet of peerless grass, with an enormous stone astronomical object in the middle; the grey wall, a triumph of proportion. A table was ready set under an awning; on it were three cups, a bowl of peaches, a bowl for refuse and an earthenware cradle for the wine-bottle. The sky, blue and white.

Much of the book's singular flavour is found in the numerous conversations, laconic yet mannered, which in their glancing obliquity have a slight hint of the dialogue of Ivy Compton-Burnett. Here, for instance, is an exchange between Park and a friendly priest, Svillig (otherwise Mgr Villa Gracil), on the thorny topic of Park's origin and identity:

> I acknowledge my ignorance.
> And we our impotence.
> So explain whatever it is right for me to know, from the rudiments.
> Well, we know you were born.
> But not when.
> Exactly. You had, and should have, a bishop.
> I can name him.
> You cannot.
> It was . . .
> Come back to the difficulty. Dare to tell me you are thousands of years old.
> Is that why I am a dead man?
> If you promise to leave that for another and probably longer conversation, I will answer 'Perhaps'. Are you thousands of years old?

How can I be?

How can you be? And yet unaccountable intelligent men say that you must be.

What a fix.

You say you are 60 (decimal numeration), he said, with a charmingly malicious smile, which obliterated the last vestige of his anger. We do not believe any of your statements of the kind.

You do not believe me? But here I am; I am in physical & mental health. I give an account of myself with its myriad particulars, which are all harmonious.

I believe you in a desperate, syllogistic way; for you are my friend. But that you were born 114 years ago I must deny; for we have proof that you are older. That you were born in Ia, on the same wild and contradictory understanding, I absolutely deny; for we have a complete list of every birth, in its proper genealogical setting (I mean of the surface race) for the last thousand years.

Like most modern fantasies that dramatise the problem of loss of identity, *Park* can be called Kafka-esque. But there is little sense of existential anguish in Gray's narrative; as the passage I have just quoted may suggest, one has rather the calm air of a scholastic disputation perceived with the weird consistency of a dream. (And a dream-narrative is what, ultimately, *Park* turns out to be.) *Park* is a puzzling story, but without deep mythic power; one recalls *Alice in Wonderland* rather than *The Castle*. It is both Gray's strength and weakness as a writer that he is above all a stylist; his effects are, as it were, on the surface, and though there are hints of symbolic overtones, I do not think one could usefully subject *Park* to a large-scale symbolic explication. But the surface of *Park* is of an unusually fascinating kind: Gray had a remarkable feeling for words, and a very curious imagination, and in this novel he achieved a unique and satisfying fusion of these qualities.

9 Chesterton and/or Belloc

The papist critic trying to reassess these two dead and illustrious figures had better put his cards on the table at once: the opposing dangers are sufficiently obvious, I think. On the one hand it is temptingly easy to genuflect before them in their established position in the front rank of English Catholic literary sainthood; to remember gratefully the spell they exercised in boyhood, to contrast their triumphant upholding of reason and right-thinking with the pestilential errors of our own day, and then, without too indecent haste, to pass on to other matters. This is implicitly to remove them from the province of criticism altogether. On the other hand, there is an equal danger of leaning over backward in a fit of unbiased (or 'undeflected') critical rigour, and dismissing them as posturing adolescents whose reputation was the result of temporary fashion and largely extra-literary considerations. However, a re-reading of some of their work recently reprinted by Penguin Books,* suggests that the truth is both duller and harder to formulate exactly than either of these two extremes would imply.

The first thing to be done, of course, is to reduce the compound monster, the Chesterbelloc, to its two components and look at them separately. The persistent coupling of their names may have had some point fifty years ago, when they seemed to their contemporaries a well-drilled propagandist musical comedy team, moving across the intellectual stage with supreme timing and precision. But in any longer view it does no good to either of them. Certain basic attitudes – apart from their Catholicism – they did of course have in common, and notably the one which seems to us most obvious and deplorable; namely, their anti-semitism. To some extent this

* G. K. Chesterton, *Essays and Poems*; Hilaire Belloc, *Selected Essays, Collected Verse*.

was a product of their cultural environment rather than anything unique to Chesterton and Belloc; in the years before the
First World War anti-semitic attitudes seem to have been extraordinarily common, both in literary circles and out of
them. As Orwell once remarked, there have been very few
English writers who were not in some degree anti-semitic;
and this was certainly true, for instance, of the socialist and
'progressive' H. G. Wells. Chesterton's attitude to the Jews
does not seem to have developed much beyond a kind of
rowdy schoolboy prejudice, but Belloc's opinions had a more
sinister tinge, for they linked up with those of the French
anti-Dreyfusards, and thus had a remote cousinship with
those subsequently associated with fascism in Europe. He was,
for instance, advocating in the twenties the kind of measures
adopted by Hitler in the thirties. And it is saddening to recall
that he lived on in silent old age right through the era of the
gas chambers and the 'final solution'. One can only regret
that the English Catholic writers who have been most assidu-
ous in perpetuating the Chesterbelloc cult should have been
so reticent about admitting – let alone condemning – their
heroes' racialism.

But it would be giving way to prejudice of another kind to
pretend that this basic flaw, once admitted, totally negates
their value as writers. It does not; or so I assume. Certainly,
the impression that Belloc gives of a greater intolerance and
potential degree of violence makes Chesterton seem, in comparison, a decidedly more genial figure. The personalities of
both men dominate their work; and Belloc appears as arro-
gant, egotistical and – what is more – a fundamentally unhappy man. Chesterton, by contrast, has a basic serenity and
assurance which blends with his exterior flamboyance to produce the popular cult-image: the lovable and convivial 'toby
jug' figure, with neo-Johnsonian overtones. Yet when one
comes to discriminations of a specifically literary kind, he becomes increasingly hard to place, for all his great output of
poems, novels, stories and essays. Much of his writing was
originally journalism, for both Chesterton and Belloc grew
up in an age when it was still just possible to combine serious
literary intentions with journalist practice. Chesterton, in
fact, was proud of his newspaper work and disliked the

aestheticism of the self-conscious artist. The daily newspaper, he wrote somewhere, was the greatest body of anonymous work to have been turned out since the cathedrals of the Middle Ages. But in the era of Northcliffe this generous attitude was already something of an anachronism.

It is true, however, that Chesterton's occasional essays are usually more interesting than his attempts at wholly imaginative writing, whether in fiction or verse. His novels are perhaps even more neglected than they deserve, for one of them at least – *The Man who was Thursday*, which is not a novel at all but a symbolic romance – deals with a potentially major theme: the whole problem of personal identity, so intriguing to our own age. But we need only compare it with, say, Kafka's symbolic fables on comparable themes, to see that Chesterton's story never rises above the level of a charade, or at least a prolonged and ingenious joke. His poetry, it must be admitted, is even less worthy of serious consideration. Reading it again, one is struck most of all by the predominance of the Pre-Raphaelite mode – a literary tradition which had become extremely tired by the time Chesterton began to write in it, c. 1900. And yet, at the same time, it must have had a certain obstinate viability to have lasted so long, for Chesterton seems never to have questioned its suitability for his poetic purposes. Indeed, one of the mildly disconcerting things about Chesterton is that though his Catholicism and medievalism represented extremely serious religious and social ideals, he was perfectly prepared to give them imaginative expression in well-worn trappings borrowed from the second-hand wardrobe of William Morris and others. As it is, Mr Wilfrid Sheed's small selection of his poems in the present volume is singularly uninspired, for it excludes both the splendid satire on F. E. Smith, and 'Lepanto', which is undoubtedly Chesterton's finest poem, containing a good deal of life and energy in its rather stagey fashion.

So we are forced to return to Chesterton's discursive prose if we are to find whatever is perdurable in his massive *œuvre*. It is in the essays that we most often find the characteristic Chestertonian vehicle and weapon, the paradox, which has been variously described as 'truth standing on her head to attract attention' and 'truth cutting her throat to attract attention'. Hugh Kenner, in his typically ingenious little book on Chesterton, has admitted his deficiencies as an artist, but has claimed that he was a 'metaphysical moralist' who employed the paradox as a mode of perceiving and under-standing the nature of reality. There is something in this: it is certainly true that Chesterton's use of paradox frequently degenerates into a mannerism, but it is equally true that he used it as earlier nineteenth-century thinkers had used other stylistic devices – in the way described in John Holloway's *Victorian Sage* – as a means of mediating a total view of life. It is well known that Chesterton 'invented' Christian ortho-doxy for himself before discovering that it really existed, and he similarly arrived at a *Weltanschauung* that was basically Thomist before he had even heard of Aquinas. (His book on Aquinas is recognised by modern Thomists as a classic of its kind, and it was written with only a casual knowledge of the relevant texts.) Whatever the limitations of his imagination, it would be a great mistake to underestimate his intelligence, which was remarkable. But for the modern reader it is prob-ably too strictly rationalistic. Every event in man's life, and everything in the universe, had for Chesterton an ultimate ontological purpose. Secure within an all-embracing and rationalistic world-picture, he could make adroit semantic analyses of his opponents' statements and wittily point out the errors and false assumptions contained in them. And this is the essence of the 'paradoxical' method. Engaged by the wit and precision of the observation, and the urbanity of the tone, one is forced to concede that some kind of point *is* being made, even if one does not agree with it: to that extent one has had, momentarily, to accept the Chestertonian *Weltan-schauung* and abandon one's own. In this way Chesterton's paradoxes have a rhetorical function, comparable to the stylistic tricks of Arnold. But they worked a good deal better in that pre-1914 Age of Reason, the period of the great debate between Chesterton and Belloc and Shaw and Wells, when men believed in the power of reason and were prepared to use it vigorously and combatively to prove that they were right and their opponents wrong, than they do now, when we are suspicious of *any* discussion of pure ideas, and a logic which deals in such clear-cut categories as 'right' or 'wrong' seems pretty crude. Whether this is a good thing or not is not at the moment my concern, but it explains why Chesterton – and the rest of his generation, Catholic or otherwise – seem such strange and remote figures nowadays. We are more concerned with a subtle and discriminating attention to particular facts than with fitting events into a total world-picture (of course, we will still have one, though it will possess the dubious advantages of being unconscious and unexamined). And here, admittedly, Chesterton is often deficient. His overriding concentration on a two-valued dialectic sometimes led him into some very unsatisfactory literary valuations. Thus, he complains in an early essay of the contemporary neglect of Scott:

> The ground of this neglect, in so far as it exists, must be found, I suppose, in the general sentiment that, like the beard of Polonius, he is too long. Yet it is surely a peculiar thing that in literature alone a house should be despised because it is too large, or a host impugned because he is too generous. If romance be really a pleasure, it is difficult to understand the modern reader's consuming desire to get it over, and if it is not a pleasure, it is difficult to understand his desire to have it all.

This is plainly nonsense, with an 'either–or' being worked to death, since there is absolutely no reason why one shouldn't enjoy romance or anything else in fairly small amounts and get bored by large quantities. The underlying notion is that good things partake of Being, that Being is good *en soi*, and the ultimate fullness of Being is God himself. Chesterton would have found it blasphemous to suggest that one *can* have too much of a good thing. It is this mistrust of subtlety, of the possibly infinite gradations of Being, that gives Chesterton's prose at its best a fine dialectic sweep and at its worst a tiresome obtuseness. Nor is this ultimately very much to do with Chesterton's Catholicism: the typically twentieth-century reader is likely to feel more at home with the poetry of Hopkins or the prose of Newman, where finer discriminations do operate.

Yet having said so much, I must hasten to add that Chesterton could be a very good literary critic. If it were a question of deciding which of his works were really worth preserving, I think I would opt for the two books on Dickens, which, though they may seem a little dated now, contain – along with Gissing's – some of the first respectable criticism to be written about Dickens. Some of the other writings on Victorian authors, too, would be well worth preserving. Indeed, instead of the present *ad hoc* collection of essays on a variety of topics that Mr Sheed has given us, I would much rather have seen a straightforward reprint of the *Criticism and Appreciations of Charles Dickens*, embodying as it does some of the best of Chesterton's criticism. In that book he adopted some surprisingly modern (and, I think, sound) attitudes. Thus, in the essay on *The Old Curiosity Shop* we find him taking a sternly anti-Intentionalist line:

> The function of criticism, if it has a legitimate function at all, can only be one function – that of dealing with the subconscious part of the author's mind which only the critic can express and not with the conscious part of the author's mind which the author himself can express. Either criticism is no good at all (a very defensible position) or else criticism means saying about an author the very things that would have made him jump out of his boots.

A fit rejoinder to what Northrop Frye has called 'the oh-come-now school of criticism'. And again, in the essay on *Great Expectations* there is a remarkable anticipation of some modern critical approaches:

> A great man of letters or any great artist is symbolic without knowing it. The things he describes are types, because they are truths. Shakespeare may, or may not, have ever put it to himself that Richard the Second was a philosophical symbol; but all good criticism must necessarily see him so. It may be a reasonable question whether the artist should be allegorical. There can be no doubt among sane men that the critic should be allegorical. Spenser may have lost by being less realistic than Fielding. But any good criticism of *Tom Jones* must be as mystical as the *Faery Queen*.

Reading the best of Chesterton's literary criticism, one can only regret that he dissipated his energy into so many other forms of writing for which he was less or not at all suited. But he was a humble man and sure of his readers, and there is no reason to think he would have regretted it himself.

If Chesterton was at his best when writing about books, Belloc was certainly at his best away from them. One need only glance at the brief essay on Jane Austen in these *Selected Essays* to see how little of a critic he was, for his essential egotism prevented him from removing his attention from himself to the work in front of him for very long. But on the other hand he was very much more of an artist than Chesterton. Re-reading his poems for the first time in several years, I was agreeably surprised, for Belloc appears in them as a good minor poet who deserves at least the same reputation as that now enjoyed by Housman: his wish to be remembered primarily as a poet seems eminently reasonable. The epigrams, of course, are deservedly famous, and one wishes we had now a political satirist who could achieve the lethal compression of 'Epitaph on the Politician':

> Here richly, with ridiculous display,
> The Politician's corpse was laid away.
> While all of his acquaintance sneered and slanged
> I wept: for I had longed to see him hanged.

There are few places outside Pope where precisely this note has been struck, and struck so well. Belloc's sonnets suggest that he was one of that remarkably small company of English poets who could genuinely think and feel and write – without apparent effort – in sonnet form. The language is almost as derivative and literary as Chesterton's, but the best of Belloc's poetry does give one the traditional romantic pleasure of hearing the voice of a vigorous and authentic personality coming through the somewhat threadbare diction and conventional rhythms. To this extent, Belloc is not merely bookish. And a similar quality redeems quite a lot of his bellelettrist prose, which is written according to prescriptions not very likely to recommend it to the modern reader, for Belloc came to literary maturity when the classically-inspired canons of 'beautiful English' and the 'fine style', largely divorced from content, were still the norm. Nowadays we see prose style as much more intimately a function of content, feeling and attitude, and are readily reminded of Max Beerbohm's comment on Pater – 'that sedulous ritual wherewith he laid out every sentence as in a shroud'. But the strange thing is that though Belloc wrote prose according to these somewhat external prescriptions, much of it is still good when judged by other standards. One might mention, for instance, the set-piece called 'The Relic' in the present book of essays, which conveys extremely well the intensely personal quality of Belloc's experience in a Spanish church.

In fact, Belloc's apprehension of the world seems to have needed the measured and calculated quality of his prose, or the formality of his verse, in order to be coherently conveyed at all. For despite his aggressively dogmatic and assertive manner, I feel that his inner life often existed on the edge of chaos and near-despair. The tension is certainly apparent in his writing. Though, like Chesterton, he whole-heartedly accepted the Catholic world-picture, Belloc did so as an act of disciplined intellectual assent, whereas Chesterton believed because the whole nature of his mind was constituted to do so. It is, perhaps, these sustaining tensions that give the sense that Belloc was both a greater artist and, for all his disagreeable attitudes, a great man. One sees, for instance, the inner isolation and unhappiness appearing for a moment beneath the rigid mask in the conclusion of his essay, 'On Unknown People':

How often have I not come upon a corbel of stone carved into the shape of a face, and that face had upon it either horror or laughter or great sweetness or vision, and I have looked at it as I might have looked upon a living face, save that it was more wonderful than most living faces. It carried in it the soul and the mind of the man who made it. But he has been dead these hundreds of years. That corbel cannot be in communion with me, for it is of stone; it is dumb and will not speak to me, though it compels me continually to ask it questions. Its author also is dumb, for he has been dead so long, and I can know nothing about him whatsoever.

Now so it is with any two human minds, not only when they are separated by centuries and by silence, but when they have their being side by side under one roof and are companions all their years.

In fact, Belloc was a good deal closer to the characteristic masters of modern literature than we may at first imagine. He, too, was a *déraciné* figure with a bewildering variety of *personae*: ex-scholar of Balliol, ex-French artilleryman, Sussex farmer, Liberal politician, anti-Dreyfusard, London man of letters, sailor. All these figures in turn inspired different aspects of his writing but never gave him anything like the conviction that a genuine set of cultural roots would have done. It is certainly true that the English connection, and in particular his friendship with Chesterton, were beneficial to him as a man, and modified the potentially sinister elements on his Gallic side. Had he remained wholly a Frenchman it is only too easy to imagine him as a supporter of Maurras, professing a purely 'political' Catholicism, and subsequently a man of Vichy. As it happens, Belloc's devotion to the culture of Western Europe as a whole, and to Catholicism as the incarnation and guardian of that culture, were clearly a form of compensation for his lack of more intimate roots. This devotion, too, was not without its unfortunate side, for it could lead him into such dangerous half-truths as the pronouncement that 'the Faith is Europe, and Europe is the Faith'. Yet it is impossible not to be moved by the extent of Belloc's knowledge and love of England and France and Italy and Spain and the Catholic parts of Germany. He knew these countries and their people and buildings intimately because he had been over most of them on foot. *The Path to Rome* is as much the record of a love-affair as a travelbook. Belloc's concept of 'Western culture' was something much more personal and existential than the purely literary and eclectic kind of 'tradition' compiled by Pound or Eliot, in their rather Adam Verver-ish fashion.

But in a final judgement it is Belloc's lack of interest in a specific literary tradition, and his tendency to oppose flatly the deeper tendencies of his age rather than to interpret and explore them, which makes him remote and inaccessible to present-day criticism. And much the same is true of Chesterton. Together with their non-Christian contemporaries they lived and argued in a world that seems almost as strange and distant as the Paris of Aquinas. Nowadays we tend to agree with Russell that 'it is better to doubt than to believe', and the conceptual apparatus of our literary criticism is made up of hints from Arnold and Richards about the 'free play of ideas' and the 'organisation of impulses'. So we go in fear of the stock response and the pre-existing *Weltanschauung*: thus far has criticism become itself ideological, with its own built-in 'deflections'. Yet this is clearly another and larger matter. Where Chesterton and Belloc are concerned, the Christian humanist is as likely as the agnostic to find them fallen idols rather than living gods in the heaven of literature. But their sleeping features deserve, at the very least, a long and respectful stare, before they are finally eroded by the winds of time.

1959

10 Man as Property

The habitual assumption that the Victorian era didn't really end until 1914 has something to recommend it if one is filling in a large enough historical canvas. All the same, it is inexact and can be misleading; it can, for example, obscure the fact that there was a genuine if limited Edwardian revolt against Victorianism. One of the more interesting manifestations of this revolt was John Galsworthy's *The Man of Property*, published in 1906. In this novel, set in the heavily respectable upper-middle-class London of the eighties, Galsworthy first introduced to the world that vast interlocking clan of Forsytes who were subsequently to become softened in the public imagination to a gallery of much-loved familiar old faces. But Galsworthy's original intention was satirical and, for its time, bold. The Forsytes, brooding over their property and the price of Consols, were rendered with a cold, derisive eye. And no one was drawn with sharper irony than the novel's central figure, Soames Forsyte, a rising solicitor in his thirties, tight-lipped, closely shaven and supercilious (in his delineation of Soames, Galsworthy made a classical embodiment of the Freudian anal-erotic type, complete with hoarding instinct). The novel describes the break-up of Soames's marriage. For all his cold nature he is passionately in love with his beautiful wife, Irene; but Irene not only doesn't love him, she finds him physically repulsive. She falls in love with the young architect, Philip Bosinney, and their affair ends tragically.

In this novel Galsworthy was attempting to make a plea for sexual freedom for women – (the misery of Irene's life with Soames is vividly, even hysterically, described – and to expose the oppressiveness of an ethos which reduces everything to questions of property. The novel is centred on two pieces of highly expensive property – Robin Hill, the country house which Bosinney is building for Soames, and Irene herself. Galsworthy establishes a parallel between them by showing Soames engaging in litigation with Bosinney over the price of Robin Hill, at the same time as he is losing Irene to him. Galsworthy emphasises the 'property' motif with some insistence: at one point Soames exercises his marital rights over Irene in what, it is implied, is a virtual rape, and this is later described as 'the greatest – the supreme act of property'. *The Man of Property* is not an entirely convincing novel; Galsworthy is a good deal better at social satire than at depicting scenes of passion – some of these are distinctly melodramatic. But the satire is sufficiently prevalent and incisive to make it a fairly memorable novel – certainly one of the best to come out of Edwardian England. Galsworthy draws the Forsytes as purely social beings: rather more than mere caricatures, but something less than deeply conceived fictional characters. Hence, perhaps, their air of existing on the same plane of reality as their furniture and hangings, stuffed and gilded objects rather than authentic persons. It is impossible to imagine them outside the inevitable setting of their tall, overfurnished houses in Kensington or Bayswater. Like, for instance, old Swithin Forsyte, who had 'an impatience of simplicity, a love of ormolu', and over whose dining-table 'a cut-glass chandelier filled with lighted candles hung like a giant stalactite above its centre, radiating over large gilt-framed mirrors, slabs of marble on the tops of side tables, and heavy gold chairs with crewel worked seats'. In passages such as this Galsworthy shows a remarkable facility for re-creating the quality of life of prosperous Victorians – whose scattered elements now clutter the Portobello Road. Yet this very facility, in some ways working against the satirical intention, might suggest a degree of concealed imaginative sympathy that could become overt.

And so it was to prove. Turning from *The Man of Property* to the succeeding volumes that make up *The Forsyte Saga*, and still more to the following trilogy, *A Modern Comedy*, which follows Soames's fortunes through to the mid twenties, one is struck and disconcerted by the way in which Galsworthy sentimentalises the Forsytes, and transforms Soames from something very like a villain into the admired and endorsed central intelligence of the sequence.

As D. H. Lawrence remarked: 'Galsworthy had not quite enough of the superb courage of his satire. He faltered, and gave in to the Forsytes.' To recognise the blatant collapse of Galsworthy's original intention is one thing, but it is another to try to explain it. And for this one can profitably consult Mr Dudley Barker's informative study.* Galsworthy was almost unique among the writers who dominated the early twentieth-century literary scene in having the background and education of a conventional English gentleman. His father was a wealthy solicitor – the model for Old Jolyon in *The Man of Property* – and Galsworthy's early life followed in a predictable course: Harrow, New College, the Bar (though he didn't practise). He loved dogs, and throughout his life religiously attended the Eton and Harrow match. At first he showed no inclination towards a literary career; he didn't start writing until nearly thirty.

The event that shattered the pattern of Galsworthy's life was his falling in love with Ada Galsworthy, the wife of his cousin Arthur. Their liaison, more or less secret, dragged on for nine years until Arthur finally divorced Ada. She married John Galsworthy in September 1905, soon after he had completed *The Man of Property*. It was Ada who first prompted Galsworthy to start writing, and his distress at her supposed sufferings at the hands of Arthur was projected in the Irene–Soames situation (Ada, who was a deeply neurotic woman, may well have exaggerated or even fabricated the story of Arthur's misdeeds – but John believed her implicitly). At all events, it is evident that the satirical impulse behind *The Man of Property* largely originated in Galsworthy's personal situation during the years in which he was writing the novel. He had accumulated a massive resentment against the treatment Ada had received from the upholders of conventional Victorian pieties – from 'Society'. His animus was that of someone who feels that he has been badly treated by his own class, not of a fundamental enemy of that class and its values. His satire, though pointed in places, was no more than skin-deep.

Once John and Ada were married it was not long before

* *The Man of Principle: A View of John Galsworthy* by Dudley Barker.

they were happily reabsorbed. Galsworthy was acquiring a fashionable reputation as a novelist and playwright: the road to the Order of Merit and the Nobel Prize for Literature lay gleaming ahead. Defiance of convention had, perhaps, made him a novelist, but once he was established he was entirely repossessed by all the fundamental assumptions of his class and upbringing. When he once more took up the Forsyte story in 1918 he was a respected elder statesman of letters, for whom the mood that had produced *The Man of Property* must have seemed remote and inaccessible. Yet he hadn't the slightest qualms about continuing the story with a totally transformed scheme of values, and a quite different view of its central character. For all his admirable personal qualities – he was a tireless supporter of good causes and gave away a large part of his earnings – it is difficult to be fair to the later Galsworthy as a writer. He continued, of course, to be an excellent story-teller, with a lively feeling for intrigue. But once he ceased to be a satirist his work lost all emotional coherence. His view of reality was hopelessly soft-centred. The sludge of sentimentality, presented in a prose shrieking with exclamation marks, is perhaps the most intolerable feature of the later sections of *The Forsyte Saga*. Even in his pre-war work a degree of sentimental evasiveness is apparent. In that wildly successful play *Strife* (1909), Galsworthy appears to be dealing seriously with a social issue – the effects of a prolonged strike in a tin-plate works. But the piece remains a nullity: insight is sacrificed to slick contrivance.

In his final years Galsworthy was wholly given over to flattering the Forsytes of the world, as though to placate them for his initial unkind treatment. To the end he retained inviolate those instinctive assumptions of the British ruling class that outsiders find so obnoxious; an effortless sense of unquestioned superiority and a corresponding condescension; one of the most insufferable scenes in *A Modern Comedy* is that in which the youngest Jolyon Forsyte encourages his American wife to 'get rid of her accent' (she, naturally, wants to).

Galsworthy tried to understand, and explain, something of what had happened to English upper-middle-class life between 1885 and 1925. He failed, for reasons which are evident from Mr Barker's book. The nearest equivalent to Galsworthy's attempt, if on a smaller scale, is to be found in Ford Madox Ford's Tietjens tetralogy. Ford, the cosmopolitan Tory, though an affected ass in some ways, had the understanding and sensibility that Galsworthy lacked, and his sequence is more penetrating and far more honest.

1963

11 The Reputation of Ford Madox Ford

If Ford Madox Ford is more widely read and discussed today than he was a few years ago, then most of the credit must go to the Americans. In the late thirties Ford's reputation was at an absolute nadir in England, only twenty years after he had been at the centre of the metropolitan literary scene. The *English Review*, which Ford edited between 1908 and 1910, was one of the most distinguished publications ever to appear in the English-speaking world: the contributors to the first issue included Hardy, James, Conrad, Galsworthy, W. H. Hudson, Tolstoy and Wells, while later numbers included the first published work of D. H. Lawrence and Wyndham Lewis. Ford may, indeed, have been half remembered as a great editor, but his own creative achievement as a novelist was resolutely disregarded. Thus, Cyril Connolly's *Enemies of Promise*, first published in 1938, contains a useful chronological list of key works of modern literature published between 1900 and 1932. If we look up the entry for the year 1915, we see titles by Norman Douglas, Ronald Firbank and Somerset Maugham, but no word of Ford's masterpiece, *The Good Soldier*. Again, Mr Connolly gives a very comprehensive list of books for the years 1924 to 1928, but says nothing of *Some Do Not* and the other sections of Ford's long novel about Christopher Tietjens, now known collectively as *Parade's End*. And *Parade's End* is certainly regarded in America as one of the major achievements of modern English fiction.

When Ford died in the summer of 1939, the *Times Literary Supplement* published a rather grudging obituary notice, which treated Ford – who was only sixty-six when he died – as if he were a forgotten minor survival from some unimaginably remote literary epoch:

Had he died even twelve years ago serious appraisals would
have been made of his practice of criticism – not, perhaps,
of his value as poet and novelist, for his work in those arts
had begun to date twenty years ago: they were steeped
deeply in the ancient ways of romance.

It is hard to believe that the writer of those words had the
slightest familiarity with Ford's major fiction, let alone any
real understanding of it. Nothing could be less 'steeped
deeply in the ancient ways of romance' than the austere, intricate, painful narrative of *The Good Soldier*. Nowadays one
can expect a more informed response. Ford has always had a
powerful English advocate in Mr Graham Greene, and under
Mr Greene's sponsorship an adequate selection of Ford's writings has been published by the Bodley Head, including *The
Good Soldier, Parade's End*, an historical trilogy, *The Fifth
Queen* and extracts from his poetry and memoirs.

Yet even where Ford is not ignored, one has the feeling
that he is more acknowledged than read. At least he does not
seem to have achieved the status of a prescribed author for A-
level English Literature texts, like Forster and Lawrence.
When I included Ford in a university course on twentieth-
century fiction, the reaction of students was a genuine appreciation of his work, coupled with mild surprise that they had
never even heard of him before.

In America, however, the situation is very different. At
least four critical books on Ford have recently appeared
there, together with a bibliographical study. And now we
have two more contributions by American scholars: *The
Life and Work of Ford Madox Ford* by Frank MacShane, and
Letters of Ford Madox Ford edited by Richard M. Ludwig.
Mr MacShane's book is a well-ordered, workmanlike study of
Ford's public career, or careers, for in the course of his life
Ford was the focus of three separate centres of literary
activity. First, in pre-war London as editor of the *English Review* and as a benevolent friend of Imagism, Vorticism and
other *avant-garde* movements. After the First World War,
Ford re-established himself as a man of letters and patron of
the experimental arts among the brilliant expatriates of

Paris. The *Transatlantic Review*, which Ford founded there in 1924, was another highly distinguished magazine, though his editorship lasted for no more than a year. Finally, Ford was something of a literary hero to the Southern Agrarian group in America during the thirties; for the last two years of his life he was a professor at Olivet College, Michigan. All these phases are well documented in Mr MacShane's biography and in the collected letters. Mr MacShane states, however, that he does not wish to add to the information about Ford's personal life contained in Douglas Goldring's more intimate biography, *The Last Pre-Raphaelite*, published in 1948. To that extent Mr MacShane's biography supplements Goldring's, but does not supplant it.

There is a sense, of course, in which this American academic devotion to Ford may owe something to the relentless need of American graduate students to find new worlds to conquer, or fresh topics to write dissertations about. There is an element of truth in this, but it would, I think, be excessively cynical to dismiss the current American interest in Ford as no more than a product of the inflationary demands of the graduate schools. The fact is that British and American literary taste is significantly different in a number of ways, and this is particularly apparent in attitudes to technique. American readers and writers – and not only academics – are keenly interested in technical considerations, whereas the British tend to find these boring and, if pushed too hard, rather an embarrassment. Hence the unending American interest in Joyce – the supreme literary technician of all time – a figure whom many English readers find too strong in gimmicks and too weak in moral seriousness. Ford, too, is an author who offers enormous technical interest to the student of modern fiction. The way the first-person narrative works in *The Good Soldier*, where the true meaning of events has to be construed from the duped and unreliable consciousness of the story-teller John Dowell, is one example of this. Another is Ford's virtuoso use of the time-shift in parts of *Parade's End*, a technique which Ford worked out in collaboration with Conrad but which, if anything, he used more adroitly than Conrad. These are questions which interest American readers more strongly than English ones.

But the American interest in Ford is far from simply academic, and involves more than a sympathetic sharing of his passionate concern with form and method in fiction. During his years in America he aroused a genuine personal devotion in a number of his fellow-writers, including poets like William Carlos Williams and Allen Tate, and this has helped to keep alive the memory of his work there. Among the pleasantest aspects of Mr MacShane's biography are the poetic tributes by American poets that form the epigraphs to some of the chapters: the whole book is prefaced with a poem in memory of Ford by Robert Lowell, who had come to know him while still an undergraduate:

> But master, mammoth mumbler, tell me why
> the bales of your left-over novels buy
> less than a bandage for your gouty foot.
> Wheel-horse, O unforgetting elephant,
> I hear you huffing at your old Brevoort,
> Timon and Falstaff, while you heap the board
> for publishers. Fiction! I'm selling short
> your lies that made the great your equals. Ford,
> you were a kind man and you died in want.

As we have seen, the English response to Ford was very different. In 1922 Ford had left England for good and he returned only on brief visits. He was not alone in finding the British post-war climate insupportable: Ezra Pound, who had looked on London as the cultural hub of the universe when he arrived there in 1908, took the first opportunity of leaving it after the war ended. So, too, did D. H. Lawrence and Richard Aldington. Expatriation has been an essential element in the literature of the Modern Movement, and the English were the hosts of some of its most distinguished practitioners: Conrad, James, Eliot, in particular, and, for some of their most formative years, Pound and Yeats. If Thomas Hardy, chronicling the life of Wessex from a house he built for himself in the heart of Dorset, can serve as a symbol of the traditional close relationship between writer and material, then James Joyce, immersing himself more and more deeply in the life of Dublin, from successive exiles in Trieste, Zürich and Paris, indicates the deliberate alienation of the modernist expatriate.

The Americans have, on the whole, regarded their expatriates with tolerance, despite the resentment of someone like Van Wyck Brooks against Henry James; or William Carlos Williams's bitter accusations that Eliot had betrayed American poetry to the enslavements of Europe. Almost all the notable American writers of the first thirty years of this century had some experience of expatriate existence; the only notable exception was William Faulkner, who throughout his life preserved a physical closeness to his subject-matter that made him remarkable among great twentieth-century writers. The British, however, have a habit of withdrawing favour from writers who decide to live elsewhere, and this I think, is one reason why Ford's reputation slumped so disastrously in the twenties and thirties. D. H. Lawrence offers something of a similar case: the general neglect of his work in the thirties must owe something to his disappearance from English literary circles, though it is also true that it suffered disastrously by being cut off from his imaginative and emotional roots. A lesser but instructive instance is the poet and novelist Richard Aldington: his novel *Death of a Hero*, which was something of an anti-English manifesto (and which, incidentally, contains a malicious portrait of Ford in his pre-war days), aroused a good deal of interest in 1929, but after that Aldington was largely neglected. His vividly interesting autobiography, one of his best books, appeared in America in 1941, but has never found an English publisher.* Ford had similar experiences with his later books, and in one of his letters he suggests that it would hardly be worth bringing out an English edition of one of his books, since it would sell so badly. To take another example: I imagine that the stature of Robert Graves would have been recognised a lot sooner if it had not been for his deliberate exile of the last thirty-seven years. (Though the career of Somerset Maugham suggests that if one is solidly established in public esteem it doesn't matter where one chooses to live.)

In his biography Mr MacShane provides some plausible clues to the British rejection of Ford. When Ford edited the

* It did, soon after this essay was published.

English Review his critical standards were so high that he offended some of the most influential reviewers and moulders of opinion by refusing to print their work. Subsequently, Mr MacShane suggests, they took their revenge on Ford by refusing to countenance him as a serious writer. Knowing the way metropolitan literary life works, it does not seem an extravagant notion. Ford was certainly not helped by his infallible capacity for making a mess of his private life – and often a sadly public mess. In 1910 he was sued by his wife for 'restitution of conjugal rights', and spent ten days in Brixton prison for defying a court order. Literary London was sharply divided over this scandal, and the majority turned against Ford, including Henry James, whom he had always regarded as a friend, and who had used Ford as a model for Merton Densher in *The Wings of the Dove*.

On all the evidence, Ford does seem to have been unjustly treated, and his troubles were most marked during the First World War, as his letters show; they were later transmuted into the tribulations of Christopher Tietjens. But the evidence is still rather scanty; Ford was a generous man and a dedicated lover of the arts and encourager of the young. But he was also a snob and something of a braggart, or as we might say nowadays, a 'role-player'. Possibly the sympathetic portrayals by Douglas Goldring and Mr MacShane need to be complemented by Aldington's representation of Ford as Mr Shobbe:

> Shobbe was an excellent example of the artist's amazing selfishness and vanity. After the comfort of his own person he really cared for nothing but his prose style and literary reputation. He was also an amazing and very amusing liar – a sort of literary Falstaff.

There may well have been something about Ford's personality that invited rebuff and irritation; at all events, like Falstaff, he was rejected. This question is not of merely biographical interest: it is desirable to know something about the context in which a writer's work was first read – or not read – if we are to grasp all its aspects.

H. G. Wells quarrelled with Ford over the running of the

English Review, but he retained a certain respect for him and defended him against a malicious attack during the course of the war. In his *Experiment in Autobiography* Wells places the half-German Ford in the company of that group of illustrious aliens who lived within a few miles of each other in Kent in the early 1900s and whose friendship Wells had enjoyed for a while; they included Ford, James, Conrad and Stephen Crane. Wells writes half affectionately, half dismissively, about their extreme devotion to the novel as an aesthetic form and what he regarded as a characteristic exoticism in their approach to life and letters. Their attitude to the novel was very different from his; and in this respect he was speaking for a great many readers. Wells and Galsworthy, Lawrence and Forster, write at very different levels of artistic seriousness, but they all write from a fairly central concern with English life and manners. Compared with these, the half-German Ford does seem exotic; Ford grew up in a cosmopolitan, highly artistic household, and when he wanted to depict Christopher Tietjens, a stolid member of the Yorkshire squirearchy, he had to do so from little extensive knowledge of that class. In fact, his friend Arthur Marwood served as an adequate model, and the character of Tietjens is a *tour de force*. Tietjens is used by Ford as the focus for a rather romantic portrayal of the crack-up of traditional English aristocratic values, which works by suggestion and implication rather than by direct realism. Americans were accustomed to imagining English society in this heightened and selective way, whereas English readers might find it a distorted picture.

As we have seen, there is one English novelist who has preserved a lifelong admiration for Ford – Graham Greene, who has written of *The Good Soldier*: 'I don't know how many times in nearly forty years I have come back to this novel of Ford's, every time to discover a new aspect to admire.' Mr Greene also admires James and Conrad, and shows this admiration in his novels. Although he has never quite been an expatriate, he has found most of his material in faraway places; when he does write about the English scene he throws a strange, exotic light on Brighton or the London suburbs. There is, I think, an unmistakable debt to Ford in Mr

Greene's fiction: a character like Scobie in *The Heart of the Matter* has a striking resemblance to Ashburnham in *The Good Soldier,* a novel whose influence is also evident in the careful construction and intense sexual anguish of *The End of the Affair.* Ford's concern with the dark side of Catholicism, as manifested by Leonora Ashburnham and Sylvia Tietjens, would also have a profound appeal for Mr Greene.

But in this creative debt to Ford Mr Greene is alone in this country. In general, Ford's exotic conception of English life, and his highly conscious artistry, mean that he still hasn't properly 'taken' with English readers. I think that before long his peculiar genius will be more widely recognised, though I doubt if he will ever be really popular in England. In the meantime, one must salute the American energy now being devoted to him, as manifested in the admirable labours of Mr MacShane and Mr Ludwig. It might even be a useful strategy for us to read Ford as if he were, after all, an American novelist of a rather special kind.

1967

12 Georgians in Peace and War

A little over fifty years ago, Rupert Brooke died of blood poisoning in the Aegean, on his way to Gallipoli. Some months before, he had anticipated the event in 'The Soldier', the most celebrated of his *1914* sonnets, which before long was to become one of the most widely read and frequently quoted short poems in the language: if the Tolstoyan theory of art had any validity, it would be one of the greatest.

> If I should die, think only this of me:
>   That there's some corner of a foreign field
> That is forever England. There shall be
>   In that rich earth a richer dust concealed,
> A dust whom England bore, shaped, made aware;
>   Gave, once, her flowers to love, her ways to roam,
> A body of England's, breathing English air,
>   Washed by the rivers, blest by suns of home.

These lines not only contributed to Brooke's personal apotheosis as the first of the 'war poets', a hero and victim of uniquely glamorous calibre; they also provided a mystical consummation to a literary and cultural movement of which Brooke had been, briefly, one of the brighter stars. In 1912 Brooke had contributed prominently to *Georgian Poetry, 1911–1912*, whose editor, Edward Marsh, had remarked in his Preface: 'This volume is issued in the belief that English poetry is now again putting on a new strength and beauty . . . we are at the beginning of another "Georgian period" which may take rank in due time with the several great poetic ages of the past.'

The Georgian movement had a number of poetic aims and

characteristics which are fully described in Mr Ross's excellently informative book.* One of the most prominent was the stress on England, both as a poetic subject and a state of mind; in the years before 1914 the word seemed to have a curious poignancy, and the small endearing features of the English rural scene were correspondingly celebrated by the young poets of whom Marsh wrote with such eager enthusiasm.

Theirs was, essentially, a little-Englander's vision, as opposed to Kipling's interest in a Greater Britain, an England beyond the seas; the poetic view is closely paralleled in E. M. Forster's novel, *Howards End*, whose central motif, the Hertfordshire house with the wych elm growing outside, is seen as an image of the continuity of English tradition. Forster's book is full of evocative, essay-like descriptions of the English countryside, and his decent worried liberalism was echoed by the more articulate of the poets. Indeed, after reading Christopher Hassall's biography of Brooke I felt that he might have been the hero of an unwritten – or suppressed – novel about pre-war Cambridge by his friend Forster. Brooke's *1914* sonnets show us the modest Georgian feeling for England being wrought to a higher pitch by the passions and expectations of war. In the later war poetry this transfigured patriotism disappears under the brutishness of trench warfare and artillery bombardments, but the Georgian mode persisted as a constant painful contrast between the remembered beauty of England and the unendurable realities of the Front. Then, with an increased sense of betrayal by the civilians at home, the soldier-poets came to feel that the Army in France was the only genuine embodiment of the England they had cherished. This sentiment was expressed by Wilfred Owen in one of his last poems, written in September 1918, only a few weeks before his death:

> This is the thing they know and never speak,
> That England one by one had fled to France,
> Not many elsewhere now, save under France.

The English war poets are given a very adequate discussion

* *The Georgian Revolt* by Robert H. Ross.

in Mr Johnston's book.* He deals in detail with five victims –
Brooke, Julian Grenfell, Charles Sorley, Owen and Isaac
Rosenberg; and five survivors – Robert Nichols, Siegfried
Sassoon, Edmund Blunden, Herbert Read and David Jones.
It is a pioneering work, since no one has tackled the subject
at this length before, and Mr Johnston deserves every credit
for being first in the field. It is a pity, though, that his book
has a number of deficiencies; for one thing, considering its
length, it is needlessly selective, and leaves out poets who
should at least have been mentioned, such as Richard Aldington and Ivor Gurney. Mr Johnston tends to write repeti-
tively, and his book is distorted rather than illuminated by
the over-rigid application of a thesis, which asserts that the
immediate semi-lyrical response of the trench poets was inadequate to a subject that demanded epical treatment. Mr
Johnston sees the nearest equivalent to such a treatment in
certain post-war works: Herbert Read's *The End of a War*
and, most particularly, David Jones's masterly *In Parenthesis*,
about which he writes very well.

Between them, *English Poetry of the First World War* and
Mr Ross's *The Georgian Revolt* – which is subtitled 'Rise
and Fall of a Poetic Ideal, 1910–1922' – provide a very handsome account of the English poetry of the second decade of
the twentieth century. Mr Johnston tends to be weak on
literary history and conducts his analyses in a rather forma-
listic critical vacuum; Mr Ross, on the other hand, writes pre-
eminently as a literary historian. He has had access to Sir
Edward Marsh's papers and is able to describe in full detail
the story of the successive volumes of *Georgian Poetry*,
from their hopeful beginnings in 1912, through the difficult
war years, and on to their decline in the early twenties; he
shows how, in the early days, 'Georgian' suggested an energetic, life-giving, innovating response to literature, whereas
ten years later, such had been the rapid shifts of history, the
word had come to mean everything that was timid, dull and
conventional. *The Georgian Revolt* is an extremely useful
piece of scholarship, though Mr Ross succumbs at times to the
scholar's weakness of being so excited by the various minu-
tiae he has turned up that he tends to forget their ultimate

* *English Poetry of the First World War* by John H. Johnston.

relevance or importance. In some ways Mr Ross has been
anticipated by C. K. Stead's admirable volume on early
twentieth-century poetry, *The New Poetic*, which came out
in 1964, too late for him to consult. Mr Stead's book is less
scholarly but more suggestive, full of helpful intuitions and a
firm grasp on the dominant interrelating themes and issues in
the poetry of the time. By contrast, Mr Ross loses sight of the
forest for some of the time in his energetic pursuit of a variety
of saplings from the Georgian grove. Both he and Mr Stead,
however, come to similar conclusions: it is insufficient to dismiss the Georgians simply as something against which Eliot
and Pound were reacting. In fact, both the Georgians, who
advocated the pursuit of straightforward rural topics in
direct, even earthy language, and the followers of Hulme and
Pound, with their more exotic and cosmopolitan interests, felt
themselves to be equally in revolt against the complacent
flaccidity of much Edwardian versifying. Mr Ross describes
the Georgians as being in the poetic Centre while the
Imagists were on the Left (within the next ten years the
Georgians, like other practitioners of bourgeois radicalism,
were to be pushed steadily to the Right).

Mr Ross points out that there were three distinct phases of
the Georgian movement. First came the original poets of the
1912 Anthology, Brooke, Lascelles Abercrombie, Gordon
Bottomley and Wilfred Gibson, who regarded themselves,
and were regarded, as being moderately radical if not *avant-
garde* in their poetic practice (one or two of Rupert Brooke's
early poems had given great offence because of their unwonted frankness of language and imagery), particularly in
their use of – relatively – direct speech. Next, during the war,
a number of soldier poets were admitted to the anthology:
Robert Graves, Siegfried Sassoon, Robert Nichols and, in a
fragmentary and unrepresentative way, Isaac Rosenberg. The
final phase came with what Mr Ross calls the 'Neo-Georgians',
such as J. C. Squire, Edward Shanks and John Freeman,
who wrote watery escapist verse that made an almost obsessive
use of moon-images; they clearly represented a loss of nerve
born of the war, and they had a lot to do with giving the
whole Georgian movement the bad name which it has never
lost.

There are some inconsistencies in Mr Ross's book, particularly in the way he expands or contracts the word 'Georgian' to suit his purposes. In the first part of his book he uses it rather in the manner of Frank Swinnerton in *The Georgian Scene*, simply to denote a given period; this enables him to say a good deal about the pre-war Pound, Hulme, and Wyndham Lewis and *Blast*, though they have little to do with what is to follow, when he restricts himself to discussing Marsh's anthologies. He might profitably have allowed himself an intermediate use of the word, rather as Mr Stead does, denoting certain poetic attitudes – of which the concern with rural England would be one – that would apply to other poets in addition to Marsh's contributors: such victims of the war as Charles Sorley, Edward Thomas and Wilfred Owen (who said that he would be proud to be classed with the Georgians), for instance. Mr Ross, like other readers, is too inclined to assume that the immediate pre-war period was one of absolutely untroubled tranquillity with no thought of war; some people felt like that, certainly, but, as George Dangerfield has shown, there was also a considerable interest in violence and a preoccupation with the threat of war; one can point to novels like Wells's *The War in the Air* and *The World Set Free*, and Saki's *When William Came*, for direct literary evidence. On the other hand, Mr Ross is very good indeed on the immediate post-war period: his long chapter called 'The Literary Scene: 1918–1922' reduces a rich and tangled period to some kind of order.

I would like, finally, to take issue with him on a small but significant detail. Although he rightly opposes the critical tendency to dismiss the Georgians as a single unified phenomenon, he does not extend a similar discrimination to the poets of the 1890s, whom he generally disposes of with a tired gesture about *fin de siècle* aestheticism. I would suggest that the poets of that period, however trifling their themes, were at least as technically accomplished as most of the contributors to *Georgian Poetry*, and sometimes more so. One of them, John Davidson, was a forerunner in the treatment of unglamorous subjects in 'everyday' language; while another, Arthur Symons, was writing Imagist poems in the early nineties. The proto-modernist Hulme recalled Symons in his

F

own Imagist poems, and another propagandist for the Modern Movement, Ford Madox Ford, spoke of Symons with respect. The fundamental point is that the *fin de siècle* poets knew about and to some extent understood the achievement of the French symbolists, whereas the little-Englander Georgians were not interested in such things. And what is of central importance in modern literature still owes an enormous amount to the subsequent discovery of the symbolists by Eliot, Pound and the other 'men of 1914'. This view would, of course, be contested by those British critics – notably Graham Hough and Robert Conquest – who regard Pound and Eliot as, at best, grossly overrated, and, at worst, charlatans. In their counter-revolutionary zeal they might have a certain interest in reinstating the truly English Georgians of the poetic centre, as opposed to the obscurantist Franco-Americans who imported an undesirable exotic deviation into English poetry. One of the virtues of Mr Ross's book is that it illuminates the Georgians so thoroughly as to make such a rewriting of literary history a good deal harder to achieve. As he says, they deserve sympathetic consideration; but he has hardly revealed a race of neglected giants.

1965

13 Kipling and the First World War

Rudyard Kipling began as the chronicler of a peace-time army. The early stories which made him famous described life in the British Army in India during the 1880s, with occasional references to wars off-stage, on the North-West Frontier or in Burma. It was not until the Boer War of 1899 that Kipling saw anything of war at first hand. And for Kipling, as for many of his fellow-countrymen, the Boer War – and specifically the early defeats of the British – came as a profound shock. The British Army, for all its proud traditions, was badly organised and ill supported by the nation at home. In one poem Kipling expressed the hope that 'We have had no end of a lesson: it will do us no end of good', but in another poem, 'The Islanders', he berates the English for their indifference to the soldierly virtues and makes his famous attack on 'The flannelled fools at the wicket or the muddied oafs at the goals'. Like other writers of the early 1900s – such as Erskine Childers in *The Riddle of the Sands* – he has a keen sense of the possibility of invasion:

> But ye say, 'It will mar our comfort.' Ye say, 'It will minish our trade.'
> Do ye wait for the spattered shrapnel ere ye learn how a gun is laid?
> For the low, red glare to southward when the raided coast-towns burn?
> (Light ye shall have on that lesson, but little time to learn).

In one of Kipling's stories about the Boer War, 'The Captive' (*Traffics and Discoveries*), a General remarks, 'It's a first-class dress-parade for Armageddon,' and during the next few years the possibility of Armageddon was often in Kipling's mind. Its likelihood was emphasised in his story, 'The Edge of the Evening' (*A Diversity of Creatures*), written in 1913, an improbable account of the capture and death of two foreign spies who have been surveying British military installations from a silent aeroplane.

For Kipling, the outbreak of war in August 1914 was something long expected, which he greeted with a sense of grim fulfilment, as in 'For All We Have and Are':

> For all we have and are,
> For all our children's fate,
> Stand up and take the war,
> The Hun is at the gate!

Despite Edmund Wilson's account of the importance of Kipling's childhood in his imaginative development, he remains one of the most impersonal of authors, offering few clues about the relation of the life to the work. Kipling responded to the First World War in several poems and stories, in a lively set of impressions of life with the Navy called *Sea Warfare*, and in the two-volume *The Irish Guards in the Great War*, published in 1923. Only the last of these directly relates to the major personal event of the war for Kipling: the death in action of his son. John Kipling was not quite seventeen at the outbreak of war, the only son of a man famous for his love of children and his skill as a writer of children's books: John and his sister Elsie had appeared as 'Dan' and 'Una' in *Puck of Pook's Hill* and *Rewards and Fairies*. Now, in August 1914, John hastened to answer Lord Kitchener's call for volunteers. He at first proposed to enlist as a private soldier, but helped by Kipling's influence with Lord Roberts, an old family friend, he was given a commission in the Irish Guards. In March 1915 Rider Haggard wrote in his diary, after a visit to the Kiplings: 'Their boy John, who is not yet 18, is an officer in the Irish Guards and one can see that they are terrified lest he should be sent to the front and killed, as has happened to nearly all the young men they know.' It was not a fate that could be averted nor, in that time of absolute, unfaltering patriotic commitment, in any sense wished away. In September 1915 John Kipling, serving in the 2nd Battalion of the Irish Guards, took part in the Battle of Loos. Casualties were heavy, and on 2 October a War Office telegram announced that John Kipling was wounded and missing. Hope lingered painfully for a few weeks, but by 12 November Kipling had given up believing that his son might be a prisoner. He wrote to Brigadier Dunsterville: 'He was reported as one of the best of the subalterns and was gym instructor and signaller. It was a short life. I'm sorry that all the years' work ended in that one afternoon but – lots of people are in our position – and it's something to have bred a man.' It was to be another two years before Kipling received an eyewitness account of John's death. His principal monument to his son was the large regimental history on which he worked for several years, where Lieutenant John Kipling appears merely as a name on a casualty list, illustrating, to the end, his father's stoical reticence. *The Irish Guards in the Great War* is a meticulously researched work, which gives a day-by-day account of the two battalions of the Guards throughout the four years of war. There are a few flashes of Kipling's narrative power, but for the most it is a sober and extraordinarily detailed record that does not make easy reading.

Their son's death caused the parents to withdraw into the privacy of grief. As Charles Carrington writes, 'Neither Rudyard nor Carrie ever talked much about their son, but their life without him was never the same; it had lost a motive force.' Kipling's bitterness about the war became more pronounced, and was expressed in a series of angry propagandist poems, directed at such targets as 'The Pope, the swithering Neutrals, / The Kaiser and his Gott'. Pope Benedict XV, who had made proposals for ending the war, was savagely condemned in 'A Song at Cock-crow'; Kipling believed that the Pope was pro-German and trying to ensure Roman Catholic dominance over Europe. The publication of Kipling's war-time poems was curiously punctuated by the appearance in *The Times* in May 1918 of a poem ascribed to Kipling called 'The Old Volunteer', which turned out to be a forgery by an unknown hoaxer. Of all Kipling's war poetry, it

F2

is the 'Epitaphs' that now seem most moving and authentic. He called them 'naked cribs of the Greek Anthology', and it is evident that Kipling used the terse, controlled form of the classical epigram to touch on feelings he was unable or unwilling to express more fully and directly. Thus, 'The Beginner' shows the lover of children reflecting on the deaths of young men who, like John Kipling, were scarcely more than children themselves:

> On the first hour of my first day
>   In the front trench I fell.
> (Children in boxes at a play
>   Stand up to watch it well.)

There is a comparable theme, treated very differently, in Kipling's short story 'Mary Postgate' (*A Diversity of Creatures*), probably his best-known piece of fiction about the war, and certainly the most controversial. It brings together public events, like the development of the Royal Flying Corps and the first German air-raids during 1914–15, and some of Kipling's deepest preoccupations: a concern with the more extreme manifestations of feminine psychology ('The female of the species is more deadly than the male'), with the suffering and death of the young, and the ethics of revenge. Mary Postgate is a middle-aged spinster who acts as lady's companion to the ageing, crippled Miss Fowler. She is devoted to Miss Fowler's orphaned nephew, Wynn, who is being brought up by his aunt. He is a cheerful, shallow youth who is fond of Mary, though he subjects her to a great deal of crude teasing. At the outbreak of war Wynn joins the Flying Corps, and after a few months is killed on a training flight:

> 'I never expected anything else,' said Miss Fowler; 'but I'm sorry it happened before he had done anything.'
> The room was whirling round Mary Postgate, but she found herself quite steady in the midst of it.
> 'Yes,' she said. 'It's a great pity he didn't die in action after he had killed somebody.'

The faded but determined maiden lady – 'quite steady in the

midst of it' – takes up the task of accomplishing the death
that Wynn died too soon for. After the funeral Mary Postgate
prepares to burn all the boy's treasured possessions; she makes
a funeral pyre of them – in describing it, Kipling takes a page
to give a lovingly exact inventory of toys and books and sport-
ing equipment – then walks into the village to buy paraffin.
She thinks she hears the sound of an aeroplane overhead, recalling the flights that Wynn used to make over the village
while he was in training. Then there is an explosion. A bomb
has fallen, bloodily killing one of the village children: 'It was
little Edna Gerritt, aged nine, whom Mary had known since
her perambulator days.'

Returning home Mary sets fire to Wynn's funeral pyre.
As she does so she hears a groan and discovers a badly injured German airman lying near by. Her response is neither
fear nor pity, but simply anger; she goes into the house to
fetch a revolver, and threatens the man with it. She ignores
his cries for a doctor, and gets on with burning Wynn's
things, deliberately letting the man die. *This* is to be the
death that Wynn had failed to accomplish, and it is specifically an act of revenge for the death of Edna. Kipling, in fact,
relates the man and the child in a bizarre but striking image:

> When she came through the rain, the eyes in the head were
> alive with expectation. The mouth even tried to smile. But
> at sight of the revolver its corners went down just like
> Edna Gerritt's. A tear trickled from one eye, and the head
> rolled from shoulder to shoulder as though trying to point
> out something.

When he calls for help, Mary musters her small German to
tell him, 'Ich haben der todt Kinder gesehn.' As the pyre
burns through, Mary waits for the German's final death
agony; she hears it, at last, with orgasmic satisfaction, and re-
turns to the house glowing with unfamiliar fulfilment:

> '*That's* all right,' said she contentedly, and went up to the
> house, where she scandalised the whole routine by taking a
> luxurious hot bath before tea, and came down looking, as
> Miss Fowler said when she saw her lying all relaxed on the
> other sofa, 'quite handsome!'

The presentation of the heroine's state of mind is masterly, and 'Mary Postgate' is one of Kipling's most brilliant stories. Nevertheless, some readers have understandably found it too horrible to take seriously, while others have tried to defuse its morally problematic quality by arguing that Kipling by no means endorses Mary's behaviour. It has also been suggested that the bitterness of the story is a result of the death of John Kipling, which is verifiably untrue, since Kipling wrote the story six months before John's death, though it is possible that the anxiety he felt about his son's future was a contributory element. I do not, in fact, think one can make very much of the story without some sympathetic understanding of Kipling's attitudes. It is well known that he was deeply interested in revenge; it forms the basis for many of his stories, such as the crude and boisterous 'Village that Voted the Earth was Flat' and the late and complex 'Dayspring Mishandled'. Kipling seems to have had not merely a detached interest but a real commitment to the ethics of revenge, considered both as a tragic destiny and a necessary ritual, and his own values may have been closer to those of the Sikh soldiers so sympathetically portrayed in 'In the Presence' (*A Diversity of Creatures*) than to those of the post-Christian liberal. Furthermore, 'Mary Postgate' was written when hatred of the Germans because of reported atrocities in Belgium, and the first civilian deaths in air-raids, was raging uncontrollably. A *Punch* cartoon by Bernard Partridge of that time shows the Kaiser rebuking a German aviator for not having killed any children: 'Well, then, no babes, no iron crosses.' The key sentence in 'Mary Postgate' is, I believe, 'Ich haben der todt Kinder gesehn'. It points, too, to the theme of another and slighter story, also written early in 1915, 'Swept and Garnished'. This is about a prosperous, self-satisfied middle-aged lady in Berlin who takes to her bed with influenza and is haunted by the ghosts of young children killed in the German advance into Belgium. At the end of the story the woman is out of bed and on her hands and knees, trying to wipe spots of blood from the floor. In these stories, Kipling is not merely expressing anti-Hun hysteria, though that is present, but is touching on something more profound and more obscure. The sociologist Peter Berger, discussing 'signals of transcendence' in his book *A Rumour of Angels*, has referred to 'the argument from damnation', which he says 'refers to experiences in which our sense of what is humanly permissible is so fundamentally outraged that the only adequate response to the offence as well as to the offender seems to be a curse of supernatural dimensions'. And, says Berger, the massacre of the innocents is an archetypal instance of such an offence. There were good reasons why such a subject was particularly sensitive for Kipling: 'Ich haben der todt Kinder gesehn' is also the theme, though expressed with serenity and not disturbance, of one of his finest stories of the previous decade, the deeply poignant 'They' (*Traffics and Discoveries*), in which a traveller finds a beautiful country house that is haunted by the happy ghosts of dead children, including, as he discovers by a fleeting touch of the hand at the end of the story, his own dead child. And 'They' is certainly a transmutation into art of Kipling's own sense of loss for his beloved eldest child, Josephine, who died at the age of seven in 1899.

Revenge was a perennial theme in Kipling's fiction, though it may well have been sharpened by the war. It is dominant in another story written early in 1915, 'Sea Constables' (*Debits and Credits*), which is full of Kipling's hatred for the 'swithering neutrals'; four naval reserve captains reminiscing after a long spell of duty discuss how one of them pursued a neutral vessel that was trading with the enemy and yet relying on the protection of the Royal Navy, and in the end left its owner to die of bronchial pneumonia. 'Sea Constables', though sharing in the same extremity of feeling as 'Mary Postgate', is far less effective. Yet the revenge theme, basic though it was in Kipling's imaginative world, was balanced by an opposed theme of reconciliation and healing. And this pervades several stories written during or after the war. One such is 'On the Gate', a curious but tender fantasy about the problems posed in heaven by the arrival of so many dead during the war. In May 1918 Rider Haggard recorded having this story read to him by Kipling: 'he read me a quaint story about Death and St Peter, written in modern language, almost in slang, which his wife would not let him publish. It would have been caviare to the General if he had, because the keynote of it is infinite mercy extending even to the case of Judas.' Kipling did not, in fact, publish 'On the Gate' until 1926, when it appeared in *Debits and Credits*. In the same volume there are several stories set in a Masonic Lodge in South London called 'Faith and Works 5837', where injured and shell-shocked men gather to relive their experiences and give each other help and support. The masonic element shows Kipling's conviction that ritual is a necessary element in preserving order in human affairs, especially at times of stress, and it reminds us of his love of in-groups of men united by a common purpose and with shared values and language, something that had fascinated him ever since as a youth he had been a privileged visitor to British Army messes in India. These stories – which in my view are often marred by an arch falsity of tone – include 'A Madonna of the Trenches', which occultly reveals the transcendent power of human love, and 'The Janeites', where a group of soldiers – not all educated men – find in the novels of Jane Austen both a satisfying source of arcane knowledge and reference, and a scheme of values that can help them withstand the horror of front-line existence. In some of these stories the theme of healing merges with another that preoccupied Kipling: the sense of man being taxed beyond endurance, which underlies several late stories in *Limits and Renewals*.

As a member of the War Graves Commission, Kipling was very familiar with the great military cemeteries in France and Flanders, and it was after visiting one at Rouen in March 1925 that he wrote 'The Gardener' (*Debits and Credits*). Like 'Mary Postgate' this fine story is deeply concerned with the psychology of a middle-aged woman; in all other respects it is opposed but complementary to the extreme negative emotions of the earlier story. 'The Gardener' opens with the words: 'Everyone in the village knew that Helen Turrell did her duty by all her world, and by none more honourably than by her only brother's unfortunate child.' The unmarried Helen brings up the boy, Michael, after the death of his parents. But in fact he is her illegitimate son; she preserves the fiction that he is her nephew, though many people suspect the truth. He joined the Army on the outbreak of war, and is killed after the Battle of Loos. Most of the story describes Helen's first visit to his grave in a huge military cemetery; she is somewhat repelled by her fellow-mourners, and is deeply disturbed by a hysterical woman who wants to talk about her dead lover. At the end of the story Helen is looking for Michael's grave, and a casual encounter dispels the pretence which she has sustained for so many years:

A man knelt behind a line of headstones – evidently a gardener, for he was firming a young plant in the soft earth. She went towards him, her paper in her hand. He rose at her approach and without prelude or salutation asked: 'Who are you looking for?'

'Lieutenant Michael Turrell – my nephew,' said Helen slowly and word for word, as she had many thousands of times in her life.

The man lifted his eyes and looked at her with infinite compassion before he turned from the fresh-sown grass toward the naked black crosses.

'Come with me,' he said, 'and I will show you where your son lies.'

When Helen left the Cemetery she turned for a last look. In the distance she saw the man bending over his young plants; and she went away, supposing him to be the gardener.

The last words echo St John's gospel, where Mary Magdalene supposes that the risen Christ 'must be the gardener'. (Mary Magdalene was forgiven much because she had loved much, and seems to have had a particular appeal for Kipling: in 'On the Gate' St Peter is accustomed to invoking what he calls 'a most useful ruling' under the initials Q.M.A, which stand for '*Quia multum amavit*'.) Together 'Mary Postgate' and 'The Gardener' show the range of Kipling's imaginative response to the war: hatred is countered with a hint of 'infinite compassion', and both are involved with the memory of a dead child. Kipling's writings about the war remind us of the strange complexity of his art, and show how completely it resists any neat and limiting formula.

1972

14 The Huxley Line

Taken together, Ronald Clark's composite biography of the Huxley family and Grover Smith's edition of Aldous Huxley's letters* cover an extraordinary chapter in English cultural history, whether one looks at it genetically or sociologically. Thomas Huxley was born in 1825, the seventh child of the manager of a savings bank. Despite his very limited formal schooling, he managed to acquire the rudiments of a medical training, and in 1846 he was commissioned as assistant-surgeon on H.M.S. *Rattlesnake*, a naval vessel which was about to start on a long voyage of exploration of the coasts of Australia and New Guinea. His real interest was in natural science rather than medicine, and the zoological discoveries he made on the voyage established his reputation and made him a member of the Royal Society before he was twenty-six. He became a vehement defender and expositor of Darwin's ideas, and his prodigious labour as researcher, populariser of science, controversialist and pioneer of state education made Huxley, for all his iconoclastic opinions, a pillar of the Victorian establishment, even if on its radical wing. He became Secretary and then President of the Royal Society; a governor of Eton; a trustee of the British Museum. And finally, towards the end of his life, one of Her Majesty's Privy Councillors; in Mr Clark's words, 'looking up from his kneeling position before the Queen when he was invested, he found that she too had wondered what the strange creature was like and had fixed her beady eyes upon him'. Thomas Huxley emerges from Mr Clark's account as one of the intellectual giants of his age and an incomparable educator; he was also a man for whom the gulf between science and the humanities – so worrying to the late twen-

* *The Huxleys* by Ronald W. Clark; *Letters of Aldous Huxley*, edited by Grover Smith.

tieth-century mind – simply didn't exist; he was, to his finger-
tips, both man of science and man of letters. On the voyage of
the *Rattlesnake*, in the midst of all his zoological investiga-
tions, he contrived to read Dante in the original with the
help of a dictionary. He was also a devoted family man, with
a deep attachment to his children, though he could hardly
have foreseen the extent to which his example and ideals
were to be propagated by a later generation of Huxleys.

Thomas Huxley's second son, Leonard, was a less emphatic
character, though a man of great intellectual and literary
competence. After spending the first part of his life as a
schoolmaster he went into publishing and became, at length,
editor of the *Cornhill*. His poems and essays had their
admirers, but his principal achievements were the large
biographies he wrote, first, of his father, and then of another
distinguished Victorian scientist, Sir Joseph Hooker. There
are versions of Leonard, presented with rather less than total
sympathy, in the fiction of his son, Aldous. Leonard's first
wife, Julia, was a niece of Matthew Arnold and a sister of Mrs
Humphry Ward; if one believes in genetic factors one must
conclude that the Huxley strain received an important rein-
forcement in this match, and the results were evident in
Leonard Huxley's sons, Julian and Aldous (his eldest son,
Trevenen, committed suicide at the age of twenty-five).
Though even without the added boost of Arnold genes,
Huxleys could still excel: one of Leonard's sons by a second
marriage was awarded the Nobel Prize for Physiology in 1963,
and, as Mr Clark shows in his fascinating book, various other
grandchildren of Thomas Huxley were conspicuously high
achievers.

The genetic element in the prolonged Huxley success story
is too speculative to be more than merely noted in passing.
What is more immediately discussable is the way in which the
Huxley family fitted into a striking pattern in late nine-
teenth- and early twentieth-century English cultural life. It
was a time when a small number of famous families played a
large part in the intellectual, professional and administrative
life of the country, and their names often recur in the
biographies and memoirs that look back on that period: the
Stephens, the Stracheys, the Darwins, the Oliviers. To appro-

priate a useful bit of neo-Marxist terminology, they exercised an active cultural hegemony, and the Huxleys were perhaps the most brilliant of all. Individual members of those families still continue to make their mark, but the high point of their hegemony had passed by the 1930s, when other cultural forces emerged. Young men from the working or lower-middle classes were beginning to find their way up the ladder, thanks to the gradual spread of educational opportunity. And Continental refugees gave a different direction to intellectual developments: indeed, the English Marxist writer, Perry Anderson, has suggested in an interesting but excessively simplified reading of recent cultural history that from the thirties onward hegemony was increasingly exercised by émigrés whose backgrounds were Austrian or Polish and whose cast of mind was inherently conservative (in Anderson's view, refugees from Germany were more naturally progressive or radical, and went on to the United States): he lists such names as Wittgenstein, Malinowski, Namier, Popper, Gombrich and Melanie Klein. According to Anderson, their influence substituted a conservative or at least sceptical view of life for the generally liberal ethos of the English hegemonic families. Anderson's argument has been sharply attacked and it is far too selective to hold water in the form in which he has advanced it; nevertheless, it does represent an attempt to understand what happened to English culture after the earlier pattern had started to break up.

The ways in which the pattern changed can be seen in the careers of Thomas Huxley's two most celebrated grandsons, Julian and Aldous. Sir Julian Huxley, the older by seven years, has carried on in an astonishingly faithful way the ideals and achievements of Thomas Huxley, and represents a living link with the ambitious young scientist who embarked on the *Rattlesnake* in 1846. After a thorough classical training at Eton he distinguished himself in zoology at Oxford. While only in his mid-twenties he became director of the biology department at the Rice Institute in Houston; then, after the First World War, he was for some years a lecturer at Oxford, and briefly a professor at King's College, London. Julian Huxley was like his grandfather in combining an immense amount of original research and writing with a passion for scientific education and popularisation, a passion for which he found endless scope during his seven years as Secretary of the London Zoo. (His taste for modern publicity methods also made him many enemies.) He was a great exponent of the larger philosophical and social questions that arose from the scientific attitude, and he wrote and lectured extensively on these topics in the atmosphere of plain living and high thinking that flourished in England during the Second World War. And, like Thomas Huxley, he was a man of wide general culture; when, in 1946, he became the first Director-General of UNESCO it was acknowledged that one of his qualifications was his familiarity with virtually all aspects of the organisation's work. Julian Huxley has happily spanned the Two Cultures, and once published a volume of poems; he has always related research to education, and has tirelessly devoted himself to public service. In all these ways he has remained true to the example of the great founder of the Huxleys, and embodied a set of essentially Victorian ideals.

In Julian's younger brother, Aldous, we see some parallels, and a significant divergence. Even as a child he seems to have been rather weighed down by his illustrious heritage, although the schoolboy letters at the beginning of Mr Smith's collection are pleasantly high-spirited. Aldous Huxley was always burdened by his physique, particularly the immensely long legs that gave him, as an adult, a height of well over six foot; here, undoubtedly, lay one cause of Huxley's lifelong preoccupation with the influence of physical factors on human personality. An even more crucial factor was the eye-disease that completely blinded him for a while in his teens, and necessitated his withdrawal from Eton; throughout his life he suffered from desperately defective vision. Although Aldous knew a lot about science, as about most other things, and had originally intended to become a doctor, after his period of blindness he turned to literature in a more decisive way than the other members of his family. At Oxford he even elected to read English Literature rather than Classics or mathematics or science, and English at that time was a suspect parvenu subject. In 1915 he got to know Lady Ottoline Morrell and the other members of the Garsington circle, and soon afterwards published his first poems. His poetry was witty and polished and heavily influenced by the dandified melancholy of Laforgue, whom Huxley had discovered for himself as an undergraduate. T. S. Eliot, with whom Huxley became friendly in 1917, had passed through his own Laforguian phase several years before and had thoroughly absorbed the French poet: he felt, rightly, that Huxley was using Laforgue in an immature and excessively derivative way. A similar remark might have been made a few years later, after Huxley had become a novelist, about his use of Gide's *Faux-Monnayeurs* in *Point Counter Point*. Given his extraordinary abilities and intellectual powers, Aldous Huxley might have been successful in any one of half a dozen fields of activity. And to a great extent he did succeed as a man of letters; after a difficult period when he was trying to get established, and supporting himself and his wife by a great deal of journalistic writing, he made a respectable breakthrough with his first novel, *Crome Yellow*, in 1921. In Proust's *Sodome et Gomorrhe*, published in the same year, there is a mysterious reference to Thomas Huxley's grandson occupying 'an unassailable position in the English literary world of today': the reference was, to say the least of it, premature, and Huxley, who had never met Proust, confessed his bafflement to a correspondent forty years later.

During the twenties Huxley achieved a great reputation for intellectual brilliance and world-weary sophistication, and he was seen, like Scott Fitzgerald, as the literary epitome of the decade. Certainly Huxley's novels of the twenties – *Crome Yellow, Antic Hay, Those Barren Leaves* and *Point Counter Point* – remain works of undeniable charm and wit and readability. Being largely *romans à clef,* they have considerable documentary interest as reflections of life at Garsington, or among wealthy English expatriates in Italy, or in the fashionable London bohemia that was exposed by Wyndham Lewis in *The Apes of God* and which provided, a little later, the setting of the early novels of Evelyn Waugh and Anthony Powell. Yet the comparison with Fitzgerald inevitably points to Huxley's limitations as a literary artist: he was, in the last analysis, more interested in ideas than in the imaginative transformation of experience, and the interest of his novels is not radically different from that of his many brilliant essays. Huxley himself admitted as much in a letter to his old friend E. S. P. Haynes in 1945: 'I remain sadly aware that I am not a born novelist, but some other kind of man of letters, possessing enough ingenuity to be able to simulate a novelist's behaviour not too unconvincingly.' By now, Huxley's novels, once so fashionable, seem to have declined to about the right level of moderate public esteem; in addition to the ones I have mentioned, *Brave New World* remains important as an anti-utopian speculation.

Huxley's collected letters, though dauntingly numerous, are not, on the whole, very interesting. He was a fluent, dutiful correspondent, much given to discussing in a relaxed, discursive way the ideas or books that currently interested him. There is enough self-revelation in Huxley's fiction to suggest that his nature was racked with a number of crucial obsessions and contradictions, but we find little trace of them in his correspondence. There is a relevant passage in a letter from D. H. Lawrence to Lady Ottoline Morrell, written in February 1929, after a visit from Aldous and Maria Huxley:

> I think the *Counter-Point* book sort of got between them – she found it hard to forgive the death of the child – which one can well understand. But, as I say, there's more than one self to everybody, and the Aldous that writes those novels is only one little Aldous amongst others – probably much nicer – that don't write novels – I mean it's only one of his little selves that writes the book and makes the child die, it's not *all* himself. No, I don't like his books: even if I admire a sort of desperate courage of repulsion and repudiation in them. But again, I feel only half a man writes the books – a sort of precocious adolescent. There is surely much more of a man in the actual Aldous.

The little Aldous that wrote the letters was certainly nicer than the one that wrote the novels, which contain many passages of gratuitous horror like the death of the child from meningitis in *Point Counter Point*. Among Huxley's later novels *Ape and Essence* indicates an extraordinary intense and obsessive loathing of human life. Ronald Clark, whose virtues as a biographer don't extend to literary criticism, admits that *Ape and Essence* is a rather extreme book, but denies that its peculiar quality reflects anything of its author's personality, saying that it merely shows Huxley's urgent concern with the fate of humanity after a nuclear holocaust. I am sure there was much more behind the book than that, but whatever it is isn't indicated in Huxley's letters.

Nevertheless, they do contain quite piquant illustrations of themes that recur throughout his fiction and essays, notably his concern with the inadequacy of the body and all the weaknesses that beset it. In 1918 he asks Ottoline Morrell, 'I wonder if you know what means Bertie Russell employed to cure his piles: for I have been slightly afflicted of late by that "distressing but almost universal complaint",' and such preoccupations recur throughout his life; in 1936 a letter to McKnight Kauffer is minutely concerned with the benefit Huxley received from 'the washing out of the intestine (by a course of colonic lavage) and the receiving of two injections of a vaccine prepared from the pathogenic organisms found in the faeces . . .' In 1954 he is giving his son and daughter-in-law detailed instructions about the right food to give small children to prevent them from becoming 'diabolic' at parties. Huxley's confident assumption of medical expertise relates to another central strand in his personality: his endless capacity for accumulating disparate fragments of knowledge. Throughout his life Huxley was an inveterate reader of encyclopaedias, in this respect being very much what Lawrence called 'a precocious adolescent', or even the grave child of Eliot's 'Animula':

> The pain of living and the drug of dreams
> Curl up the small soul in the winter seat
> Behind the *Encyclopaedia Britannica*.

In his essay 'Books for the Journey', Huxley describes the virtues of any single volume of the *Britannica* as a travelling companion (Mr Clark denies the allegation that Huxley had a special box fitted into his car to enable him to take the whole set of the encyclopaedia around with him): Huxley acknowledges, however, that 'a stray volume of the *Encylo-*

paedia is like the mind of a learned madman – stored with correct ideas, between which, however, there is no other connection than the fact that there is a B in both'. His own mind was rather like that, hence his tiresome practice of strewing his books with extensive deposits of quite unstructured random information, which has never been subjected to any kind of imaginative fusion. When Aldous was a boy, his elder brother, Julian, had quoted to him a remark made by a weary listener to Macaulay's table-talk: 'Sir, his information is greater than society requires.' Other modern writers, such as Joyce, Beckett and Borges, have had similar inclinations, but unlike Huxley are able to integrate their encyclopaedism into the texture of their writing.

In the final years of his life Huxley was busily involved with a whole range of interests and activities which in any ordinary view of the world would seem mutually irreconcilable, but in Huxley's comprehensive scheme of things all somehow fitted together: orthodox medicine and the most way-out forms of fringe therapy; hypnotism and E.S.P.; spiritualism and Eastern mysticism, and, notoriously, experiments with mescalin and L.S.D. which he saw as directly opening the doors to transcendent modes of being (in fairness to Huxley, one must point out that he took only small quantities of these drugs, at long intervals, and under expert supervision). This phase produced some curious and entertaining letters, where his lifelong encyclopaedism reached heights of inspired nuttiness that are heavily reminiscent of *Bouvard et Pécuchet*:

> I spent some days, earlier this month, at Glen Cove in the strange household assembled by Puharic – Alice and Mrs P, behaving to one another in a conspicuously friendly way; Elinor Bond, doing telepathic guessing remarkably well, but not producing anything of interest or value in the mediumistic sitting she gave me; Frances Farrelly, with her diagnostic machine – which Puharic's tests have shown to be merely an instrument, like a crystal ball, for concentrating E.S.P. faculties; Harry, the Dutch sculptor, who goes into trances in the Faraday cages and produces automatic scripts in Egyptian hieroglyphics; Narodny, the cockroach man, who is preparing experiments to test the

effects of human telepathy on insects. It was all very lively
and amusing – and, I really think, promising. . . .

Such an assembly might have occurred in one of Huxley's
novels of the twenties, though described in a spirit of mockery that is quite lacking here. Thomas Huxley's grandson had
come a long way, but without ever repudiating the spirit of
scientific inquiry.

From an English point of view Huxley's long residence in
Los Angeles looks like a crucial influence. Compared with his
brother, Julian, who was playing an active part in war-time
and post-war English society, and functionally deploying his
own polymathic interests in the service of UNESCO, Aldous
had undergone a marked process of cultural marginalisation,
just as his friend Lawrence had a generation earlier. Aldous
Huxley had tried to be a novelist, whilst really being, as he
admitted, some other kind of man of letters. It was, perhaps, a
mistaken endeavour, for the English hegemonic families were
not very good at imaginative literature; though they had a
modest gift for *belles-lettres*, their genius was for science and
administration: only Virginia Woolf (née Stephen) made
very much impact as a literary artist. Otherwise literature fell
into the innovating hands of Celts, Americans and other
kinds of alien, whose achievement is apparent in the splendid
history of the Modern Movement, to which Huxley contrib-
utes a footnote rather than a chapter. At the end he had
become, in a thoroughly genial way, not just a representative
of a great English family, but that traditional type, the English eccentric. And even in Southern California that was
something rather special.

                                                    1970

15 The *Waste Land* Manuscripts

In 1956 Eliot wrote, apropos of John Livingstone Lowes's *Road to Xanadu*, 'poetic originality is largely an original way of assembling the most disparate and unlikely material to make a new whole'. 'Assembling' is not a word one usually applies to writing poetry, but it is very relevant to Eliot's own methods. C. K. Stead has shown how the separate parts of 'The Hollow Men' were previously published in different combinations, until Eliot finally shuffled them into the right order. And we have his own account of how ' Burnt Norton' was made up of fragments discarded from *Murder in the Cathedral* during the course of production. Eliot's basic method of composition was more traditionally Romantic than is often realised, with a frank reliance on unconscious sources of inspiration to produce brief poetic passages, or perhaps just single lines, of great isolated intensity. The next, and equally arduous, stage in the assembling of a whole poem was akin to the methods of an artist in mosaic or collage. Fragments or phrases not suitable for one poem would be carefully kept until they could be used in another, sometimes for years on end. It is this aspect of Eliot's art that is most fascinatingly revealed in the long-lost manuscripts of *The Waste Land*, a poem whose most crucial line is certainly 'These fragments I have shored against my ruins'.

For a long time students – and teachers – have wistfully assumed that if only those legendary manuscripts would turn up, then the worst difficulties might be resolved, since Eliot's *ur*-version must have been more lucid and coherent than the final product of Ezra Pound's ruthless editing. That notion, at least, is now dispelled. The first draft of *The Waste Land*, brought back by Eliot from his rest-cure at Lausanne in the autumn of 1921, was, as he once deprecatingly told an interviewer, 'just as structureless, only in a more futile way'. The original manuscript consisted of several extended sections – in blank verse, quatrains and heroic couplets – plus a number of shorter fragments, that Eliot hoped could be somehow 'worked in' to the final version. If Eliot's original design had a unity it was of a very loose kind, for the work that he brought back from Lausanne was essentially a set of separate poems; even after *The Waste Land* was published in 1922, reviewers tended to refer to it as 'poems' rather than a 'poem'. Mrs Eliot's admirable edition shows clearly the streamlining effect of the editorial cuts, by no means all of which were made by Pound, as Eliot modestly implied. It was a pencil stroke in Eliot's own hand that excised the original opening, a low-pressure chatty passage about Boston low-life, thereby ensuring that the first line was 'April is the cruellest month' rather than 'First we had a couple of feelers down at Tom's place'. Most of the material that was cut, whether by Eliot himself, or by Pound, deserved to go. But I think Eliot was mistaken when he removed, at Pound's suggestion, the original epigraph from Conrad's *Heart of Darkness*:

'Did he live his life again in every detail of desire, tempta-tion, and surrender during that supreme moment of com-plete knowledge? He cried out in a whisper at some image, at some vision, – he cried out twice, a cry that was no more than a breath – 'The horror! ! the horror!' ' '

If *The Waste Land* had been prefaced with this quotation it might have been evident from the beginning that the poem is, at bottom, an anguished reliving of subjective experience, and not the 'impersonal' meditation on cultural decline that so many commentators – whether sympathetic or unsympa-thetic – have assumed it to be. Conrad's lines point to the real subject of the poem; the word 'surrender' had a peculiar sig-nificance for Eliot, and Conrad's use of it seems to be echoed later in *The Waste Land*, in 'The awful daring of a moment's surrender' (and perhaps in 'Tradition and the Individual Talent', where Eliot says of the poet, 'what happens is a con-tinual surrender of himself as he is at the moment to some-thing which is more valuable').

There is one other place where Pound's excision may have been misplaced. Part IV, 'Death by Water', was originally much longer. After a very inferior set of opening quatrains, the verse develops into a mostly well-written account of a disastrous voyage by a New England fishing vessel, with deliberate echoes of Tennyson's and Dante's Ulysses. There are striking anticipations of the *Quartets* of twenty years later:

> Kingfisher weather, with a light fair breeze,
> Full canvas, and the eight sails drawing well.
> We beat around the cape and laid our course
> From the Dry Salvages to the eastern banks.
> A porpoise snored upon the phosphorescent swell,
> A triton rang the final warning bell
> Astern, and the sea rolled, asleep.

Later in this section the verse becomes more intense, recalling the quotation from Conrad, and looking back momentarily to the final lines of 'Prufrock':

> One night
> On watch, I thought I saw in the fore cross-trees
> Three women leaning forward, with white hair
> Streaming behind, who sang above the wind
> A song that charmed my senses, while I was
> Frightened beyond fear, horrified past horror, calm,
> (Nothing was real) for, I thought, now, when
> I like, I can wake up and end the dream.
> – Something which we knew must be a dawn –
> A different darkness, flowed above the clouds,
> And dead ahead we saw, where sky and sea should meet,
> A line, a white line, a long white line,
> A wall, a barrier towards which we drove.

Not all the deleted lines are as good as this. Some cutting, particularly of the sailors' talk, was probably required, but it is a pity that the whole section had to go; the parallel between the New England fishermen and Phlebas the Phoenician was effective, and the Phlebas passage by itself (an adaptation from the closing lines of one of Eliot's French poems of 1918, 'Dans le Restaurant') stands rather too abruptly. Eliot, in fact, wanted to delete that too, when the first part of 'Death by Water' went, but Pound dissuaded him. Characteristically, though, Eliot hung on to a couple of phrases from the deleted lines, which later turned up in 'The Dry Salvages' and 'Marina'.

On the other hand, Pound's editing greatly improved 'The Fire Sermon'. This section originally opened with a long set of Popean couplets, which were adroit enough in their way, but which only reiterated points made more tersely elsewhere about the emptiness of fashionable life. As an exercise in the smart neoclassicising of the twenties – there are musical parallels in Stravinsky or Prokofiev – they have a certain curiosity value, but it wasn't really Eliot's kind of thing. Nor, for that matter, were the quatrain poems, like 'Sweeney Erect', that he wrote between 1917 and 1919, largely as a result of reading Gautier under Pound's influence. In the original draft of 'The Fire Sermon' the account by Tiresias of the seduction of a bored typist by the 'young man carbuncular' was told in a long sequence of such quatrains. Pound's cuts boldly ignored the rhyme scheme, so that the lines ended up as the section of continuous and irregularly rhyming verse that appeared in the published version. One of the minor puzzles in that version is the peculiar syntax of the lines about

> the evening hour that strives
> Homeward, and brings the sailor home from sea,
> The typist home at teatime, clears her breakfast, lights
> Her stove, and lays out food in tins.

It now looks as if this elision was the result of inadequate suturing after the editorial cuts. The manuscript read

> The typist home at teatime, who begins
> To clear away her broken breakfast, lights
> Her stove, and lays out squalid food in tins . . .

Pound's marginal comment on these lines was 'verse not interesting enough as verse to warrant so much of it'. Certainly the taut and rapid final version is a vast improvement on the laboured quatrains. At first, there was a good deal more about the young man, whom Eliot seems to have regarded with immense distaste but with a certain novelistic interest, describing him as a layabout who frequents the Café Royal, and a crude but confident womaniser. If some readers find these lines deplorably snobbish and anti-life, one can only say that the original version was far more so; the young man's departure might have read like this, if it were not for a cautious comment by Pound:

> – Bestows one final patronising kiss,
> And gropes his way, finding the stairs unlit;
> And at the corner where the stable is,
> Delays only to urinate and spit.

Eliot was much closer to his central concerns in some fragmentary and unused lines about London, seen, as elsewhere in *The Waste Land,* as a Baudelairian inferno. A line, cancelled by Eliot himself, which read 'London, your people is bound upon the wheel', reflects one of the central configurations of his imagination: 'I see crowds of people, walking round in a ring' and 'Here we go round the prickly pear'.

The most interesting material lies not so much in the cancellations as in the early fragments, in some cases written several years before the 1921 draft, from which Eliot extracted lines or images for use in *The Waste Land*. 'The Death of Saint Narcissus' is one such, which provided the source for 'Come in under the shadow of this red rock'. Perhaps the most powerful lines in *The Waste Land* are those beginning 'A woman drew her long black hair out tight', and in this edition we find a draft of them in a manuscript which Mrs Eliot suggests, on the evidence of handwriting, may have been written in 1914, or even before. In another manuscript, of the same early date, there is a version of the opening lines of 'What the Thunder said', astonishingly combined with a Laforguian conclusion in the manner of Eliot's first poetic exercises written at Harvard in 1909:

> After the ending of this inspiration
> And the torches and the faces and the shouting
> The world seemed futile – like a Sunday outing.

Such pivotal lines look both forward and back, emphasising the imaginative unity of Eliot's work. So, too, does a seemingly later fragment called 'The Death of the Duchess'. I found this exciting, because it provided a precise link between two passages of Eliot's verse which have always struck me by their resemblances, although quite separate in time: the edgily dramatic words of the two neurotic women in 'Portrait of a Lady' (1910) and in 'A Game of Chess' in *The Waste Land* (1921). 'The Death of the Duchess' takes its point of departure from *The Duchess of Malfi*, in the scene where the Duchess is surprised in her bedchamber by her evil brother Ferdinand. This draft by Eliot contains most of the lines later incorporated into the middle section of 'A Game of Chess', whilst being an unmistakable attempt to recapture, perhaps even imitate, the manner of 'Prufrock' and 'Portrait of a Lady'. There is a similar nervous but intense sexuality:

> With her back turned, her arms were bare
> Fixed for a question, her hands behind her hair
> And the firelight shining where the muscle drew.

At one place Pound has scribbled in the margin: 'cadence reproduction from Prufrock or Portrait of a Lady'.

When the *Waste Land* manuscripts were first discovered I feared that they might disintegrate the poem as we have always known it. But Mrs Eliot's edition reassuringly makes this look unlikely: *The Waste Land*, in its final version, is so obviously superior to the drafts – apart from the special case of 'Death by Water' – that they are not likely to affect our reading of it. What they can provide is the traditional Romantic pleasure of seeing how a great poet's mind works.

1972

16 Modern Reactionaries

It looks as if the point of departure for Mr Harrison's book*
was a minatory passage in Lord Snow's Rede Lecture, which
condemns some of the most admired modern writers for
being 'not only politically silly, but politically wicked'. The
brunt of the criticism is made in a quotation from an unnamed scientist friend of Snow, who asked bitterly: 'Why do
most writers take on social opinions which would have been
thought distinctly uncivilised and démodé at the time of the
Plantagenets?' Snow largely endorses this indictment, which
forms a substantial element in his attack on traditional literary culture; over the last few years it has had a fairly wide
circulation, and it is time it was shown up as demonstrable
nonsense. Presumably Snow would agree that attitudes to the
Spanish Civil War were a certain test of political virtue or
wickedness: in 1937 a poll of writers showed that only five –
the most prominent of these being Evelyn Waugh and
Edmund Blunden – supported General Franco. Sixteen, including both the 'reactionaries' Pound and Eliot and the
'progressive' H. G. Wells, declared themselves neutral. The
remaining one hundred vigorously supported the Spanish
Republic; among them were such dedicated upholders of the
literary *avant-garde* (regarded with disfavour by Snow) as
Samuel Beckett, Ford Madox Ford and Herbert Read.

Mr Harrison is nothing if not level-headed, and although
he is evidently in sympathy with Snow's general approach, he
carefully avoids scattering wild charges. He is specifically concerned with five writers: three of them, Yeats, Pound and
Wyndham Lewis, were attacked by Snow in the Rede Lecture; to these he adds the names of Eliot and Lawrence. All
five were more or less closely linked with the great creative
outburst of the Modern Movement in the years immediately

* *The Reactionaries* by John R. Harrison.

before and during the First World War. All of them were disenchanted with liberal democracy, inclined to an authoritarian and hierarchical social order, and during the twenties and thirties showed some degree of sympathy for Italian or German Fascism (Pound, of course, showed something more than mere sympathy). Thus stated the facts are incontrovertible, and Mr Harrison gives a fair account of them, although he certainly makes a gross overstatement when he alleges that 'Yeats, Pound, Lewis, Lawrence and Eliot all saw themselves as leaders of society, and they put forward their recommendations as practical policies'. It is a weakness of Mr Harrison's approach that he is unable to distinguish between a political programme and a poet's dominating personal myth.

His underlying concern is not merely to describe, nor to indict, but to seek causes and explanations, and to show why these men held such opinions: 'This leads one to examine not only their social and political principles but their artistic principles. In the very close connection between these two sets of principles, and their very deep concern for the arts, lies the answer to this question.' Here Mr Harrison is following Orwell, who wrote that 'a writer's political and religious beliefs are not excrescences to be laughed away, but something that will leave their mark even on the smallest detail of his work'. (Snow has expressed it more vehemently: 'there is, in fact, a connection, which literary persons were culpably slow to see, between some kinds of early twentieth-century art and the most imbecile expressions of anti-social feelings'.) This is the kind of statement that certainly looks as if it ought to be true, but so far nobody has shown in an incontrovertible way just what the connections are between *Weltanschauung* and style. Mr Harrison makes a number of bold stabs at it, but although he is a fairly good historian of ideas he is an extremely poor literary critic, and he makes no progress at all in providing the 'answer' that he confidently looks for. At the beginning of his book he condemns the formalism that is only interested in how an author says something and not in what he says. This is a fair criticism, but Mr Harrison simply inverts it by, as it were, scooping out the ideas from the work of men who were primarily novelists or poets, disregarding any concrete imaginative and verbal embodiment. In effect we are given a series of studies, written in a pained but just tone, of the various ways in which Yeats, Pound, Lewis, Eliot and Lawrence deviated from the norms of the liberal-democratic ideal: Yeats's cult of the aristocracy and hard, heroic men; Pound's conviction that usury was poisoning society and that it was best combated by the dynamism of a Mussolini; Lewis's belief that great art could only flourish in a fixed, hierarchical order with no democratic untidiness about it; Eliot's clerical-agrarian traditionalism; and Lawrence's predilection for dark gods, blood-relations, natural leadership, and the occasional necessity of homicide.

When he comes to talk about style, Mr Harrison shows a marked naïvety. He observes of Yeats's later manner: 'As his "tendency" became more authoritarian, his verse in general became monosyllabic, terse, the lines short, the rhythms muscular.' As comment this does no more than reflect the obvious; it certainly doesn't say anything very searching about the precise relation between Yeats's literary and political attitudes. Elsewhere Mr Harrison allows himself a bolder speculation:

It is also likely that Milton's political and literary principles have a common basis. The austerity of his style, the linguistic discipline imposed by his 'latinisms', the bareness and harshness of much of his poetry, are the literary counterparts of his Puritanism. Much of *Paradise Lost* evidently dramatises his Parliamentarian sympathies, even if in a puzzling way.

As I read this I felt like a comic-strip character, with a balloon growing out of my head filled with large question marks. I should like, sometime, to thrust a text of *Paradise Lost* at Mr Harrison and ask him to prove it. (If he had said *Paradise Regained* it might have made a bit more sense.)

The fact is, Mr Harrison talks quite freely about literary style while seeming to have only a hazy idea of what it is. At one point he remarks of Wyndham Lewis: 'His writing has little emotive power and this is intentional.' On another page he mentions the 'linguistic brilliance' of *The Apes of God*: if this novel – and the best of Lewis's other fiction – makes any

kind of impact as literature, it is presumably because the
writing has a good deal of emotive power, of a highly idiosyncratic kind.

Where Mr Harrison is more successful is in tracing broad
cultural and intellectual currents. I think he overestimates
the influence of T. E. Hulme, but it is certainly true that
something like Hulme's distinction between the aesthetic and
the vital did play an important part in the artistic principles
of the Modern Movement, and provided links with the
cultural-political attitudes of French right-wing neo-classicism, and so with certain strands of fascism. (Lawrence would
not fit easily into this classification, however.) At the same
time, it is worth recalling that one of the things Wyndham
Lewis *disliked* about fascism was its preoccupation with
action and the vital. Mr Harrison is right to stress the aesthetic dimension in the authoritarianism of the writers he
deals with; in an important sense, they were the heirs of Ruskin in wanting a society where the arts could flourish. Mr
Harrison acknowledges this, but seems implicitly to accept
the aesthetic–vital dichotomy, by suggesting that such a
society would be something other than the liberal ideal of a
good society: 'that is, one in which the majority of its members live full, free and satisfying lives'. Have the basic lessons
of Ruskin and Morris no relevance here?

At the same time, he might have said more about the aesthetic and even sensuous appeal of fascism for artists who find
the drabness of an egalitarian society uninspiring. That
appeal was, of course, both limited and one-sided. The official
public style of fascism was largely Philistine, and the typical
fascist bureaucrat would have denounced Mr Harrison's
authors as purveyors of *Kulturbolschewismus*. Nevertheless,
the appeal did exist, at least until the rise of Nazism; in 1934
Roy Campbell described fascism as 'human and not mechanical'. The movement Mr Harrison describes is best seen as a
part of the widespread revolt against liberalism in the be-
tween-wars period, its other aspect being the affection felt by
many intellectuals for Soviet totalitarianism: for a time, at
least, the system that murdered Isaac Babel and Osip Man-
delshtam was much admired by many of the literary intelli-
gentsia. If, by now, we are happy to accept and defend

liberalism, it is not because the disabilities that seemed so evident in the twenties and thirties – those underlined, for instance, in Eliot's social criticism – are any less manifest, but because the history of the last thirty years shows that any of the likely alternatives are unspeakably worse. All the same, a problem that Mr Harrison several times touches on is likely to recur: the major artist may not feel at home in an egalitarian and democratic society, simply because there is something anti-egalitarian about the kind of peculiar excellence that produces great art. In the recent past, some artists turned nostalgically to elitist, authoritarian orders, and were self-deludingly bemused by fascism. That is one attempt at a solution. A more recent, and diametrically opposed, approach is the endeavour by Raymond Williams and his disciples to reconcile high art with an egalitarian culture. But I think it would be a mistake to assume that the earlier impulse now belongs wholly to history. In a long and closely argued essay on Philip Larkin published in the December 1964 issue of the *Review*, Colin Falck attacked Larkin's total and seemingly egalitarian acceptance of the contemporary world: 'In the typical landscape of Larkin's poems the whole chiaroscuro of meaning, all polarities of life and death, good and evil, are levelled away.' He concluded:

> In rejecting Larkin's particular brand of 'humanism' I may seem to be asking for the kind of 'right wing' violence to which D. H. Lawrence was sometimes led. I think perhaps I am. The last and truest humanism in art is the truthful expression of emotion, and this is something prior to all questions of politics: it concerns only the honesty or the corruption of our own consciousness. If this means barbarism, then let us have barbarism. Barbarism has come to be associated with obscurity, but no true expression can be really obscure. Let us have lucid barbarism. If we cannot face it in art we shall have to face it soon enough in life.

Mr Harrison may, perhaps, feel he should now turn his attention to whatever is implied in Mr Falck's portentous reflections. (They seem roughly parallel to the fascist streak which various critics have noticed in Norman Mailer; one

can refer to Mailer's assertion of the value of individual violence against the mechanical uniformity of the modern world
– 'There's still some love if you can use a knife'.)

A book which, like Mr Harrison's, raises these central questions about our literary culture is of undoubted value. As he
deals with such contentious questions, one is grateful for his
sympathy and fair-mindedness, and for a style which, though
pedestrian, is lucid and, at times, pleasantly astringent. Nevertheless, his work is sharply limited by the critical disability to
which I have referred, and by a certain insensitivity of mind.
It is also, in places, remarkably superficial. The statements on
modern Irish history in the section on Yeats are very muddled; nor is it clear how far Mr Harrison has consulted Conor
Cruise O'Brien's recent key essay on Yeats's relations with fascism. In the account of Wyndham Lewis he makes no use of
Lewis's letters – published in 1963 – nor of Geoffrey Wagner's
admirable study of Lewis, which unravels Lewis's tangled
and self-contradictory political views; he relies too heavily, in
any case, on *The Art of Being Ruled*, a rather early book.
There are other instances of Mr Harrison not having done
sufficient homework; but I shall merely refer, finally, to his
sluggish refusal to provide an index.

1966

17 Wyndham Lewis

It was Wyndham Lewis who described Pound, Eliot, Joyce and himself as the 'Men of 1914', thereby providing literary historians with a useful label, and emphasising the importance of Lewis's magazine *Blast*, which ran for two numbers in 1914 and 1915. As well as its copious contributions by Lewis and Pound, *Blast* provided the first British publication of Eliot's poems; and though Joyce was not a contributor, he was genially mentioned in the first issue. Fifty-five years later three of the Men of 1914 seem securely established, and much energy has been devoted to drawing, and redrawing, the maps of their achievement. Two of them, Joyce and Eliot, have attained not only greatness but academic respectability, and the shapeliness of their literary careers has been of great help to the exegetes: the path from *Dubliners* to the *Wake* may go dauntingly far, but it is clear and unbroken; whilst the way in which Eliot's poetry and prose support each other to form a complex but clearly defined totality is becoming more and more apparent. Pound is a harder case, certainly: between the historians who are concerned with him as an influence and entrepreneur, and the cranks and ideologues who have turned him into a cult, the measure of Pound's strictly creative achievement remains problematical. Nevertheless, the *Cantos*, still in progress after more than fifty years, can be seen as a continuous development of some sort, even if it leads, at the end, into a blind alley. In contrast with these three, Lewis stands as the author of a vast, untidy *œuvre* with no clear centre or pattern to it, and his reputation remains shadowy and unfocused. Whereas the output of Joyce, Eliot and Pound, particularly when streamlined for pedagogic purposes, can be made to look like a river or at least a substantial stream, Lewis's work is like a broad, ill-defined delta, with many channels, some deep, others shallow, quite a number of stagnant pools, and a good deal of uninviting marsh. It was not enough for Lewis to be both a painter and a man of letters: as a writer he directed his overpowering energies into all the main literary forms; primarily fiction, but marginally also into verse and drama, as well as producing many books of literary and art criticism, and philosophical and political speculation. Lewis, in short, wrote too many books for his own good, and contemporary readers are still disinclined to do the basic work of sorting over the heap.

Now, however, they have Mr Pritchard to help them: his short and unpretentious study does a remarkably useful job.* He knows Lewis's work well, and he has a firm grasp on its context in twentieth-century English literature. Furthermore, he writes with admirable clarity and exactness, and is in the strict sense a critic, not just an explicator or exegete. That is to say, Mr Pritchard is very insistent that some of Lewis's books are better than others, that a few of them are very bad, and that even in the good ones some bits may be better than other bits. At the beginning of his book he gets Lewis right by placing him in the company of the great Victorian sages like Carlyle, Ruskin and Arnold; literary men who felt themselves entitled, indeed called upon, to turn their critical attention to every kind of social or intellectual activity. At the same time, as John Holloway has shown, they did not proceed by advancing arguable proposi-tions; rather, they tried to make the reader share their view of the world by the whole quality and movement of their writing, working emotionally and imaginatively rather than intellectually. They were, in short, literary artists even at their most argumentative and polemical. This is abundantly true of Lewis, who recalls them in many ways: he admired Ruskin and Arnold – *The Art of Being Ruled* is full of quotations from *Culture and Anarchy* – and his prose, in its singularity and vehemence, can be very reminiscent of Car-lyle. During his intensely productive phase in the twenties Lewis did not make any deep distinction between fictional and non-fictional kinds of writing, since discursive works like *The Art of Being Ruled* and *Time and Western Man*, and novels like *The Childermass* and *The Apes of God*, were all

* *Wyndham Lewis* by William H. Pritchard.

intended to be fragments of one huge literary enterprise.

In his early, pre-1914 phase, Lewis was more purely an artist; *Blast*, for all its stridency of manner, was the vehicle of a dynamic formalism. (Despite Lewis's dislike of Marinetti, he seems to have been much more influenced by the futurists than is generally acknowledged; Apollinaire's manifesto, *L'Antitradition futuriste*, published in Milan in 1913 and reproduced in the *London Magazine* for November 1968, anticipates both the tone and the typographical peculiarities of *Blast*.) Lewis's earliest stories had been published by Ford Madox Ford in the *English Review* in 1909, although they were not collected until *The Wild Body* came out in 1927. These stories, and Lewis's first novel *Tarr*, most of which was written before the war, are sympathetically discussed by Mr Pritchard. It is in this early fiction that Lewis first adopted the stance of what Walter Allen has called the Black Cartesian: mind and body are regarded as totally separate, the former being reluctantly imprisoned inside the absurd and inefficient mechanism of the latter. The dichotomy is exploited to savagely comic effect; the humour arises, in Bergsonian terms, from the organic being transformed into the mechanical. In this fiction Lewis is writing in a tradition that goes back to the Jonsonian comedy of humours, with Smollet and Dickens as later exemplars; to convey his bleak view of the world Lewis evolved a very idiosyncratic prose style, which is intensely energetic and jerky, full of staccato rushes of substantives. The first version of *Tarr*, published in 1918, was intended by Lewis to be the literary equivalent of a cubist painting, and its fragmentary prose still reads very oddly: Lewis evidently considered that this experiment was not a success, and he later rewrote the book in rather more conventional terms. (Mr Pritchard compares extracts from the two versions, showing the superiority of the later one.) Lewis's prose is well adapted to his way of looking at the world, but it does, I think, possess an accumulative monotony; its intensity is too exclusive, too lacking in modulation or nuance. And this is not merely a stylistic defect but is essential to Lewis's vision. We all have moods, no doubt, of seeing humanity as absurd and pointlessly animated puppets, but Lewis in all his fiction up to *The Revenge for Love* never lets

us see them as anything else. It may be that the naturalistic
bias of prose fiction is too strong to sustain this exclusively
two-dimensional vision, which may require a medium as
stylised as the stage comedy of Jonson. Mr Pritchard, to be
sure, is aware of this limitation, but he wants to deal with it
by jettisoning Lewis's fiction of the twenties, *The Childermass* and *The Apes of God*. I am quite happy to abandon
The Childermass; although it contains some magnificent
writing, particularly at the beginning, a great deal of it con-
sists of not very intelligible argument and localised satire, the
kind of thing that Lewis did a great deal better in wholly
discursive terms in *Time and Western Man*. On the other
hand, I think I would rather keep *The Apes of God* than
Tarr or *The Wild Body*, since it aims to be pure satire and
nothing else and one is less troubled by a sense of willed limitation. It is, of course, far too long and utterly intolerable to
read right through more than once: nevertheless, it contains
some of Lewis's most brilliant prose and is well worth preserving as an anthology of bravura satirical passages.

With *The Revenge for Love* in 1937 Lewis revealed that
he could write a genuine, even moving novel: the apparatus
of puppet-fiction was not dismantled, but the puppets showed
an unexpected capacity to suffer, just as they do in such
roughly contemporary novels as Evelyn Waugh's *A Handful
of Dust* and Nathanael West's *Miss Lonelyhearts*. Mr Pritchard writes very perceptively about the qualities of this fine
novel, and Lewis's later ones, like *The Vulgar Streak* and *Self
Condemned*. The last of these, incidentally, takes the same
sort of place in Lewis's development as the *Pisan Cantos* in
Pound's: in both works a lifelong dedication to objectivity
and impersonality is cracked open by the intensity of personal
suffering. Mr Pritchard interestingly compares Lewis's relation to his hero, René Harding, with Lawrence's to Birkin in
Women in Love. However opposed Lewis and Lawrence may
have been, the one staking everything on the intellect and
the visible world, the other crusading for feeling and the dark
gods, they had quite a lot in common. Both were lonely, in-
dividualistic prophets, passionately convinced that the world
was out of joint and that they were called on in their writing
to set it right; both were equally at odds with the values and

personalities of the English literary establishment.

Mr Pritchard, whose manifest common sense sometimes declines into timidity, writes best about Lewis as a novelist and next best about him as a literary critic, in which role Lewis could be very good indeed. The few pages on Pound in *Time and Western Man* still seem to me quite seminal, and the criticism of Joyce in the same book, though less penetrating, is still important, as Mr Pritchard shows (a pity, though, that he didn't refer to Joyce's comeback in *Finnegans Wake*, where Lewis is mocked as the author of *Spice and West-End Woman*). So, too, are the chapters on Faulkner, Hemingway and Eliot in *Men Without Art*. Prudently, Mr Pritchard doesn't try to relate Lewis the painter to Lewis the writer, though I wish he had tried. After all, the principal motif in *Time and Western Man* is Lewis's insistence on the superiority of the eye over the ear (and, by extension, of art over music, and space over time): the whole book is pervaded by Lewis's presentation of himself as, like Gautier, *un homme pour qui le monde extérieur existe*. Mr Pritchard recognises the brilliance of *Time and Western Man*, though he doesn't seem sure how to do it justice. It is here, rather than in the arid and rambling *Art of Being Ruled*, that Lewis may claim to have done for the 1920s what Arnold did for the 1860s in *Culture and Anarchy*. Lewis's targets may have lost their potency, just as Arnold's have: philosophically no one worries much about Whitehead or Alexander or even Bergson any more, and if Pound and Joyce are still live fish, Gertrude Stein isn't. And the book amply displays Lewis's faults of method: the arguments that lead nowhere, the portentous connections that don't connect, and, above all, the repetitiveness that makes him go on asserting for paragraph after paragraph, even chapter after chapter, what he has already made abundantly clear. But for all that, it remains, like *Culture and Anarchy*, a superbly entertaining book, where one is constantly diverted by the spectacle of a prodigiously well-stocked mind in action, lashing its victims one after another in full enjoyment of its own exuberance.

Again, although Mr Pritchard is clearly right to dismiss the ephemeral political works that reflected Lewis's brief flirtation with fascism in the thirties, I feel he should have dwelt more fully on the works of cultural criticism that followed *Time and Western Man*, such as *The Diabolical Principle, Paleface* and *The Doom of Youth*. Uneven though they are, and in some respects objectionable to liberal feelings, they remain admirably vigorous examples of how not to be taken in by fashionable manifestations in either minority or mass culture. In his later years Lewis was friendly with McLuhan and one sees the influence of his critical spirit in *The Mechanical Bride*, though hardly, I think, in *Understanding Media*. This spirit is sadly lacking in our own confused and pretentious cultural scene, and we have need of a latter-day Lewis with equivalent courage and energy and polemical zeal; one would like to read him on, for instance, Bob Dylan or Susan Sontag or Andy Warhol. Since Lewis wrote *The Doom of Youth* the youth cult has swollen immeasurably throughout the Western world, and is badly in need of fresh puncturing.

If, as I have implied, Mr Pritchard is not a flawless critic of Lewis, he is still a very good one: his coolness is to be preferred to the spirit of resentful special pleading that has characterised Lewis's disciples in the past. Most important, he is aware of, though I don't think he sufficiently stresses, the paradox that lay at the heart of Lewis's literary personality. Although a scarifier of romantic pretensions and sensationalism, Lewis's own stance as an isolated and heroic artist – 'the lonely old volcano' in Auden's phrase – who is persecuted but undefeated, is essentially a late-romantic attitude. And although Lewis may have wished to write like Arnold, he was always an individual crusader, who could not appeal, as Arnold did, to a community of educated opinion to support his criticisms. Lewis's aesthetics placed a high value on the deadness and immobility of art as against the untidy flux of life, and in general he preferred contemplation to action; yet everything that he wrote is pervaded by his own restless and often violent energy: all too evidently his own taste was for polemic rather than contemplation. Mr Pritchard sums it up very well:

But the strange, almost paradoxical, doubleness of response that had always characterised Lewis' obsessive dealings with matters of the self and the will persists: on the one hand, there is a condemnation of action and the self-willed 'actor' – Vincent Penhale for example; on the other a fascinated admiration for such energy and a recognition at least implicitly, that he, Lewis, possessed it himself.

If Lewis is to remain important as a literary artist, then I think he will have to be understood in terms of this paradox; just as, with Eliot, the doctrine of impersonality now seems to have concealed a great intensity of personal suffering. The essential Lewis is likely to be confined to a fairly small number of books from his large output; the pruning operation that Mr Pritchard has carried out, severe though it may seem to Lewis's admirers, is surely essential if he is to survive.

1969

18 Roy Campbell: Outsider on the Right

It is nearly ten years since Roy Campbell died in a motor accident in Portugal at the age of fifty-six. A frequently expressed opinion about Campbell is that he was a fascist who fought for Franco. His literary reputation has suffered accordingly, although many readers would agree that he was a lyrical and narrative poet who deserves to be remembered for such early works as *The Flaming Terrapin* and *Adamastor*, and for his exquisite translation of the poems of St John of the Cross, even if his characteristic rhetoric, which derives largely from French and Spanish poetry, often falls strangely on English ears. One should also mention Campbell's abilities as a satirist, which were most effectively expressed in his epigrams and a number of pungent passages in *The Georgiad*, his long neo-Augustan satire on London literary life in the late twenties. Campbell himself considered his masterpiece to be *Flowering Rifle*, a 5,000-line satirical epic about the Spanish Civil War which he published in 1939; although of considerable documentary interest, and a revealing vehicle for Campbell's obsessions, its poetic qualities are very uneven, since the satire constantly declines into repetitive hectoring and crude abuse. In this essay I shall not be offering any extensive literary consideration of Campbell's work; most of the essential points have been made by Mr David Wright in a British Council pamphlet on the poet, and in a brief but admirably just discussion by Mr G. S Fraser.[1] My present purpose is to examine those aspects of Campbell's career which embody ideas and attitudes that have seldom been so fully expressed in English, though they are not at all uncommon in continental intellectual and literary circles. That many of these ideas are deplorable does not make Campbell's expression of them any the less interesting.

Some years before he died Campbell was referred to in the *Observer* as a 'right-wing Hemingway', and since the deaths of both writers this remark has seemed more accurate than such journalistic labels usually are. Campbell and Hemingway shared a great capacity for self-dramatisation, which expressed itself in a love of violent activity and displays of physical prowess; they both appeared before the world as men of action and tried to hide the fact that they were highly cultivated literary artists. They were both vigorously involved in the Spanish Civil War, if on opposed sides, and were passionate devotees of bullfighting. A principal difference was that Campbell was a more deeply ideological writer than Hemingway, even if the ideology was never expressed abstractly, or very coherently formulated.

Campbell's sense of himself as an outsider is apparent in many of his early poems. He saw himself as the lone wolf, going his own way in the face of popular opinion, despising the herd-like masses. There are a number of strands in this *persona*, which became more emphatic over the years. In its most traditional sense it is simply Byronic, where the writer projects himself as a brooding, disdainful solitary; this notion is combined with the later nineteenth-century concept of the isolated *poète maudit* – as described, for instance, in Frank Kermode's *Romantic Image* – and both these elements were given intellectual stiffening by the anti-democratic sentiments of various modern conservative thinkers. Such a state of mind is vividly conveyed in 'Tristan da Cunha', a poem which David Wright describes as Campbell's 'Resolution and Independence'. Campbell had once seen the lonely island on a voyage from Durban, and his poem, though seemingly descriptive, makes it, in Mr Wright's words, 'an emblem of the poet, solitary, anachronistic, and disdainful':

> We shall not meet again; over the wave
> Our ways divide, and yours is straight and endless,
> But mine is short and crooked to the grave:
> Yet what of these dark crowds amid whose flow
> I battle like a rock, aloof and friendless,
> Are not their generations vague and endless
> The waves, the strides, the feet on which I go?

G

Many of Campbell's characteristic attitudes become more ex-
plicable when one reads his two autobiographical volumes,
Broken Record (1934) and *Light on a Dark Horse* (1951). His
early years in South Africa were spent in intimate association
with nature, in a wholly pastoral, pre-industrial world; he
learnt, as a child, to ride, fish and shoot, and became profici-
ent in every form of outdoor activity. (He remarks in *Light
on a Dark Horse* that his earliest distinct memory was of seeing the sea through the legs of a horse – a highly symbolic
combination which anticipated his adult love of horses and
boats.) This way of life engrained in Campbell a rugged in-
dividualism and a belief in the excellence of physical action,
although he was distinguished from the average young col-
onial boy by a talent for writing and drawing, and a passion
for books, in which he was encouraged by his father, a cultivated Durban doctor. His formative years instilled certain
deep habitual prejudices in Campbell which he never lost
and which left him unable to understand the complexities of
modern, industrial, urban civilisation, and gave him little desire to do so. In *Broken Record* he describes himself as an
outsider both in space and time: 'The only value my impressions of Europe can have for the general reader is that of an
outside critic. Take me for the inhabitant of another planet
and you may see this value.'[2] He claims that he is more truly
European than the modern European, and his argument reminds one of the sentiments of the Southern Agrarians in
America:

> I am presenting an outsider's point of view: you may take it
> as that of the pre-Victorian man, or of a pagan who never
> was put through any mill except that of the pre-industrial
> European culture of an equestrian, slightly feudal type, a
> sort of inhabitant of the moon, a foreign being who can-
> not imagine what meaning such words as 'rights', 'pro-
> gress', 'freedom' and 'liberty' have at all. . . .[3]

Campbell's rejection of the values of urban, democratic
society broadly parallels that of other modern writers; in
Geoffrey Wagner's words:

Lawrence, Yeats and Campbell were all men who hun-
gered for the human relationship in an increasing urban-
ised society. Yeats loved aristocrat and peasant, while
Broken Record is a *cri du cœur* for the feudal relationship
of serf to lord, working inside which the poet could so
manipulate mythology.[4]

Yet if Campbell's reactionary nostalgia and hatred for the
contemporary world were by no means unique (they can be
traced at least as far back as Carlyle), there was something
very personal about his mode of expression. The fact that he
spent most of his adult life in Provence, Spain and Portugal
gave him a Latin rather than an Anglo-Saxon caste of mind:
in the peasant communities of southern Europe an alternative to the modern urban world still seemed a living possibility (similar notions were expressed in the 1930s by Ford
Madox Ford, who was a friend of the Southern Agrarians, but
also, in contrast to Campbell, a strong anti-fascist and supporter of the Spanish Republic). At the same time, he found
support for his distinctive attitudes in such writers as Mistral,
Maurras and Montherlant. Campbell energetically adopted
the French right-wing cult of neo-classicism, and an accom-
panying admiration for the traditional Roman and Mediter-
ranean virtues, together with an idiosyncratic kind of
Catholicism that was mingled with Mithraic and other pagan
elements. Given such an intellectual and cultural background, it is not to be wondered at that Campbell has seemed
a strangely exotic figure, and has evoked a response from English readers that is as much baffled as hostile.

Indeed, one constantly runs up against paradox and even
overt contradiction when trying to see Campbell in focus. He
was a confessed admirer of Maurras;[5] and yet Maurras might
well have regarded this expatriate South African of mixed
Irish, Scottish and Gascon descent, who wandered from country to country, and who spent some years working as a cowboy
and fisherman in Provence, as something of a *métèque*.
Campbell himself liked to give the impression of a simple
and inarticulate ex-soldier, who would far rather sit drinking
and telling tall stories with a group of cronies than join in the
high-flown discussion of literary questions. Yet he was, in fact,

a man of wide reading, with a thorough knowledge of several languages and literature. (The third volume of Campbell's *Collected Poems* contains translations from Latin, French, Spanish and Portuguese; he was also well acquainted with Provençal poetry.) And as much as he despised academics and men of letters, he had a serious devotion to literature; this is very apparent from his little book on Lorca,[6] which was his one venture into literary criticism. It shows a remarkable knowledge of the Spanish literary tradition, and apart from one or two characteristic personal interpolations, its sober, rational tone is in utter contrast to the violence of Campbell's satirical verse and polemical prose. And yet, having written of Lorca with real admiration in this book, and expertly translated many of Lorca's poems, Campbell could still direct a gratuitous sneer at him a few years later. In one of the notes to the revised version of *Flowering Rifle,* he refers to some leading Nationalists who had been executed and remarks: 'They were intellectuals on a higher scale, and died better than the cowardly Lorca.' Since Campbell had previously admitted the obscurity surrounding Lorca's death, this is an extraordinarily presumptuous comment; he also remarks: 'If the author of this poem, a better poet than Lorca, so Borges the leading S. American critic points out, had not been resourceful, he would have died like Lorca, but at the hands of the Reds.'[7] It is such inconsistencies, of tone if not of reference, arising from the alternation of the various aspects of Campbell's *persona*, that make him hard to assess. Some of his admirers have tried to smooth over the less agreeable aspects of his make-up, and generally simplify his literary personality, by making him out to be an unsophisticated and even naïve poet, with no interest in politics, who supported Franco purely for religious reasons. Admittedly, a poet's relation to a particular ideology is liable to be oblique and idiosyncratic, and Campbell was never a merely propagandist writer; nevertheless, the general caste of his thought was already established well before the outbreak of the Spanish Civil War.

In *Broken Record* there are several expressions of admiration for fascism, which Campbell saw as 'religious, not fanatical; human and not mechanical'. To have admired fascism in

1934 was not, perhaps, very heinous; at that time, before the full emergence of Nazism and the horrors of full-scale totalitarianism, fascism could seem an imaginatively liberating force by those who, like Campbell or Yeats, disliked the modern world. Later, Campbell soft-pedalled this admiration, and even claimed that the Spanish Falange was not a fascist organisation.[8] He made little attempt to conceal his anti-semitism:

> I am no pogromite myself. One can forgive the Jews anything for the beauty of their women, which makes up for the ugliness of their men. But I fail to see how a man like Hitler makes any 'mistake' in expelling a race that is intellectually subversive as far as we are concerned.[9]

In *Flowering Rifle* there are many anti-Jewish references, some of them extremely unpleasant.[10] In later years, Campbell retorted to charges of fascism by saying that, unlike most writers of his age-group, he had fought in the British Army against fascism during the Second World War, and been badly wounded in the process. It is certainly true that Campbell had no sympathy at all for Nazism – which he regarded as 'brown bolshevism' – and the totalitarian glorification of the state. Throughout his life, however, he regarded Soviet communism as the real enemy. One can, I think, argue that, because of his early conditioning and particular way of thinking, Campbell never properly grasped the nature of fascism, nor the ultimate implications of racialism. It is inconceivable that Campbell, who was personally generous and warmhearted, could have knowingly aligned himself with the mass butchery of the Final Solution, even though much of his ignorance was culpable.

Catholicism was another important element in Campbell's make-up. In *Light on a Dark Horse* he described how he and his wife, who were then living in Spain, were converted to Catholicism just before the outbreak of the Civil War:

> Up to then we had been vaguely and vacillatingly Anglo-Catholic: but now was the time to decide whether, by staying in the territorials, to remain half-apathetic to the great

fight which was obviously approaching – or whether we should step into the front ranks of the Regular Army of Christ.[11]

The military terminology is characteristic; Campbell professed a militant kind of Catholicism that since the Second Vatican Council has been disapprovingly labelled 'triumphalism', which makes a devotion to the visible institutions of the Church and all its material interests at least as important as the practice of the traditional Christian virtues. This strain was emphasised by Campbell's experience of the anti-religious atrocities committed by Spanish leftists in the summer of 1936, and as a result he regarded the Nationalist cause as a hallowed crusade (he made a vow to give up drinking wine until Franco's victory). Campbell's poetry was much admired in English Catholic circles, and he was given an esteemed place in the Catholic literary pantheon that includes G. K. Chesterton and Hilaire Belloc (although I think it is true to say that Campbell's exoticism and truculence of manner were regarded a little uneasily). Like other British Catholic writers, Campbell made no attempt to distinguish between the universal truths of Christianity and their particular cultural embodiment; for him, Catholicism was inextricably bound up with the Latin cultural traditions that he so admired, and his writings contain many polemical attacks on Protestantism. Some of the sharpest passages in *Flowering Rifle* lampoon the Church of England because of its alleged sympathy with the Spanish Republicans:

> Who smile to see true Churches overthrown
> And made as void and ugly as their own
> When they of Saints and Angels stripped their Abbey
> To fill with whiskered imbeciles, and flabby,
> Frock-coated wiseacres in Alabaster –
> The harbingers of Progress and Disaster . . .[12]

Charity was not a virtue that came easily to Campbell, and he made little attempt to love his enemies, although he could respect those of them that he thought of as brave fighters, like George Orwell or the Asturian miners. In *Broken Record* he attacked the humanitarian image of Christ, asserting that Christ 'had violent hatreds and furious eruptions'. The fact was that Campbell's Catholicism, though sincerely held, was tinged with the pagan fantasies of 'Latinity', and in particular with Mithraism. Certainly, his orthodox Catholic admirers might have been disturbed by such lines as these:

> Fill high the holy Cup
> That Christ has bled to crown,
> Against the sunrise hold it up
> And, empty, hurl it down!
> Life is a girl superbly built
> And kicking in your hold –
> But plunge your dagger to the hilt
> If ever she grows cold! [13]

In a note to *Mithraic Emblems* Campbell stressed the elements in Mithraism that anticipate Christianity, and in his poems he often refers to Christ as the 'Solar Sire', an equivalent of the Mithraic *Sol Invictus*. There are many bold conceits for Christ in Campbell's poems; he more than once sees Christ both in terms of Mithras slaying the sacrificial bull and of modern bullfighting:

> and then the Red
> Torero (Him who took the toss
> And rode the black horns of the cross –
> But rose snow-silver from the dead!)[14]

More extravagantly, in *Flowering Rifle* Campbell compares God the Father to Colonel Moscardò, the heroic defender of the Alcazar at Toledo, whose son had been shot by the besieging Republicans:

> That God was never brilliantined or curled
> Who out of Chaos saw his battles won,
> And gave, like Moscardò, his only Son,
> To save the charred Alcazar of the world. [15]

Elsewhere in *Flowering Rifle* Campbell compares the ascending Christ both to an aeroplane and to a spermatozoon:

And even in our own ejected seed
Creation is the Devil-Darer's deed ...

These instances of Campbell's metaphorical exuberance do
not indicate religious heterodoxy, but they do suggest the
ease with which he transformed the central mysteries of
Christianity into the materials of his personal poetic myth.
He saw Catholicism very much on his own terms, and one can
imagine the dismay with which he would have regarded the
transformation in the Catholic Church following the Second
Vatican Council.

In addition to Catholicism and French neo-classicism,
another important influence on Campbell was his friend,
Wyndham Lewis, painter, novelist and critic. Lewis was a
subtler and more complex figure than Campbell, and
attempts to describe him as a straightforward apologist for
fascism go wide of the mark. Lewis was always seeking a
hierarchical static society, in which art could flourish; and although he writes approvingly of fascism in *The Art of Being
Ruled* (1926), he also shows himself very sympathetic to the
Soviet approach; they both had the virtues of being ordered,
elitist systems, in contrast to democratic untidiness. In 1930 –
three years before the Nazis came to power – Lewis published
a book praising Hitler, which he subsequently repudiated,
and although he never cared for what he saw as the comic-
opera elements in Italian fascism, he adopted for a time in
the mid-thirties a thoroughly pro-Axis position, seeing the
European fascist powers as 'have not' nations struggling for a
place in the sun against the joint hegemony of Soviet Russia
and the Western democracies. This was a short-lived position
on Lewis's part, as Geoffrey Wagner shows in his masterly
study of Lewis. But it was at this point, corresponding to the
outbreak of the Spanish Civil War, that the ideological align-
ment between Lewis and Campbell seemed to be most intimate.

The two men had been friends since the early twenties,
and in 1930 they collaborated in a pamphlet, *Satire and Fiction*, which Lewis published when the *New Statesman* refused to print Campbell's enthusiastic review of Lewis's huge
satirical novel, *The Apes of God*. There are several admiring

references to Lewis in *The Georgiad* and *Broken Record,* and
Lewis returned the compliment in his novel, *Snooty Baronet*
(1932), where there is a portrait of Campbell as 'Rob
McPhail', a South African who lives in Provence and works as
a fisherman and bullfighter; he is described as 'one of the few
authentic poets now writing in English', and Geoffrey Wagner has called McPhail 'perhaps the first thoroughly sympathetic character Lewis had created in his satire'. Lewis seems
to have given a faithful account of Campbell's way of life in
the south of France in the early thirties, although he is fairly
derisory about Mithraism and tauromachy, which Campbell
took very seriously. Campbell and Lewis had a common inclination to the politics of neo-classicism, as expounded by
Lewis in such books as *The Art of Being Ruled, Time and
Western Man* and *The Childermass,* and a deep contempt for
egalitarianism and the flux and relativism of a debauched
democratic society which overturned all hierarchical distinctions. Campbell praised *The Apes of God* for its stress on the
'masculine intellect' as opposed to 'the sentimental idealisa-
tion of "youth" for its own sake, of the feminine in the male,
and the male in the feminine, the romanticism of the negro-
philist . . .' In the 'Author's Note' to *Flowering Rifle* he
echoed this sentiment when he condemned the humani-
tarianism which 'sides *automatically* with the Dog against the
Man, the Jew against the Christian, the black against the
white, the servant against the master, the criminal against the
judge'. Even though Lewis was not an exclusive intellectual
influence on Campbell, he undoubtedly helped to give a particular articulation to Campbell's existing ideas and attitudes.

In 1936, soon after his escape from Toledo, Campbell compared Lewis in a letter to the defender of the Alcazar: 'Intellectually, you are Moscardò to the whole of Europe . . .' In his
reply Lewis wrote: 'I gloried in the title of *Moscardò.* You
may rely on me to behave on all occasions in a manner no
way inferior to that of the "Eagle of Castile".'[16] A few
months later Lewis published *Count Your Dead: They are
Alive!,* a vigorous apologia for Franco, which denounces the
alleged pro-Soviet leanings of the Western democracies; it
seemed that Lewis and Campbell were united in upholding a
position which – outside Catholic circles – had few intel-

lectual defenders in the English-speaking world. Nevertheless, their positions were to diverge before long. Lewis's later
development makes it clear that his fundamental attitude to
politics was very different from Campbell's, as the latter was
ruefully to discover. Although Lewis was extremely interested in politics and wrote copiously on the subject, his basic
criteria were aesthetic rather than social or ideological: he was
primarily concerned with the kind of society in which great
art could be produced, and he was prepared to abandon political and ideological positions according to his latest assumptions and insights. After his support for fascist nationalism in
the thirties, he swung completely in the opposite direction
during the Second World War and declared himself in
favour of total internationalism and what he called 'cosmic
man'. Lewis liked to present himself as an unchanging,
monolithic figure, stemming the flux of a sickly, time-bound
romanticism, but he was decidedly volatile and inconsistent
where particular political questions were concerned. Thus,
although he was bitterly anti-Soviet in the thirties, after the
qualified admiration expressed in *The Art of Being Ruled*, we
find him praising Stalin in his war-time letters, then becoming anti-Soviet again with the growth of the Cold War in the
late forties.

Campbell, by contrast, was massively single-minded, and
throughout the Second World War remained convinced that
communism was the major enemy, and that Franco's crusade
had been a wholly just and noble cause. (He claimed that
after the Yalta agreement he threw away his British and
American medals in protest against the betrayal of Eastern
Europe to Russia; at a public occasion connected with the
Festival of Britain in 1951 he wore only his Spanish Nationalist medals, saying that they were the only decorations he
could wear without a sense of shame.) He must have been
dismayed at his friend's blatant shifts of opinion, as when
Lewis wrote to Mrs Campbell in 1944:

I was glad to hear from Augustus that he has exchanged his
requeté uniform for that of the Home Guard. The best
Catholic opinion now – and I speak from very near the

horse's mouth[17] – is that the requetés were on the wrong side in the land of the flowering rifle.[18]

Lewis, on his part, must always have had doubts about aspects of the poet's *persona*. Since a distaste for 'action' was at the core of Lewis's aesthetic philosophy, we can assume that Campbell's determined immersion in the role of man of action did not greatly appeal to him (one recalls Lewis's scathing remarks about Hemingway in *Men Without Art* (1934)). It is certain that he was not very sympathetic to Campbell's religious attitudes, whether Mithraic or Catholic: in 1942 he wrote to Augustus John: 'It is really capital news that he has got out of Spain, where he was liable, because of his over-fervent papist nature to get involved in all kinds of abominable nonsense.'[19] In the epilogue to Lewis's book of short stories, *Rotting Hill* (1951), there is a portrait of Campbell *in propria persona* which combines sympathy with a certain detached observation, producing an effect close to pathos (the account corresponds exactly with the present writer's recollection of Campbell at about that time):

> Roy Campbell passed and he raised his large coffee-coloured hat. He walked as if the camp were paved with eggs, treading slowly, putting his feet down with measured care. 'Tis his war-wound imposes this gait on him of a legendary hidalgo. He was followed by a nondescript group, some say his audience. I noted a poetaster, a photographer, a rentier, and a B.B.C. actor. He is the best poet for six miles or more around. But he suffers from loneliness I believe. He is like a man who rushes out into the street when the lonely fit is on him and invites the first dozen people he meets to come up and have a drink. He led his band into 'The Catherine Wheel'.[20]

Campbell continued to admire Lewis, although he made no secret of his disappointment at Lewis's post-war advocacy of internationalism and 'cosmic man'; in *Light on a Dark Horse* he wrote of Lewis: 'I gradually came more and more under his influence till I started generating ideas of my own, and he went "cosmic".'[21] In a long review of a reissue of

Tarr,[22] Campbell wrote of Lewis's books with unrestrained enthusiasm, saying that although Lewis had now lost faith in Western culture, he had once been its most vigorous defender, and that Lewis's current attitudes in no way affected the value of such works as *The Childermass* and *Time and Western Man*. Here, as on other occasions, Campbell was trying to fit Lewis into his own frame of reference, with its sharp polarities. In fact, as Wagner has shown, Lewis could never have accepted a purely Maurrassian view of Western culture; his lifelong admiration for oriental art, for instance, would complicate such an interpretation. At all events, Lewis appreciated Campbell's review; he wrote: 'To find you still at my side is a matter of the greatest satisfaction to me: and I hope we shall always remain comrades-in-arms against the forces of philistia.'[23]

Yet although these influences were of great importance in Campbell's intellectual formation, there can be no doubt that the crucial event in his life was the outbreak of the Spanish Civil War. At a time when the writers of the world were almost unanimous in their support of the Spanish Republic – and when even 'reactionaries' like Pound and Eliot declared themselves neutral – Campbell sided unhesitatingly with Franco. Although the literary response to the Spanish war is usually thought of in terms of the English leftist poets of the thirties, it is worth recalling that Campbell wrote more, in sheer bulk, about that war than any other poet.[24] He saw it as the ultimate encounter between light and darkness, tradition and chaos, Christianity and atheism, Europe and Asia, that he had confidently expected in *Broken Record* (Campbell often referred to Marx and Freud as Asiatic underminers of European man). But ideological questions apart, Campbell had little reason to love the Republicans. In the summer of 1936 he had been beaten up by militiamen in Toledo and narrowly escaped with his life; after the outbreak of the Civil War he was again imprisoned and apparently in danger of execution. According to Campbell's own account he escaped from prison by killing a warder – one of the local *Cheka* – when the prison was hit by a Republican bomb aimed at the Alcazar.[25] Campbell then escaped with his family in a lorry full of militiamen, under the fire of the besieged Nationalists in the Alcazar. They were evacuated from Valencia in a British ship, together with Robert Graves, and after some months in England went to Portugal. From there Campbell returned to Spain and joined the Nationalist forces.

A number of recent writers have suggested that Campbell, despite whatever claims he may have made, did not in fact fight with Franco's Army; he has been variously described as a propagandist or war correspondent.[26] Campbell himself, however, is quite explicit on the point; in his autobiographical letter to a French admirer he wrote:

> Pour les tortures qu'ils m'ont infligées, j'avais quelque chose à dire aux rouges: le moment que ma famille était sauf, je me suis engagé dans 'los novios de la muerte', 'les fiancés de la mort', le premier régiment l'Europe. C'est la légion d'Espagne, le régiment de Cervantes, de Lopez et de Garcilaso: on admet quelques étrangers mais ce n'est pas comme la légion française *étrangère* avec des bordels, etc.[27]

An unsigned biographical note in *Hommage à Roy Campbell* states that Campbell fought with the Carlists and was wounded at Talavera de la Reina; the latter detail seems unlikely, since Talavera was captured by the Nationalists as early as September 1936. Campbell does, however, refer elsewhere to injuries received during the Spanish war.[28] A recent letter to the present writer from the poet's widow indicates that Campbell's active service may indeed have been short-lived: 'He did a bit of fighting but they told him they wanted "plumas mas que espallas".' He later returned to Portugal and there wrote *Flowering Rifle*; Mrs Campbell describes it as having been written in three weeks, during which time the poet lived entirely on tea and did not sleep at all.

Many of the descriptions in *Flowering Rifle* and in other poems about the war reflect Campbell's first-hand experience of the front, even if not all of it was obtained in a combatant capacity. Much of *Flowering Rifle* is, however, not about Spain at all, but carries on Campbell's feud with the English intellectual establishment that had begun in *The Georgiad*;

it is full of vitriolic abuse of English liberals or progressives, whom Campbell vilifies under the generic title of 'wowsers' or 'charlies', and particularly the left-wing poets of the thirties, whom he later fused in a composite target called 'MacSpaunday' (composed of MacNeice, Spender, Auden and Day Lewis). Apart from any question of justice, much of this feuding is too private to make effective satire, and *Flowering Rifle* is marred, in a literary sense, by repetitiveness and by Campbell's inability to impose any large-scale organisation on his poem. It remains, however, the fullest example we have of Campbell's personal and poetic mythology; in the absoluteness and even brutality of its attitudes it is more reminiscent of some kinds of Renaissance literature than the work of a twentieth-century sensibility. The dominance of Campbell's myth is such that he takes little heed of verifiable fact, and Hugh D. Ford has listed some of the wild assertions that occur in *Flowering Rifle*; in the notes to the 1957 revision of the poem Campbell was still confidently asserting that Guernica was destroyed, not by German aircraft, but by the re-treating Republicans. Elsewhere he improves on the official Nationalist claim that the war cost one million dead, by stating that the dead numbered nearly three million.[29]

In later years Campbell remained unfalteringly true to the authoritarian, Latin traditionalism that he had acquired in Provence and Spain, and which he had found so splendidly embodied in Franco's crusade. Thus, from 1949 to 1951 he was co-editor of the *Catacomb*, a small literary and political magazine whose ideals were pro-European, royalist, ultramontane Catholic, and virulently anti-socialist though not specifically neo-fascist, and which published contributions by Montherlant and Salazar, and articles on such writers as Bonald, Mistral and Maurras. It was underpinned by the assumption that the Spanish war might have to be fought all over again on a larger scale, since Western Europe was in imminent danger of being overrun by Soviet communism.

With the passing of the years it should be possible to see Campbell's total achievement, and the myths that inspired it, in some kind of perspective. On the one hand, his admirers should recognise that Campbell, however much he liked to appear as a simple apolitical poet, was an ideologically committed writer, many of whose attitudes were dangerous and sometimes vicious. On the other hand, those who refuse to do justice to Campbell's poetry because of their dislike of his ideas – even though the best of his original work was written before 1936 – should recognise that a writer can be important despite reactionary and illiberal attitudes. This problem has to be faced with Pound and Céline and Drieu La Rochelle: unlike them, Campbell did at least bear arms against fascism.

1967

19 Keith Douglas

Remember me when I am dead
and simplify me when I'm dead.

Since his death in action in 1944, Keith Douglas has indeed been remembered, though in imperfect ways, and these two volumes* are intended to replace various earlier memorials to his work and life: the 1946 edition of *Alamein to Zem-Zem*, his prose journal of the desert war, which contained a number of his poems in strangely bad texts; the incomplete *Collected Poems* of 1951; and Ted Hughes's *Selected Poems* of a few years ago. The new edition of the poems prints in chronological order all of Douglas's surviving poems and drafts, together with an introduction by Edmund Blunden, who was his tutor at Merton. At the back of the volume are several pages of notes, which are prefaced by the remark that they 'are not intended to provide a comprehensive list of alternative versions, nor a commentary; this would be tedious'. Maybe; but the fact that a job seems tedious to the editors, and to most likely readers, is not in itself a good reason for not doing it, particularly since this book is supposed to be the definitive edition of Douglas's poems and is not likely to be supplemented. If Douglas had been a poet born in, say, 1720 rather than 1920, then any self-respecting modern editor would, as a matter of course, give his edition a full textual apparatus and as full a commentary as he could. The notes in this edition are admirably informative as far as they go, but with three editors involved in producing a volume of 160 pages, one feels they might have pushed themselves just a little further and been more systematic, even if the idea that the texts of twentieth-century authors ought to

* *Collected Poems* and *Alamein to Zem-Zem* by Keith Douglas, edited by John Waller, G. S. Fraser and J. C. Hall.

be produced with the same scholarly care as those of earlier periods still seems startlingly novel.

Keith Douglas has, then, been remembered in ways one hopes he would have approved of, and Donald Hall's assertion that he left 'the finest poems written in our language by a soldier of the Second World War' will only be seriously questioned by those who would make a similar claim for Alun Lewis. Yet the completeness with which this reputation has been established may have fulfilled the second of his injunctions – 'and simplify me when I'm dead' – in a rather unsatisfactory way. Reading through the *Collected Poems* I made a number of discoveries. The first of them was that most of Douglas's poems about the Middle East were, indeed, as good as they are usually said to be, and as I remembered them as being from anthologies and the issues of *Poetry London* where several of them first appeared in the late forties and early fifties. Douglas was, indeed, a poet of tremendous technical accomplishment, a quality already very evident in the first poems in the collection, which he wrote as a schoolboy at Christ's Hospital, and he had an impressive sense of economy. Yet although he wrote magnificently when on form, his form was only precariously maintained, and when he was off it his language could collapse into an awkward prattling. The process is remarkably apparent in the poem from which I have already quoted, 'Simplify Me When I'm Dead'. After the opening injunctions it continues:

> As the processes of earth
> strip off the colour and the skin:
> take the brown hair and blue eye
>
> and leave me simpler than at birth,
> when hairless I came howling in
> as the moon entered the cold sky.

There is an admirable concentration about this, and a line like 'when hairless I came howling in' makes a splendid effect. The poem relaxes a little in the next three lines, with a dry, Eliotic wit:

Of my skeleton perhaps,
so stripped, a learned man will say
'He was of such a type and intelligence,' no more.

Then, in the following six lines, we have a disconcerting decline into clumsiness and rhythmic incoherence:

thus when in a year collapse
particular memories, you may
deduce from the long pain I bore

the opinions I held, who was my foe
and what I left, even my appearance
but incidents will be no guide.

It seems that Douglas's precociously formed technique had
great bravura qualities but rather little staying power, although in making such a judgement one must remember that
if he had lived and had continued developing as promisingly
as he had between 1940 and 1944, then most of the poems in
this volume would be regarded as no more than juvenilia in
the perspective of a normal life's work.

If one aspect of the 'simplification' of Douglas's posthumous reputation has been to assume that he was a more
evenly accomplished poet than was the case, another has
overemphasised him as a dry, precise, intelligent poet, in
sharp contrast to the sticky neo-romanticism that dominated
English verse during the 1940s. Douglas had a rare intelligence, and a happy mastery of the rational virtues; but a
reading of the *Collected Poems* shows how much literary
romanticism he had absorbed, even if it was not of the shrill
Apocalyptic variety; doubtless such currents of feeling were
running strongly in Oxford in 1940, as we can see from the
exactly contemporary work of Sidney Keyes and John Heath-
Stubbs. Here, for instance, is the opening of Douglas's 'An
Oration', written in that year:

In this city, lovers beneath this moon,
greater here than elsewhere and more beautiful,
who loves conspiracies and lovers, here you walked.

It was you who spoke in the dark streets, stood in the
    shadows
or where the lamps lit your white faces and red lips.

Douglas was acutely sensitive to prevailing influences, at least
in his pre-Army days, and before this genteel romanticism he
had shown himself very aware of Auden, or, at least, of that
astonishingly homogeneous thirties idiom which was Auden's
main legacy. It is conspicuous in 'Dejection', written at school
and published in *New Verse* in 1938:

> Yesterday travellers in summer's country,
> Tonight the sprinkled moon and ravenous sky
> Say, we have reached the boundary. The autumn clothes
> Are on; Death is the season and we the living
> Are hailed by the solitary to join their regiment,
> To leave the sea and the horses and march away
> Endlessly. The spheres speak with persuasive voices.

The prevalence of this manner means I can read Douglas's
early poems with a peculiar pleasure that has little to do with
their actual literary merit; it is simply that I find the possible
variations of this idiom – well exemplified, for instance, in
Robin Skelton's anthology of thirties poetry – exceedingly
fascinating in a largely extra-literary way. Yet critical honesty
constrains me to say that of all the poems that Douglas wrote
at school and university the most exquisitely achieved is 'Encounter With a God', dated 1936, which owes little to fashionable styles, and is an extraordinarily poised and mature
composition for a boy of sixteen.

Douglas was always poised, but in battle his poise shifted
from the knowing, carefully nurtured self-consciousness of
the articulate schoolboy and undergraduate to something
much tougher, the total preparedness for experience of the
hardened young tank officer, although, as we see from the late
poems and his journal, traces of the earlier attitude always
persisted. Douglas's war poems inevitably invite comparison
with the parallel work of the First World War, though the
immediate effect of the comparison is to force me into somewhat oblique reflections about the relation between literary

form and collective experience. It is, of course, true that in
the desert Douglas was fighting a very different war from the
trench poets of 1914–18, and that he knew far more than
Owen, Sassoon or Rosenberg (who is alluded to sympathetically in Douglas's 'Desert Flowers'), for their transmutation of
experience was very much a part of what he knew. There is
no sense of shock, of protest or anger, and not a great deal of
pity, merely a calm, disdainful acceptance of the worst experience can offer, which does not strike a sufficiently emphatic attitude to be called stoical.

Yet Douglas's way of responding to war, it seems to me,
could hardly have been expressed in the former war, not because people could not feel like that, but because there was
no effective way for them to express their feelings in words.
Thus, the best poetry of that war tends to be polarised between the pity of Owen and the anger of Sassoon; only
Rosenberg, who had read Donne very thoroughly, comes
close in a few poems to a deeply felt complexity of attitude.
Yet Douglas, though formally a fairly conservative poet, had
grown up in the mainstream of modernist poetics, whose
basic attitudes were to be found in Eliot's poetry and criticism, and enshrined in a more systematic way in the tenets of
the New Criticism: the essential poetic qualities were wit,
irony, ambiguity, complexity, tension, all that is implied in
the capacity to treat of several different – even conflicting –
aspects of experience at the same time. One of Douglas's best
poems, though marred in some lines by his recurrent clumsiness, is 'Time Eating', which begins:

> Ravenous Time has flowers for his food
> in Autumn, yet can cleverly make good
> each petal: devours animals and men,
> but for ten dead he can create ten.

It is a poem I have known for a long time, and these words
never fail to call up in my mind a famous sentence from a
critical essay of Eliot's: 'The poets of the seventeenth century, the successors of the dramatists of the sixteenth, possessed a mechanism of sensibility which could devour any
kind of experience.' The resemblance is, no doubt, for-

tuitous, and merely brought to mind by the emphasis given
to the verb 'devour' in both passages (in strictly poetic terms
there may be a closer parallel elsewhere in Eliot: 'The tiger
springs in the new year. Us he devours'). Yet the association
can remind us how closely Douglas adhered to the concept of
'wit' and unity of thought and feeling that Eliot outlined in
his writings on the Metaphysical poets, at least in the apparent intentions underlying the late poems, if not always with
perfect success in their realisation. Such a Poem as 'Dead
Men', for instance, is both a powerful crystallisation of his
experience of the desert war and a textbook exercise in the
use of 'serious wit'. The opening recalls the rather lax
romanticism of Douglas's Oxford period, though sharply controlled by an astringent vocabulary ('inveigles', 'infer',
'tacit'); from there the poem moves steadily to a confronta-
tion with the fact of death that recalls Eliot (and, perhaps,
Donne behind him), with possibly a conscious echo of 'Oh
keep the dog far hence':

> Tonight the moon inveigles them
> to love; they infer from her gaze
> her tacit encouragement.
> Tonight the white dresses and the jasmin scent
> in the streets. I in another place
> see the white dresses glimmer like moths. Come
> to the west, out of that trance, my heart –
> here the same hours have illumined
> sleepers who are condemned or reprieved
> and those whom their ambitions have deceived;
> the dead men whom the wind
> powders till they are like dolls: they tonight
>
> rest in the sanitary earth perhaps
> or where they died, no one has found them
> or in their shallow graves the wild dog
> discovered and exhumed a face or a leg
> for food: the human virtue round them
> is a vapour tasteless to a dog's chops.

The poem develops its opposition between love and death

until the last stanza, where two opposed attitudes are juxtaposed without resolution:

> And the wise man is the lover
> who in his planetary love resolves
> without the traction of reason or time's control
> and the wild dog finding meat in a hole
> is a philosopher. The prudent mind resolves
> on the lover's or the dog's attitude forever.

Elsewhere Douglas picks up this opposition between love and death, as in 'Vergissmeinnicht', which is his best-known poem, though not necessarily his best: 'And death who had the soldier singled / has done the lover mortal hurt.' Most of his late poems are filled with the presence of death, though Douglas is capable of treating it with considerable coolness, as in the final lines of 'Mersa', which is a finely chiselled piece of poetic description:

> I see my feet like stones
> underwater. The logical little fish
> converge and nip the flesh
> imagining I am one of the dead.

Arguably, Douglas carried the coolness too far, almost to the point of callousness, but it must have been a very necessary fiction to preserve his psychic poise, a difficult business for a man of his evident sensitivity: as he wrote in 'Aristocrats', another fine poem: 'How can I live among this gentle / obsolescent breed of heroes, and not weep?' Doubtless many elements made up this characteristic poise in Douglas, beyond his literary dedication to the poetics of complexity and irony; the ethos acquired at an English public school, perhaps as well as the pervasive attitude manifested in all the services during the Second World War: anti-heroic, understating, consistently sardonic.

This tone and underlying state of mind also permeates *Alamein to Zem-Zem*, which is an absorbing document even though it falls short of the distinction of Douglas's best poetry. Whereas the principal battle narratives of the First World

War described a war of immobility and largely passive endurance, broken by episodes of extreme and often suicidal action,
like the infantry assaults that opened the Somme offensive,
Douglas's book gives a graphic account of a highly mobile,
wholly mechanised kind of fighting. Its stress on the intimate
relation between the tank soldiers and their vehicles reminded me a little of the Futurist praise of the machine that
was often expressed in the years immediately before 1914. In
the desert war the individual tank commander, although receiving orders by radio, was very much on his own, and was
able to determine his own actions and fate to a very large
extent. It is this freedom that makes *Alamein to Zem-Zem* so
different from the narratives of the earlier war, which were
mostly written by infantry officers who felt themselves to be
part of a vast predetermined process. In some ways Douglas
recalls the gaily chivalric standards of the old days of heroic
warfare, although his tone is always realistic, and his sense of
the total confusion of a battle when seen from the point of
the participants recalls the classical descriptions of Stendhal
and Tolstoy and expresses a similarly anti-heroic sensibility.

As one might expect from a journal, as opposed to a considered narrative written after the event, Douglas offers vivid
description, a great sense of immediacy and involvement, but
not very much perspective. It does, in fact, possess all the
journalistic virtues, and is likely to remain a uniquely valuable
narrative of the desert war. The poise, the coolness and
toughness do at times become a little fixed, a little too much
of a deliberate attitude. I do not know whether Douglas had
read Robert Graves's *Goodbye to All That*, but in places he
seemed to be aspiring to a similar nonchalance in dealing
with the unspeakable:

That night we were issued with about a couple of wine-
glasses full of rum to each man, the effect of which was a
little spoiled by one of our twenty-five-pounders, which
was off calibration and dropped shells in the middle of our
area at regular intervals of seconds for about an hour. The
first shells made a hole in the adjutant's head, and blinded
a corporal in B Squadron. I spent an uncomfortable night
curled up on a bed of tacky blood on the turret floor.

The difference is that Graves achieved his calm at great cost, after war-time experience that was far longer and more intense than Douglas's, followed by ten years of learning to live with what he had undergone. Possibly if Douglas, too, had survived he might have returned to his experiences and produced an account that fully possessed the literary power that *Alamein to Zem-Zem* promised. Nevertheless, one is glad to have it reprinted in a uniform edition with the *Collected Poems*.

Taken together, they form a fitting memorial to this extraordinarily attractive and talented young man, who significantly developed the possibilities of literary response to modern warfare. One would like to think that it will not fall to anyone else to develop them still further.

1968

References

Chapter 1

1. See H. M. McLuhan, 'Tennyson and Picturesque Poetry', in John Killham (ed.), *Critical Essays on the Poetry of Tennyson* (1960).
2. John Killham, *Tennyson and 'The Princess'* (1958).
3. Leslie A. Fiedler, 'The New Mutants', in B. Bergonzi (ed.), *Innovations* (1968).

Chapter 2

1. Ian Fletcher, in I. Fletcher (ed.), *Romantic Mythologies* (1967) p. 181.
2. W. B. Yeats, *Autobiographies* (1955) p. 302.
3. M. Beerbohm, *Works and More* (1946) p. 115.
4. G. S. Fraser, 'Walter Pater: His Theory of Style, His Style in Practice, His Influence', in G. Levine and W. Madden (eds), *The Art of Victorian Prose* (New York, 1968) pp. 201–23.
5. *Autobiographies*, p. 302.
6. A. Symons, *Studies in Prose and Verse* (1904) p. 125.
7. Ruth Z. Temple, in R. Ellmann (ed.), *Edwardians and Late Victorians*, English Institute Essays 1959 (New York, 1960) p. 42.
8. I. Gregor, 'Comedy and Oscar Wilde', *Sewanee Review*, LXXIV (1966) 501–21.
9. *Studies in Prose and Verse*, p. 124.
10. Quoted in F. O. Matthiessen, *The Achievement of T. S. Eliot* (New York, 1959) pp. 27–8.
11. W. B. Yeats (ed.), *The Oxford Book of Modern Verse* (Oxford, 1936) p. ix.
12. Quoted in T. S. Eliot (ed.), *Literary Essays of Ezra Pound* (1960) p. 365.
13. G. F. Maine (ed.), *The Works of Oscar Wilde* (1948) p. 925.
14. M. Lindsay (ed.), *John Davidson: A Selection of His Poems* (1961) pp. xi–xii.
15. For a further account of Gray, see my introduction to his *Park: A Fantastic Story* (Aylesford, 1966). For a comparison of Gray and Symons as translators from the French, see Ruth Z. Temple, *The Critic's Alchemy* (New Haven, 1953) pp. 322–30.
16. H. Jackson, *The Eighteen Nineties* (Harmondsworth, 1950) p. 47.

17. In *The Early H. G. Wells* (Manchester, 1961).
18. *Oxford Book of Modern Verse*, p. xi.

Chapter 4

1. Q. D. Leavis, 'Gissing and the English Novel', *Scrutiny*, VII (June 1938) 73–81.
2. Austin Harrison, 'George Gissing', *Nineteenth Century and After*, LX (Sep. 1906) 453–63.
3. Jacob Korg, *George Gissing: A Critical Biography* (Seattle, 1963) p. 153.
4. Arthur C. Young (ed.), *The Letters of George Gissing to Eduard Bertz, 1887–1903* (1961) p. 121.
5. Ibid., p. 122.

Chapter 6

1. Leon Edel and Gordon N. Ray (eds.), *Henry James and H. G. Wells* (1958) p. 103.
2. See Gordon N. Ray, 'H. G. Wells Tries to be a Novelist', in Ellmann (ed.), *Edwardians and Late Victorians*, pp. 106–59.
3. Richard M. Ludwig (ed.), *Letters of Ford Madox Ford* (Princeton, 1965) p. 29.
4. Harry T. Moore (ed.), *The Collected Letters of D. H. Lawrence* (1962) I 51, 54.
5. Originally delivered as a lecture in 1911 under the title of 'The Scope of the Novel', this piece was collected in *An Englishman Looks at the World* (1914) as 'The Contemporary Novel'; it was reprinted in 1958 in *Henry James and H. G. Wells*.
6. *The Long Revolution* (1961) p. 278.
7. Jan Kott, *Shakespeare Our Contemporary* (1964) p. 94.
8. *Boon* (1915) pp. 134, 145.
9. *Youth* (1960) p. 60.
10. *Experiment in Autobiography* (1934) II 616.

Chapter 18

1. David Wright, *Roy Campbell* (1961); G. S. Fraser, *The Modern Writer and His World* (Harmondsworth, 1964) pp. 287–90.
2. *Broken Record* (1934) p. 54.
3. Ibid., pp. 143–4.
4. Geoffrey Wagner, *Wyndham Lewis* (1957) p. 88. There is a fuller discussion of this position in John R. Harrison, *The Reactionaries* (1966).
5. As he remarks both in *Broken Record*, pp. 48, 49, 188, and *Light on a Dark Horse* (1951) pp. 302–3.
6. *Lorca: An Appreciation of His Poetry* (Cambridge, 1952).
7. *Collected Poems* (1957) II 199 n.
8. Ibid., II 246 n.

9. *Broken Record*, p. 156.

10. Campbell altered some of the most offensive when his revised version of the poem appeared in vol. II of his *Collected Poems*. Thus a couplet about gold which in the 1939 text read:

The least fastidious Element we knew,
That loves the chill, webbed hand-clasp of the Jew,

in the 1957 version becomes:

The dirtiest of the elements in chief,
That loves the chill, webbed hand-clasp of the thief.

These revisions point to a prudential toning-down rather than a real change of attitude.

11. *Light on a Dark Horse*, p. 317.

12. *Collected Poems*, II 204.

13. From 'Herdsman's Song', *Mithraic Emblems* (1936) p. 130. Campbell did not reprint this poem in his *Collected Poems*.

14. *Collected Poems*, I 127.

15. Ibid., II 174. The impact of the simile is perhaps a little lessened when one learns that the executed youth was not, in fact, Colonel Moscardò's only son.

16. W. K. Rose (ed.), *The Letters of Wyndham Lewis* (1963) p. 239.

17. At this time Lewis was teaching in a Canadian Catholic college.

18. *The Letters of Wyndham Lewis*, p. 374.

19. Ibid., p. 338.

20. *Rotting Hill* (1951) p. 302.

21. *Light on a Dark Horse*, p. 224.

22. *Time and Tide*, 7 July 1951.

23. *The Letters of Wyndham Lewis*, p. 543.

24. There is a useful account of Campbell's contribution in Hugh D. Ford, *A Poet's War* (1965).

25. There are accounts of these incidents in *Light on a Dark Horse* and in a long autobiographical letter by Campbell printed in *Hommage à Roy Campbell* (Montpellier, 1958), a posthumous tribute to Campbell by various French and English admirers; no editor's name appears on this book.

26. See Hugh Thomas, *The Spanish Civil War* (1961) p. 231 n; Ford, *A Poet's War*, p. 199.

27. *Hommage à Roy Campbell*, pp. 73–4.

28. *Light on a Dark Horse*, p. 40.

29. *Lorca*, p. 37. Hugh Thomas, in *The Spanish Civil War*, p. 632, estimates the total number of deaths from all causes as not more than 600,000.

Index

Sustained discussions of an author are indicated in bold type

PEI